More praise for *The Distance to the Moon*

"Why are we as a nation so beguiled by these conveyances and their operations that we've been willing to pave over our amber fields of grain in order to better accommodate them? . . . It's positively folkloric: the automobile is the handiest tool ever devised for the pursuit of that unholy, unwholesome, all-American trinity of sex, speed, and status. Isn't that enough? Well, James Morgan suspected that it might all be a lot more complex than that, and in *The Distance to the Moon* he goes to considerable lengths to explore the matter."

—Bruce McCall, *The New York Times Book Review*

"Morgan's latest book about touring cross-country in a brand-new Porsche should strike a nostalgic chord among many readers. Few who read *The Distance to the Moon* will be able to drive down the street afterward and not notice cars more than they did before. . . . Morgan has a talent for telling a story about his own experiences and making readers think about their own pasts—whether he is writing about an old house, as he did in *If These Walls Had Ears*, or about cars. . . . By reading about his grand chance to drive a $41,000 Porsche across the country, we who have lusted after cars feel as if we are riding along. And what a journey we have."

—Karen Haymon Long, *The Tampa Tribune*

"[A] bittersweet travelogue . . . The long stretches of highway shift [Morgan's] soul into a somber, ruminative gear. . . . [*The Distance to the Moon*] is a thoughtful, eloquent contribution to the road book canon, written for an age when Kerouac's beatific wonder has been vanquished by Samuel Beckett's isolation and confusion."   —Jeff Turentine, *Forbes FYI*

"It begins like a book about a sports car . . . But as the pages flipped by, and Morgan's clean, well-lighted prose recounted significant interviews with people who shaped the interstates, people shaped by them, car nuts and urban planners, I realized he was riding deep into a complex of issues important to everyone. . . . Morgan traverses the landscape of sexual relations, of men and women brought together in back seats only to roar away from one another and the hassles of commitment. . . . But he also travels through a national policy landscape, the ideology of gun control, [and] he interviews little guys who love cars and the big guys who made pavement the nation's Manifest Destiny. . . . Then he returns his Porsche to the manufacturer and slinks home . . . leaving us amused and better informed about highways and the American heart. *The Distance to the Moon* is a deceptively male, usefully personal book; it takes the road more traveled and shows us where that leads."

—Celia Storey, *Arkansas Democrat Gazette*

A Road Trip into the
American Dream

Riverhead Books

New York

The

Distance

to

the

Moon

James
Morgan

Riverhead Books
Published by The Berkley Publishing Group
A division of Penguin Putnam Inc.
375 Hudson Street
New York, New York 10014

PORSCHE and BOXSTER are registered trademarks of Dr. Ing. h.c. F. Porsche AG. The PORSCHE® BOXSTER® image on the spine is used with permission of Porsche Cars North America, Inc.

A continuation of credits appears on page 321.

Copyright © 1999 by James Morgan
Book design by Claire Naylon Vaccaro and Jennifer Ann Daddio
Title page photograph by Joseph Duraes
Cover design by Miguel Santana
Cover photograph © Robert Mizono/WorkBook Co/Op Stock

First Riverhead hardcover edition: May 1999
First Riverhead trade paperback edition: June 2000
Riverhead trade paperback ISBN: 1-57322-816-8

The Penguin Putnam Inc. World Wide Web site address is
http://www.penguinputnam.com

The Library of Congress has catalogued the Riverhead hardcover edition as follows:

Morgan, James.
The distance to the moon : a road trip into the American Dream / James Morgan.
p.   cm.
ISBN: 1-57322-135-X
I. United States—Description and travel.   2. Morgan, James, date.—
Journeys—United States.   3. Automobile travel—United States.   I. Title.
E169.04.M663   1999
917.304'92—dc21   98-54716   CIP

Printed in the United States of America

10   9   8   7   6   5   4   3   2   1

For my sons,

David and Matthew

Contents

Will the future understand ... how much of our lives was spent in automobiles, and how largely their little curved caves of painted metal, speeding through a landscape of imploring advertisements and commercial desolation, and the powerful instant responses of their knobs and pedals, and the fine points of their amenities and costliness, and their aura of controlled explosion were part of our coming-of-age, our mating, our fulfillment of obligations, our thrusts of dreaming? An average American male became a man at the age of sixteen, with his possession of a driver's license, and every seventeen years thereafter he drove the distance to the moon.

— JOHN UPDIKE

The Distance to the Moon

Love Story

I am not a "car person," not in the way we usually think of the term. I don't read car magazines or go to car races or collect antique cars or change my own motor oil. It's very easy for me to go days without thinking about cars, except for the mundane questions of whether I've got enough gas to get where I want to go and, if I'm headed somewhere special, whether the car looks too dirty to be seen in. Other than that, I seldom give cars a conscious thought. But that's not to say my unconscious isn't working overtime.

I recently spent a year writing a book about the history of a house. The house happened to be the one my family and I live in now. I was focusing, by definition, on intensely domestic issues. It was toward the end of my writing that book that I began noticing a strange thing about myself. I was becoming very restless. I would look out the window a lot, and my need for breaks became more and more frequent. I would find excuses—*any* excuse—to jump in the car and run to the grocery store.

But the weirdest thing took place early in the mornings, before I even began writing. I always fix a pot of coffee and read the newspaper before I go upstairs to work. Usually, the classifieds are of no interest to me. In the spring of 1995, though, as I neared the final stretch on the house book, I found myself turning to the classifieds after I had finished the rest of my paper. The category I always went to was automobiles—specifically "Import Autos for Sale." And within that narrow confine I would run my finger down the page until I found "Porsche, 911."

There was a time in my life when I openly lusted for such a car, but that was eons ago, before I was even out of high school. What is it the Bible says? "When I became a man I gave up childish ways"? I thought the old urge had passed. I thought it had vanished, along with movie-star worship, into the thick blinding mist of adult responsibility.

So when, at age fifty-one, I felt it resurfacing like a Stephen King mania, I suddenly realized I needed to ask myself some very hard questions.

What you're about to read is a love story. Like all love stories, it sometimes makes no sense. The affair is between us and our automobiles. That, after all, is the epic entanglement that's defined this century and reshaped the face of America.

What brought me to this subject were two seemingly distinct events. The first occurred a few years ago while I was writing an article about the suburbs. During my research for that piece, I first encountered the outrage of the self-styled "new urbanists"—the increasingly influential architects and designers and historians and planners who believe that, beginning after World War II, our frantic devotion to the automobile took us down the path to ruin. "The automobile," says Vincent Scully, the venerable Yale architectural and urban historian, "has been the agent of chaos, the breaker of the city."

It doesn't take a degree in urban planning to know that the car has had its drawbacks. Smog, noise, gridlock, crashes, vanity plates—all of these have become part of our everyday lives, thanks to our love for automobiles. But the new urbanists have taken our inchoate daily experience with cars and shaped an entire philosophy around it. To them, the automobile is the evil force responsible not just for boarded-up downtowns but also for a variety of other ills—aesthetic, economic, moral, political, communal. "There is a growing sense of frustration and placelessness in our suburban landscape," says Peter Calthorpe, an architect and author of *The Next American Metropolis*, "a homogeneous quality which overlays the unique nature of each place with chain-store architecture, scaleless office parks, and monotonous subdivisions."

For the new urbanists, the antidote is an America reshaped into the way it was in good old pre–World War II days, when human beings ruled the world and the automobile knew its place. Instead of living in the automobile-glorifying suburbs, with their wide sidewalkless streets and their sad extravagant houses with three-car-garage façades, we all would go back to living in turn-of-the-century (the *last* century) neighborhoods: narrow, human-scaled streets on easy-to-follow grid patterns; sidewalks; parks; front porches; small yards; mass transit; varieties of housing; close-by schools and churches and offices and stores. Cars would be parked at the backs of houses, via alleys and rear driveways. In other words, the new urbanists would take us home again.

When I first encountered the new urbanists, my head told me they were really on to something. But my heart told me they were stuck in rush hour without a cell phone—because around the same time I also began feeling the first resurgent longings for the Porsche. (That's the second seemingly distinct event I was referring to earlier.) And here I'd like to say in my defense that lust of any kind is like a roof leak: You can't control, or sometimes even determine, where it's coming from. It simply shows up and washes over you.

For me, the lust began in Hazlehurst, Mississippi, in the fall of 1955. My father had moved us there during a bad time in his life, when his career had gone off track. To support his family he'd had to accept the job of managing a grocery store for his rich brother-in-law, my uncle Alex, the husband of my mother's sister May.

It wasn't until I'd grown up that I learned that my father and mother had been miserable in Hazlehurst. Back then, at the age of eleven, I was oblivious—deliriously so. I was a sixth-grader attending my third elementary school, and I'd already discovered that there were benefits to moving around. Life in one place eventually began to feel stale, but you could reinvent yourself by moving. I was actually enjoying being the new kid in school, the one the girls whispered about before class and during recess. My developing persona included a touch of Elvis, a dash of *Blackboard Jungle,* and a whole lot of a brooding actor named James Dean, who had become an icon that very fall by perishing in the violent crash of his silver Porsche Spyder. I kept a picture of the wreckage taped to my bedroom wall. It was the first thing I saw in the morning and the last thing I saw at night.

Four decades later I still can remember the impact that photograph had on me. The car lay twisted next to a barbed-wire fence, the hood flayed open and hanging out like a tongue. The whole driver's side was mangled, especially the front quarter panel, and the left front tire was tucked awkwardly into the wreckage. In the rear, the trunk was popped and gaping. To an eleven-year-old romantic, Dean's aura somehow metamorphosed the twisted steel so that it was no longer wreckage—it was sculpture. Signifying exactly what, I've not yet sorted out.

But ever since I saw that photograph, I've lusted, at least on some level, for a Porsche.

Thirty years had passed since I even entertained the notion of owning such a car—thirty years since I graduated from college with a degree in English and began learning about the *real* world. It was, I soon gathered, a place where people lusted for Porsches but settled for Chevy Vegas. The gap between them was an emotional schism you just had to find ways to bridge. And I had found ways, for a very long time.

With the hindsight of age I now know that cars can define the seasons of our lives. Unless we move often, even houses can't do that. Our houses speak to the parts of our souls that yearn for permanence, that want the seasons to slip by mercifully unnoticed. Cars are like songs. They're as much about change as the *Billboard* Top 40.

Besides the Porsche, the car I first identified with was one I never drove. My father was a Ford man, which meant that at a certain rebellious age I was attracted to Chevys. In Hazlehurst in the mid-1950s, we lived on a busy thoroughfare called Extension Street, which was simply the part of Highway 51 that fell within the city limits. My father saw to it that I was kept occupied, and I remember spending many hand-blistering afternoons in the fall of 1956 raking the oak and pecan leaves in the front yard. To amuse myself, I began counting the 1955 Chevrolets that passed our house. The 1955 Chevy was a milestone of sleek and sporty design, and it was snapped up by drivers everywhere. Television ads for the car provided a sound track of wanderlust: "See the U.S.A./In your Chevrolet!" That's my first memory of intense car consciousness. It's possible that I invested the Chevys with the romance of James Dean's doomed Porsche, but I think they were two entirely distinct events that, by chance, happened at the same time. I was simply a boy about to come of age in a country ready to be reborn for the road. I counted more than three hundred '55 Chevys passing the house that fall.

The car in which I learned to drive was my father's stripped-down baby-blue 1955 Ford, standard shift, with rubber floor mats and no radio. No *wonder* I was a dreamer. But that Ford was the car that first carried me into the world alone, free from the watchful eyes of parents, and so for me it retains a certain emotional stature. That car was succeeded by a used red-and-white 1958 Ford, which Dad simply showed up with one day. He probably thought I would love it, but I had a nagging sense that it was sporty to the point of tackiness. Then when I was a senior in high school, he bought us a *new* 1962 Rambler—beige, stick shift, rubber mats. At least it had a radio. But the best thing you could say about the Rambler was that its seats would lie back almost flat. I seized on that. In order to retain any status at all among my friends—in order to avoid becoming who my father's car would force me to be—I began billing that dull Rambler as the "Beige Bed." It was spin control, to say the least, though I have to say the old Rambler did have its moments.

More fitting to my self-image was another pivotal car—a maroon 1960 Thunderbird that belonged to my cousin Alex (called Alex Boy), the son of my aunt May and uncle Alex. It came along about the time I entered high school and for years occupied an important place in my private separate universe—a universe in which I wasn't destined to drive Ramblers. At first I saw the T-Bird only in the summers, when I was visiting in Mississippi. Alex Boy was in a mental hospital being treated for schizophrenia, and his beautiful car was just gathering dust in May and Alex's garage. I lobbied them to let me drive it, and finally they gave in—but only if I acquired a Mississippi driver's license. In Hazlehurst in those days, driver's tests were administered only once a week, and the morning May and Alex said yes was the morning the test was being given. I went in with no preparation and failed it. That afternoon, my friend David Sanders drove me to Jackson, thirty-five miles away, and I took the test again. This time I scored a hundred. From then on I drove that T-Bird whenever I was in Hazlehurst, and even took it with me to college a couple of semesters.

Forty years later, Alex Boy is dead (never having left the hospital) and the car, which no longer runs consistently, still usually rests in the same garage. Many other family members have sat back in that T-Bird's buttery leather seats since my day. But every time I'm in Hazlehurst, the very sight of that car reminds me of a certain season—the end of high school, the beginning of real life. I felt like a movie star in that car—felt, when I was behind the wheel, that it was *I* who'd been born rich, instead of my cousin.

My first taste of the freedom of the road came in the summer of 1964, when my friend David and I drove his black Pontiac Bonneville from Miami to the New York World's Fair, then up through New England and back down to the tip of Florida. It was a wonderful two-week trip. I still remember hurtling all night along the backroads of places like Virginia and Pennsylvania and New York State, guided only by the high beams and the green glow of the radio (from which Roy Orbison whined his paean to a pretty woman—"Mercy!") and consciously comparing my carefree life on the road with the dreaded duties that faced me at home: work, school, and the sure sense that I was moving, before my time, toward marriage.

Marriage brought with it an icy blue 1962 Chevrolet Super Sport, of which I always felt undeserving: I hadn't earned it; I had married into it. And it was so sleek that it gave people the false impression that we were solvent. In fact, we were just a college student and a secretary, and we were driving a lie. We couldn't afford the gas-guzzling Chevy and had to trade it for a demeaning 1965 Volkswagen in a shade of beige billed as "Sea Sand." Years later, having finished college and started careers, we went in together on another Chevy, a brand-new midnight-blue 1969 Super Sport, and later a pathetic little silver 1972 Vega at which I squinted my eyes and pretended I was seeing James Bond's Aston-Martin. At one point we seemed to be the only people on our street in Minnesota who couldn't afford a Volvo. Eventually, my first wife and I divorced. Though I wouldn't know it until later, she planned to marry her rich boss and escape our marginal existence. But before the divorce was final, she went with me to pick out a white 1976 Fiat Spider convertible in which I would launch another season of life—my new singlehood.

Since the 1976 Fiat Spider, the litany has been as much about farce as drama. I kept the Fiat two years, then sold it in order to move to Chicago, where I lived without a car until once again I began feeling the urge to escape. I bought another Fiat Spider, a cream-colored 1981 model that seemed to fit, as much as I could afford, my role as articles editor of *Playboy* magazine. The problem was that this convertible proved hopelessly impractical for a family man, even a broken-family man whose two sons visited only occasionally. It was the only car my second wife and I owned, and when my sons from my first marriage came to visit, I had to rent a bigger car while still making payments on the Fiat. It was absurd. We finally traded it in and bought a 1983 Audi 4000, the first almost-luxury car I'd ever owned. Worried that its four doors underscored a certain creeping of age, I ordered a stick shift, telling myself it made the Audi feel like a sports car.

My next car was a 1984 Jeep Wagoneer that I picked up, with 20,000 miles on it, from my boss at *Playboy*. He was a tall Jewish intellectual from the Bronx who'd traded his company car, a Mercedes station wagon, for the Jeep when he decided he wasn't in touch with his readers. He drove the thing for two years, back and forth between his office on Michigan Avenue and his home in suburban Skokie. By then he felt sufficiently in touch to order another Mercedes, so I bought the

Jeep when I was leaving *Playboy*, with its steady salary, for wildest Arkansas, where a four-wheel-drive vehicle was a requisite part of my new cowboy self-image as an entrepreneur at a start-up magazine. I drove it for eight years and 90,000 miles, until I burned up the engine one December day in 1993 while eating a McDonald's chicken sandwich and listening to loud rock and roll during a pounding rainstorm on the interstate, and so could neither hear the awful sound the engine was making nor see the smoke.

To replace the Jeep, my third wife and I bought a white 1994 Plymouth Voyager van, because by then I'd made a U-turn in life: At age forty-five, with grown children of my own, I'd gone and married a woman with two young daughters. My new wife already owned a 1984 Toyota van, but she thought our new car ought to be another van because hers was getting old.

So now, when I look out my window at the driveway, I have to face an embarrassing, reproachful fact: Here in mid-life, at age fifty-two, despite a long and winding road of facts *and* dreams that rolls out behind me, I've become something totally antithetical to any viable image of myself. I've become a two-van man.

I was having a conversation with a woman recently, and the subject turned to cars. "*You're* not the kind of man who would allow himself to be defined by a car," she said, flatteringly. "No *way*," I said, thinking of the vans in my driveway and the Vega in my past. I didn't tell her about my lifelong passion for the Porsche, or about the questions that now were nagging inside my head: *Would owning a Porsche fulfill me? Would it make me into someone else?*

Having the Porsche dream pop back into my life was a little like bumping into an old flame at a high-school reunion. I'm not the same and neither is she, but it warms my heart to know there's still a spark between us. And sometimes age works the opposite of the way you'd think. Instead of being more cautious, we become less so. In our heads the middle-age voices shrill their litany of warnings and chidings and fears: *Better save more for retirement! What if you get sick? The house needs a paint job!* And then from out of the hysteria comes a laconic voice your ears have never detected before—a voice that sounds, the more you listen to it, like the voice of pure Reason: *Screw it. It's now or never. Life isn't a dress rehearsal.*

I soon found myself actually trying to figure out how to buy a Porsche. Understand, I'm a freelance writer. I knew there was no way, short of selling my house, that I could afford a new one. But as vague longing turned to full-fledged fever, I ran across an article in which several car experts suggested ways that non-Rockefeller heirs could own certain high-ticket automobiles. They suggested buying Porsches from the late 1970s. The cars were still sound, the experts said, and the prices were affordable—anywhere from $11,000 to $18,000.

My heart pounded with possibility. Never mind the fact that if I'd had an extra $18,000 lying around, I already would have jettisoned the old van in the driveway. There was just something about getting a *Porsche* for the price of a Plymouth that made the deal feel—well, reasonable. Not everyone saw it that way. My neighbor John, who is a bona fide car nut but also an eminently practical man, threw a slight damper on my plan. "Eighteen thousand dollars?" he said. "For a twenty-year-old car?"

For weeks I devoured the classifieds, underlining and circling— but never calling any of the numbers listed. As long as I kept the cars safely in my imagination, I didn't have to actually commit myself. Nor did I have to face the potential limitations of a twenty-year-old vehicle. Instead, I became nigglingly discerning: *No way I'm going to buy orange! Too much mileage! What, no air conditioning? Way too pricey! Too inexpensive to be good!*

To help me sort out the ticklish issues of engine displacement and compression ratios, John brought me an old Porsche *Buyer's Guide* from his own automobile library. I pored over the book like a teenager reading *Playboy*—probably exactly like that, as a matter of fact. I never read a word of the text, I only looked at the pictures. The Porsche has a beautiful shape, especially the 911. At night before I drifted off to car dreams, I admired the sleek thrust of its front and the perfect slope of its rear. I appreciated the flare of its wheel wells and the solid feel of its footing. I paid special attention to the late-seventies models, and was thrilled to learn that I liked their non-fussy lines best of all. I imagined myself in the cockpit of one of them, shifting higher and higher as the engine whined behind me, while in front the white line of the road was a blur I consumed like a drug.

Then one night as I was lying awake obsessing, a disturbingly rational thought entered my mind: *This is nuts. This is a compulsion you'd better see about.* I began looking harder at my resurgent Porsche lust, remembering how and when it had resurfaced. I examined the feeling I'd had while finishing the house book. It wasn't just that I'd wanted to jump in my car and make a run to the grocery store. It was that, on some level, I wanted to leave for the grocery store and never come *back*. To be honest, it was a feeling I'd experienced for much of my life, whenever home threatened to suffocate me. I knew it wasn't that I didn't love my wife and family. I knew it wasn't that I didn't love my home.

But if it wasn't those things, what was it?

If you look at all into the literature of cars, you'll find a bookshelf worthy of Dr. Johnson. Well, at least of *Junior* Johnson. There are a lot of car books. Many deal with the technical aspects of automobiles, and just as many more cover the often mercurial personalities of the founders of the auto industry. A few of the books, usually written by academics, explore the infinite number of subjective, ego-salving qualities car lovers derive from their automobiles.

Such analyses seem to go without saying. Of *course* driving a Porsche would make me look (and maybe even feel) successful, sophisticated, etcetera, etcetera. But I had to believe the attraction went deeper than that. It seemed to me that since the heroic days of World War II, cars had become the most powerful means we have of expressing our personal mythology. When I was a kid, I would go to see a movie and then I would come home and play whatever the movie was about—cops and robbers, army, cowboys. As grown-ups, we can't do that. But still we can climb into the cockpits of our sports cars and utility vehicles and become the heroes, or the antiheroes, we want to imagine ourselves as. The car is our alternative to mowing the lawn. The car is *the open road,* with everything that implies.

And that implies a lot. Many years ago, I wrote a master's thesis on the circular journeys of escapism and search taken by Hemingway's heroes. I argued that his characters were always looking for a safe haven—a home. Then once they'd found it, it inevitably began to feel oppressive to them. Had that thesis been an autobiography? The reason I wrote the house book in the first place was because I had lived in so many houses in my life—twenty-five, to be exact—and I wanted finally to connect to something old and real and permanent. Now here I was, having lived in this house going on eight years and in this city for eleven, dreaming of getting in a car and driving away. We hear often about "sense of place," but I wonder if, in the human heart, there's such a thing as too much "place." And I wonder if it's especially true in the American heart.

For a few months when I was a teenager, the radio filled my soft Miami nights with a song called "Tell Laura I Love Her." It was one of those melodramatic ballads, popular before the Beatles set irony to music, which featured lyrics about car races and class rings and lovers' spats and horrible wrecks on the railroad track. But there's a line from this particular song that has remained with me through the years, precisely because it spells out so simply the sweet complexity of what kids of my postwar generation were brought up to think of as the American dream.

> I wanted to buy her everything
> A house, a car, a wedding ring.

As my old teachers would say, What's wrong with this picture? In the American psyche, the house and the ring speak to our needs to belong and to be safe. The car taps into the opposite side of our nature, the side that yearns to escape all confinements. And yet they're all a part of the impossible baggage we lug around with us. We dream of security while we dream of freedom. We dream of stability while we dream of the road. We search for home, only to find that home smothers. Our most fervent desires are marked by a profound and confounding restlessness, a passionate ambivalence in which the house and the car are the opposite faces of the same coin. The house and the car, home and the road—they're the flip sides of the American dream.

This country was *founded* on our quest to define ourselves, to seek our *own* destinies, and searching seems to be in our blood. "In the United States," Alexis de Tocqueville wrote in 1835, "a man builds a house in which to spend his old age, and he sells it before the roof is on." Tocqueville attributed American rootlessness to the opportunities afforded by our "classless society," opportunities so vast and so grand that we can't be satisfied no matter how much chasing and hoping we do. The result, said Tocqueville, is a hand-wringing mixture of "anxiety, fear, and regret."

By the time the twentieth century rolled around, some people thought we were all out of opportunities. "The free lands are gone, the continent is crossed," wrote historian Frederick Jackson Turner in 1896, "and all this push and energy is turning into channels of agitation. . . . This, then, is the real situation: a people composed of heterogeneous materials, with diverse and conflicting ideals and social interests, having passed from the task of filling up the vacant spaces of the continent, is now thrown back upon itself, and is seeking an equilibrium."

In other words, the twentieth century dawned on an American people pent-up and frustrated, born for adventure but no longer knowing where to find it. No wonder the automobile captured this country's spirit so. The very year Turner penned those prophetic words, two boys from Springfield, Massachusetts—Charles and Frank Duryea—began building and selling automobiles, officially launching the industry that would change this country forever.

That, I believe, is what our love affair with the automobile is all about. It's about our bone-deep need for clean breaks and fresh beginnings, for self-reinvention, for fleeing the numbing grind of everyday existence. That's why we love road trips and why the very thought of lying in a motel bed watching HBO and ordering room service is so appealing: It's a hiatus from real life and from who real life forces us to be. It's also why the aching wants of the boy I once was had the power to resurface years later and take hold of my middle-age imagination.

I slept no more on that car-crazed night, but suddenly my obsessions had found a focus. I began conceiving of a road trip, a journey, in which I would drive my particular (and rebelliously foreign) American-dream car into America's restless heart to see what I could fathom about where we've been and where we're heading—and why. The American dream has defined us, and our pursuit of it has been the stuff of daily life. But the new urbanists would say we've paid a terrible price for it. Has it been worth it? Has attaining all this freedom made us happy? Can cars also define the seasons of a *nation's* life? And what *is* it, exactly, that thrills me so about that legendary California car wreck? Here in the late winter of what Henry Luce called "the American century," these seemed questions well worth asking.

I wrote up a proposal to pursue these ideas as a book, and my agent sold the project quickly. Suddenly I was committed to buying a Porsche. Then my neighbor John came over with bad news. He has a rich friend who owns several Porsches, and the friend told John a cautionary tale about a man who'd bought an old one. As soon as the guy owned the car, it turned out to have engine trouble. "Cost him ten thousand dollars to fix it," John said. It was the first time I'd ever thought about maintenance.

I began to worry, but John had a solution. "My buddy says you ought to buy a new one—just take out a loan for seventy thousand dollars. You could drive it for a year and still not lose money." I really couldn't blame John. A guy starts talking about buying a Porsche, pretty soon people think he's flush.

I mulled the whole mess over for a week or so. Real life has a way of leavening dreams. Journeys inevitably present detours. Already the numbers weren't working as projected, and I hadn't even received the book advance. For a time I considered giving back the money—except that my family needed it to live on.

Then one day my wife, Beth, came up with the brilliant idea of appealing to Porsche, Inc.—the Company itself—to see if they would give me a car. I saw it as throwing myself on the mercy of the gods, but Beth, a savvy marketer, saw it as an opportunity for Porsche as well as for me. I tracked down the phone number of Porsche headquarters and soon had the name of the head of public relations, a man named Bob Carlson.

"Dear Mr. Carlson," I began. "I'm writing to you with what I hope you'll see as an opportunity for both of us." I went on to explain the trip I was planning to make, and I asked for Porsche's assistance in finding an old but reliable 911 from the late 1970s, which I hoped they'd make available to me "on favorable terms."

Three days later I got a call from Carlson. He told me they'd all had a barrel of fun reading my material and were going to consult with their ad agency to see how such a book might benefit their company. "But I have one question," Carlson said. "Does it really have to be an *old* Porsche?"

It was a question most men only dream of hearing. I swallowed hard and said I thought yes, and mumbled something about a theme I had in mind—how we seldom achieve our dreams fully, the way we imagine when we're starting out (my rationale for not being able to afford a new one). I may have even used my favorite reference for that idea—the aged fisherman in Hemingway's *The Old Man and the Sea*. For eighty-four days he'd caught nothing, and then he finally reeled in the biggest fish of all. Because his boat was tiny, he lashed the great fish to the side of his skiff. Then, on the way back to shore, the sharks ripped so at the fish's flesh that all the old man brought home was a skeleton.

But what a magnificent skeleton it was.

Carlson said he'd get back to me. I figured I'd never hear from him again. Then, one month later on a morning in November, my phone rang and Carlson was on the other end. "Jim," he said, "we'd like to give you a car—"

I was stunned speechless.

"—to use while you're on your trip." My heart sank. It's amazing how quickly greed replaces groveling. "Afterwards," he continued, "we can work with you if you want to buy it." My heart soared again.

"But we'd really prefer that you use a *new* car," he said. "You can have a 911—or you can drive our new Boxster, which won't even be available in this country until the spring of ninety-seven."

"Boxster?" I said, reeling. "What's a Boxster?"

"The reason I thought you might like the Boxster," said Carlson, "is that it's the direct descendant of the 550 Spyder that James Dean was driving."

I said nothing for a long moment—the longest moment in the universe. I thought of the curiously romantic wreckage that set me on this road in the first place. I thought of my father and his sad stripped-down Rambler. I thought of Miami, where we moved when I was thirteen and where Dad taught me to drive in the 1950s, at the height of the country's love affair with the automobile. I thought of road trips our family had taken in the old days—the mom-and-pop motels we'd stayed in, the speed traps we'd been snared in, the songs we'd sung, the endless car games we'd played. I thought of teenage nights in steamed-up cars, and cold adult mornings with a pregnant wife and a VW with no heat. I thought of my beautiful blue Super Sport and the depressing end it came to. I thought of my carefree Fiats, shrinks on wheels. I thought of all the other cars, the other trips, the exuberant escapes and happy homecomings.

Was it all just texture, or was it essence? I wanted to know.

Carlson was waiting for an answer.

"Can I have a silver one?" I said.

ONE

Lewis & Clark & Me

The first time I saw Miami was from the air, staring out the window of a TWA prop airliner as the pilot circled wide over the blue Atlantic. As the plane banked and began its approach, we cruised low over Miami Beach, and soon we were a silver sliver in the aqua gleam of Biscayne Bay. Finally we made a rushing shadow over miles of red-tiled, green-palmed, blue-pooled postage stamps. From the sky, the city looked like a pastel paradise in a heat shimmer of dancing whites. The whites, blinding sun streaks amid the color, turned out to be roads—the very roads I soon would learn to drive on.

That was thirty-nine years ago, on a January day in 1958. It felt like summer to me then, and in memory it does so still. Not just for me, but for the country itself. On any external scale of this consumer-mad century, it's astonishing to consider just how young we were then. Our family had owned a TV set for less than three years. We had one black rotary phone on a party line. In the years still to come, my friends and I would hang out at what was only the second Burger King in the nation. It was a time when it still was possible to focus.

Which may be why I remember Miami so well. Miami opened my eyes—opened my *senses*. I loved the surface of the place. Mississippi had been all pine-tree green and Pearl River brown. In Miami, red and purple flowers tumbled out of window boxes. Houses took on tints I'd seldom seen outside the Sunday comics. Thick lush lawns sprouted thin trees heavy with fruit. In my mind's eye, the lemons outside my bedroom window looked gold, like the stars in a Van Gogh night.

In Miami, I encountered Jews, Italians, Puerto Ricans, Cubans, Chinese, Filipinos, Romanians, Greeks—even New Yorkers. I learned to sing Havah Nagila. I ate, for the very first time, the following foods: bagels, lox, cream cheese, avocados, Reuben sandwiches, submarine sandwiches, kosher dills, pastrami, Swiss cheese, lobster, stone crab, black beans, Key lime pie. I also discovered mangoes, a fruit so sweet and ripe and dripping with juice that they're almost disturbing in their sensuality. I've always thought of mangoes as sex plucked from a tree.

On Sunday afternoons, especially in the early days, I stood outside open-air Miami Beach "pavilions" and watched sun-blond girls in bikinis dance with swarthy men wearing pastel pants and tattoos. On the grainy beach I watched musclemen wipe oil on the backs of girls on bright blankets. I watched blue-veined jellyfish wash ashore, puffed up and full of promise, only to deflate and litter the sand like last night's condoms. I watched sunburned kids dig moats around castles, while women with umber skin stood ankle-deep in the surf, wearing swimsuits and furs.

Before I could drive, I hitchhiked everywhere. That too was part of the giddy appeal of Miami in the fifties—the notion that you could skim safely across this vast surface like a stone, day or night, skipping from ride to ride until, in no more than three different vehicles, you'd traveled from my house on 103rd Street in Miami Shores south to 79th Street, then east across the causeway to Miami Beach, and then up or down depending on at which beach you were meeting your friends.

There was a technique to hitchhiking, which made me feel enormously street-smart: Whenever possible, I hitched at traffic lights, where I could walk out to stopped cars and tap on the window and say, "Going to Seventy-ninth Street, sir?" That way I also had a chance to case the person behind the wheel. If I simply stuck out my thumb on the street, no telling who might pick me up. These were pre–Gay Rights days, and nobody I knew was much ahead of his time. Once when I was fourteen, a car stopped and I ran for it, only to find the male driver wearing nothing but a swimsuit the size of a fig leaf. Inside the car, I kept my hand on the door handle. Finally he popped the inevitable question: "Have you ever had a blow job?" He was glancing my way, and when I said no, he asked, "Do you want one?" I told him to put me out right there—but I got great laughs once I got to the party I was hitching to.

Over all of this lively exterior hung the fabled Miami moon, huge and full and bright and golden. For the first couple of years, I would jog home the twenty blocks across Miami Shores from my new girlfriend's house to mine, watching my midnight shadow sprint beneath the moon. Later, when I could drive, the moon became a luminous crashing whitecap on the dark Atlantic, or a postcard ripple on gentle Biscayne Bay. It was easy, on nights like that—inside that parked car, face-to-face with moonglow innocence—to believe that nothing touched by such a heavenly light would ever go bad.

Miami, Miami. Miami *had* to be my starting point.

In the weeks prior to the trip, I'd been reading Stephen Ambrose's *Undaunted Courage,* about Lewis and Clark's expedition to find a water route through the Northwest territories to the Pacific. The feeling that I needed to read that book came to me in a dream. Certainly I had heard about it, but I hadn't thought it at all relevant to me. What could a river trip into uncharted territory nearly 200 years ago have to do with a 1997 traveler sailing along on interstates in a $45,000 convertible and paying chain motels with a hologrammed piece of plastic?

But I soon discovered a certain kinship with the young Meriwether Lewis. He loved to "ramble," Thomas Jefferson said about him, and even his mother jokingly complained about his "roving propensities." When he was eight years old, his family moved from Virginia to Georgia, which was frontier then. Ambrose paints an engaging portrait of a young boy enthralled with life on the road, "on the march with horses, cattle, oxen, pigs, dogs, wagons, slaves, other children, adults—making camp every night—hunting for deer, turkey, and possum; fishing in the streams running across the route of march; watching and perhaps helping with the cooking; packing up each morning and striking out again." It's an image sure to stir the adventurous American blood.

As my own journey drew nearer, and as I read farther into the book, I found myself identifying more and more closely with Lewis and Clark. I began to see myself as stepping off the safe base of home into an untamed land. Like Lewis and Clark, who had been careful to prepare themselves for encounters with potentially hostile strangers, I was about to venture from the familiar East across a vast continent toward a mythic West. Two people, no doubt influenced by certain recent news headlines, even asked if I was taking a gun, and for half a second I considered it. It was the classic American journey, never mind the motels. In fact, we three (Lewis & Clark & Me) all were headed straight for that northwest destiny called Oregon. I had designated Portland, that paragon of new-urbanist thinking, as the perfect counterpoint to 1950s Miami. Together they formed opposite poles of experience in the saga of our love affair with the automobile.

One detail in *Undaunted Courage* that particularly struck me was how hard it was for Lewis and Clark to pack. Even after President Thomas Jefferson had given Meriwether Lewis's expedition the green light, months passed while Lewis ran up and down the East coast and then along the Mississippi River, getting boats built, ordering guns and ammo, hiring men, taking on provisions, and choosing trinkets as potential bribes for the Indians.

I can't imagine such a packing job. For years I was the most anxious packer I knew. I made lists and tried to cross-index them to make sure each shirt would go with a minimum of two pairs of pants and sport coats. And then there were the ties and shoes and belts and socks. Infinite combinations. I would throw up my hands and go fix a drink. Then eleven years ago I gave up on variety, opting instead to simplify my wardrobe and therefore my life. I now stick pretty much to khaki pants or jeans, blue shirts, white socks, and cordovan loafers. My packing has been made considerably easier.

Still, I couldn't seem to get ready for this trip, and my difficulty had nothing whatsoever to do with that great wild land I was about to venture into. It had to do with profound American ambivalence: Going away is one thing; leaving home is another. No wonder my reluctance manifested itself as a packing problem. Packing is an effort to take your home along with you, to surround yourself with familiar things, to lessen the chance for surprises. I was going to be in Miami in early May—and then in Missouri and Nebraska and Colorado and Idaho and Oregon and wherever else I might decide to go for the next six or so weeks. How do you pack for that? And how roomy was this Boxster, anyway?

All my friends were upbeat about my going. The Porsche people, like Jefferson, seemed a tad impatient with my last-minute delays. The car arrived in Charleston harbor and was originally to be delivered to Little Rock, but I wasn't ready. I couldn't make myself focus. I couldn't even hold the thought of getting ready in my head.

Also among my pretrip reading was John Steinbeck's *Travels with Charley*, which I last had looked at as a senior in high school. I was struck by something I hadn't understood the first time through. Steinbeck talks about how hard it was to leave home: "As the day approached, my warm bed and comfortable house grew increasingly desirable and my dear wife incalculably precious." I saw myself in Steinbeck's words. As a high school senior, I had been thrilled at the prospect of getting away from home. And I was excited this time, too—not many men my age get to have such an adventure. But after a lifetime of leave-takings we can grow attached—debilitatingly so—to familiar ground. I asked Beth to go with me for the first few days. I told her I wanted to show her *my* Miami, but really I wanted her to be with me, to help me get started. She knows how to get people to tell their stories. Once she agreed to go, I felt better.

Then I laid eyes on the Boxster and began to feel like a man cheating on his wife.

I picked up the Porsche in Dallas on a rainy Saturday, the twenty-sixth of April. When I first saw the car, I couldn't tell if I was looking at the back or the front. (It turned out to be the back.) I'd never seen anything like it. The car was bigger than I'd expected—not simply a glorified Miata, like the new BMW roadster appeared to be. Its rump was big, and its wheelbase wide. From my first vantage point, the dominant feature was a slightly less than round—more eye-shaped— single exhaust pipe, chrome, protruding from the rear of the car in dead center. It made the Boxster look like a rocket. Driving this, I might indeed find an untamed land. The car had 202 miles on it, thanks to the lucky men who tested it prior to my driving it cross-country.

Two days later I got my first taste of the adventure I was about to embark on. It was the day before I was to leave, and I was stopping at the optometrist to check on some new eyeglass frames. Witherspoon Optical is in a small, fancy shopping mall, and as I pulled into the parking area in the Boxster, I noticed a red Jeep Cherokee coming out of a spot. I waited, with my left blinker on, for the red Jeep to drive away. But after pulling out, the Jeep didn't move. Instead, the driver, a woman, waited as she motioned for me to go ahead and turn into the space. I waved my thanks and pulled in.

When I got out of the Porsche, the red Jeep was still behind me, but I didn't pay much attention to it. Then I heard these words: "Since I gave you my parking space, I think I ought to get a ride in your car." The driver of the Jeep had lowered the passenger window and was talking to me. She was a beautiful brunette.

"Your parking space?" I said. "I thought you were leaving."

Turns out she was dropping an injured friend off at the restaurant next door. The friend's crutches were in the backseat. I began explaining that this wasn't my car, that Porsche had lent it to me, that I was writing a book "about America and The Automobile." She eyed me over her sunglasses. Clearly I wasn't deserving of the Boxster.

By the time the Woman in the Red Jeep (as she soon became known in my fantasies) drove off to find another parking space, a crowd had gathered. My optometrist, John Witherspoon, and a couple other people stood around admiring the car. Then three more men walked up—one in a suit, one in a sport coat, and one in jeans. "What is it? We *want* it!" said Sport Coat.

"Porsche," John answered. "The new Boxster."

"Is it yours?" said Suit, addressing me. And this was only my first experience with what would become the crucial moment in scores of encounters across the country. In this case, I could've said yes, but I knew John knew otherwise. I wasn't psychologically prepared to say yes yet anyway. I'd been driving this car for two days. In my mind I was still a two-van man with a Vega in his past. I was still routinely clacking the ignition key on the right side of the steering column, instead of inserting it in the trademark Porsche ignition on the left dash. To be honest, I wasn't 100-percent sure of what it was I was seeking on this expedition. Was this sociology, or psychology? Was this Bruce Chatwin meets Frederick Jackson Turner, or was it simply Walter Mitty meets Jack Kerouac?

"Porsche lent it to me," I said to Suit. "I'm driving it across the country, researching a book."

All the assembled stared at me in silence for a long moment. Then Sport Coat spoke up. "What's the name of this book—*How to Be over Fifty and Still Get a Lot of Pussy?*"

I resolved not to share that story with Beth. Unfortunately, I couldn't help telling our friend Sarah. "Har! Har! Har!" laughed Sarah, and just as Beth walked into the room, Sarah was in the midst of saying, "Of *course*—that car's a *pussy machine!*"

Beth gave me a look and asked what was so funny. "Oh, just this weird thing that happened today," I said limply. And I told her.

That night, scarcely twelve hours before we were to leave, Beth and I had an argument. We were in bed in the dark. The gist of the argument was this: She wanted me to admit that I knew the Boxster was a "pussy machine," and I steadfastly refused to do it. "That's not what this trip is about," I said. "I'm writing a book about the *American dream*. This is about *restlessness* and *mobility* and—"

"The car's a *pussy* machine."

"I don't know what you're talking about. I'm just trying to understand why we love our *cars*." I put a pillow over my face.

That was my story and I was sticking with it. I expected to lose either way, but stonewalling seemed the path of least pyrotechnics. "Let's get some sleep," I finally said when I thought there was half a chance of that. "We're heading for Miami tomorrow."

————

The American road trip as literary enterprise has a long, rich history. It's become a wagon train in time—a new Conestoga ever visible over the horizon, the ruts of the pioneers indelible in the path ahead. Walt Whitman celebrated the healing qualities of the road long before there were even automobiles. "O public road . . ." he wrote. "You express me better than I can express myself." His friend Emerson proclaimed, "There is no truth but in transit." Mark Twain wrote about all sorts of trips, domestic and foreign, fictional and real. *The Adventures of Huckleberry Finn* tells the story of one of the greatest American road trips, even if the road in question is a little wet.

Once the car had established itself in the American culture, the road-trip book soon followed. In 1916 the novelist Theodore Dreiser wrote one of the first prominent ones, *A Hoosier Holiday,* drawn from his pilgrimage with a friend and their chauffeur from Manhattan to Dreiser's native Indiana. The term "road book" didn't stick until the 1950s, after Jack Kerouac's *On the Road*. For my generation, that was the book that mapped out the highway as a route to self-discovery. Every decade since, almost like clockwork, somebody has produced some great journal of the road. John Steinbeck did it in 1962 with *Travels with Charley*. Robert Pirsig did it in 1974 with *Zen and the Art of Motorcycle Maintenance*. William Least Heat Moon did it in 1982 with *Blue Highways*.

The very existence of such a genre is part of why I was making this drive, but I didn't presume to follow in those writers' now classic tire tracks. For one thing, my goal would be somewhat different from theirs. All of them sought out a "real" America far from the interstates. They meandered along country lanes and backwater blacktops, stopping occasionally to chat with refugees from the age of the general store. It's an America I know and cherish, but it's not the America I was after this time.

The America I was looking for is a moving target, one traveling faster than the speed of reason. The *other* real America. For that one, I had to search the interstates and the suburbs and the shopping malls. I had to haunt the motels and the drive-throughs, the truck stops and the convenience stores. I had to go where the traffic took me.

But home holds on like Super Glue. Beth and I finally got away about 3:00 P.M. on April 29, a Tuesday. After mowing the lawn, paying bills, buying traveler's checks, and delivering a project I'd been working on for weeks, I threw a bunch of clothes and shoes into a big hang-up bag with millions of pockets on the outside and jammed it into the front luggage compartment of the Boxster. Folded up, it was thick as a giant's burrito. I tossed my Timberland boots on top of it loose for good measure. Beth had a bag about the same size, which I put in the rear luggage compartment. I carried my laptop (I was planning to write on the road, which shows how little I knew about what I was in for) in an old Land's End briefcase and piled my books and tape recorder and notebooks and files in a leather L. L. Bean bag. Both were stowed in the rear. On the way out of town, Beth and I stopped at Service Merchandise, where we bought a camcorder, audio and video cassettes, and a small surge protector. Finally, I had to swing by Alltel to get an adapter to my phone cord so it would fit into the Porsche cigarette lighter. So much for careful Lewis and Clark preparations.

We made it to Nashville the first night, and to Jacksonville, Florida, the second. The Porsche notched 1,000 miles on I-24 between Nashville and Chattanooga. In Nashville, the bellman (we landed in the midst of the Vanderbilt graduation ceremonies so could find only a $100 room in a fancy hotel) asked, "How you like your Boxster?" I swallowed and began to live the lie—I told him I liked it fine. He said he'd never seen one "in person" but had watched them being tested on the Gordon Liddy show. In Jacksonville, as we were leaving a restaurant after a late dinner, a very young woman in a very short dress that showed to fine advantage her impossibly long legs shouted at us as we passed: "Wow! I *want* that!" I waved with the insouciance that comes from two martinis and tried not to meet Beth's eye.

We rolled into Miami in early evening. Rolling into Miami is a process that takes an hour or so. Coming from the north on Interstate 95, you notice about forty or fifty miles out that the traffic is becoming feverish. The cars close in around you, and every one of them is speeding, rushing headlong toward the end of the earth. Just south of West Palm, a Lexus passed me like a streak. I was going 85 m.p.h. just to keep up with the cars around me. We had the top down, and Beth was screaming into the cell phone, trying to book us a hotel room. I decided to catch the Lexus and see how fast it was going. I backed off at 100 because the traffic was too thick. The Lexus was still pulling away.

Suddenly a man in the next lane was trying to get our attention. "What *is* it?" he shouted into the wind. He pointed at our car.

"Porsche!" I yelled back.

"Boxster?"

I nodded. "Wow!" he said, and gave me what by then I knew was the universal road symbol of high approval—the thumbs-up. I had learned that over the past two days. No one had ever given me the thumbs-up in my Plymouth van.

Then, as the man pulled away, he suddenly pointed to the front of my car. He shouted something, which I understood to be that either my hood or gas tank was open. I looked at the dash—no red lights. "Maybe I should pull over," I said.

"Don't," said Beth, who is more streetwise than I am. "This may be a carjacking." By then the man in the next lane had sped away—a little too fast, it seemed to us. I kept going, with just a glance in the rearview to see if there was anyone suspicious in that raging current of cars.

The traffic didn't slow much once we hit the city limits. Interstate 95 runs right through the city, with exits peeling off every half mile or so. People were cutting across lanes to catch their off-ramps. The left lane was supposed to be for car pools and buses only, but most cars in that lane were occupied by just one person. Maybe it was too late in the day, or maybe it was too late in the century. The traffic roared on like a flash flood, 85 m.p.h. being the approximate minimum speed.

We exited at the Julia Tuttle Causeway, 36th Street, slinging ourselves around the cloverleaf toward Biscayne Bay. It had been fifteen years since I'd seen that magical sight—the blue-green water, the swaying palms, the rich green gardens tumbling with color. Even in the evening light the buildings along Miami Beach were gleaming white. It all brought back that first time, thirty-nine years before, when I flew in low over this amazing place and saw a new reflection of myself.

Miami was born with the automobile. In February of 1896, the Duryea brothers from Springfield, Massachusetts sold the first gasoline-powered vehicle in the United States. A whole decade earlier, a German inventor named Karl Benz had combined a tricycle with an internal combustion engine, creating the first true automobile. In 1889 an article on Benz appeared in the magazine *Scientific American,* which was seen by the Duryeas. Frank Duryea was a bicycle maker, and he and his brother Charles set to work producing their own automobile. I found a picture of Charles in a magazine. He's sitting upright, looking like one of those guys on the Smith Brothers cough drop box, and the contraption he's riding in is essentially a buggy with a tiller where the reins would've been.

In the same winter that Charles and Frank Duryea were starting to manufacture their horseless carriage, another man with wanderlust and the means to indulge it was drawn to a small Indian settlement at the tip of Florida. The man was Henry Flagler, cofounder of Standard Oil and builder of railroads. In the early 1890s he had developed Palm Beach, an orange-scented mecca for the wealthy. But a killing frost in the winter of 1895 to 1896 had descended upon the paradise, freezing the orange trees. One of Flagler's men brought him a spray of lemon blossoms from groves ninety miles to the south, where the Calusa Indians lived by a river they called Mayama—Big Water. This place was below the frost line, so Flagler immediately extended his railroad and designed a city to meet it.

Sixty-two years later I got my first glimpse of the place. My father had taken a job in Florida, and the rest of my family had moved the previous fall. I had stayed with my aunt May in Hazlehurst to finish the semester of my eighth-grade year and come to terms with leaving my girlfriend. I thought back to that warm winter day as Beth and I drove into a heated Miami evening. I still remembered the way the Miami roads looked from the air then. Now we were on those streaks of blinding glare, and, like everything else over four decades, there were so many more of them. The streaks now crisscrossed and curlicued, split and came together and split yet again. I imagined seeing them from the air today and thought they must look like a ski run in the sunshine after the skiers had gone and their tracks were a glistening record of human movement, however random and purposeless.

Down here on the slopes, however, the skiers never seemed to go home anymore. There was something about the blinding streaks that compelled them to stay.

When I lived in Miami, we didn't use the 36th Street causeway much. That brought us too far down. South Beach was then a forgotten land inhabited by forgotten people. Now, of course, it's been reinvented as a playground for the world's trendsetters and their wannabes. We wanted to see it in all its Art Deco glory, so Beth found us a room at the Colony Hotel, in the midst of the madness.

It was 7:30 on a Thursday night when we finally arrived. I drove slowly along Ocean Drive, south to north. To our right was the

Atlantic Ocean; to our left was something just as timeless. The Deco hotels were lit like cruise ships, and along the strip of sidewalk in front of them was a jam of humanity right out of Dante. Crowded around tables the size of Frisbees, they posed in a pageant of pretension. Everyone watched to see if everyone was watching. Black-tied waiters served pastel drinks, while girls in bikinis and musclemen in Speedos Rollerbladed through the scene.

I missed the hotel the first time by, so I cruised past for a block or two. And at this point I *was* cruising. Cruising is different from driving. Driving is a mechanical act done for pure utility or for personal gratification, and sometimes for both at once. Cruising is show. All the road's a stage, and the cruiser is an actor giving a performance. In fact, I would guess that there are as many different kinds of cruisers as there are actors. I tend to be a method cruiser, one who recalls emotions and reactions from past experience and uses them to create a compelling cruising stance. For example, I love the scene in *Rebel Without a Cause* when James Dean and his nemesis are getting ready to do the chickie run toward the cliff. Dean—at least in my memory, and I don't want to be dissuaded—kind of hangs his hand *over* the steering wheel, as though preparing to drive with his wrist. That's not a good way to speed toward a precipice, but it's an excellent cruising stance. You can also do it with both hands (wrists), though that looks a little too much like teenagers slow dancing. I like to drape my right wrist over the wheel while positioning my elbow on the door. You have to shift your body slightly so that your right shoulder is raised and your cruising arm is straight. If your shoulder is too low and you have to drape your wrist at an angle, you risk coming off limp-wristed. With your arm straight and your hand hanging loosely over the wheel, you convey just the right devil-may-care attitude.

Before leaving Little Rock, I had pondered what kind of cap went best with the Boxster. I always need a cap because otherwise the sun sneaks in over my sunglasses and I can't see a thing. Besides, without one I'd burn my balding head. Usually I wear one of two caps—the one from Merrimack College, where my son David went to school, or the one from University of Maryland, where my son Matt goes. I had thought about buying one of those black Nikes, like Tiger Woods wears, but I never got around to getting one, and I was soon happy about that. All across the country, kids were suddenly wearing black Tiger Woods Nike caps. Such is the power of modern media mythology. In the end I just brought the two caps I always wear.

I don't remember which one I was wearing that night we first cruised South Beach, but it was working. Beth had on cat-eyed sunglasses and her black Gap cap with the movie director bill, and, besides my cap, I had on a black T-shirt and new Matsuda glasses and shades that made me look like I was from someplace besides Little Rock. I had my hand draped over the wheel and my elbow on the door, and surrounding us was the gleaming silver bullet with the Nevada manufacturer's license plate. All along the strip we could see the heads turn. Rollerbladers almost lost their balance.

Our theatrical entrance reminded me of a story I'd run across the winter before, during research in the automotive history section of the Detroit Public Library. There I read a yellowing account of the very first car driven on the streets of Detroit a hundred years ago. The name of that first Motown driver was Charles Brady King. The year, again, was 1896. The Duryeas out in Springfield were just the fastest of the scores of auto tinkerers working in machine shops across the country in those heady days. By 1895 there were enough such dreamers to support a trade journal, *Horseless Age*. According to the piece I read, that magazine's first issue reported seventy-three "known experimenters working on steam, gas, or electric autos." In Detroit, thirty-two-year-old Charlie King was one of them. He and a handful of cronies were putting the finishing touches on their own machine. King, an acknowledged "mechanical genius" who worked for a railroad-car company, had been determined to build an automobile since seeing his first one at the Chicago World's Fair in 1893. The actual site of King's creation—essentially the birthplace of the Detroit auto industry—was the machine shop of one John Lauer on lower St. Antoine Street. From the account I read, there was much secrecy about the mysterious comings and goings behind Lauer's garage doors.

And then, finally about 11:00 P.M. on March 6, 1896, everything was ready. That's what touched something visceral in me about King's story—the fact that he couldn't wait, that he had to get on the road the very first moment he was able. When he did, people poured out of their homes to see him. He drove through downtown Detroit that night—down St. Antoine to Jefferson Avenue, then west to Woodward and north to Cadillac Square. There his horseless carriage experienced engine trouble, and King delighted onlookers by hopping out and sliding under the thing and tweaking it back into business. The next day's newspaper reported that the sighting of this first car on the city's streets "caused a deal of comment, people crowding around it so that its progress was impeded. The apparatus seemed to work all right and it went at the rate of five or six miles an hour at an even rate of speed."

Just like Beth and me in South Beach.

We pulled up to the Colony, and several people came running to help. That's when the smiling valet manager told me the fee was $14 a day for parking, for three days. I winced and peeled off a $100 bill just like a Porsche owner.

I had come to Miami this time with questions. I wanted to talk with old friends about those days when the roads were new, at least to us, and whether they had meant the same to them as they had to me. I also wondered if a guy I'll call Jack was still alive. I didn't see how he could be, the way he had taken to the roads in those early days. He was a year older, and I hadn't known him well, but he'd been part of a wider group I'd run with. Even in junior high he'd driven a motorcycle, and I remember him whizzing by with his thin blond hair flying back like Isadora Duncan's scarf.

I hadn't been with Jack often, and never just the two of us, but whenever I had, the roads became extremely dangerous. The night I remember best involved two cars careening in tandem down Biscayne Boulevard at 50 or 60 miles an hour. I was probably in the eleventh grade. Everyone in our car and the one beside it was drinking, and as the other car, a convertible, pulled ever closer to ours, one boy— Jack—stood up wobbly in the backseat of the convertible and stepped over the rushing blur of pavement through the open rear window of our car. I was sitting by that window, and Jack thrust his right leg across my face and then stepped away from the convertible with his left leg and somehow clung to the top of the car while he pretzeled his body to fit both legs through the window. He then slid into the car, into the safe laps of the three of us in the backseat, and he was giggling like the madman he most surely was.

I suppose Jack's mania could be explained in a thousand ways, but what I recall is how he seemed drawn beyond reason to the road. The road made him crazy, or so it appeared to me.

On our first full day in Miami, I took Beth across the causeway to Miami Shores, the little community where I had spent such a pivotal time in my life. As we drove through the manicured boulevards, I remembered the note a friend from those days, whose name is Carla, wrote to wish me a happy fifty-second birthday. It must have been as disturbing a note to write as it was to receive. Our birthdays are six days apart; we've known each other since we both were thirteen. In her note, she mentions Miami Shores, the "village" we lived in, as having been "in so many ways like a small town."

But Miami changed. Miami didn't stay as sweet as it was, to paraphrase the rose-colored yearbook inscriptions we all wrote to one another back then. Though Miami Shores still looks surprisingly clean and lush, I couldn't help noticing the barricades. When I lived there the blazing roads were an endless crisscross grid, open from one end of the village to the other. Now the cross streets are closed off, blocked at one end by decorative barriers of tropical foliage that disguise their true mission. "All the Haitians in North Miami were coming down to the Shores and burglarizing houses," a cab driver named John told Beth and me on a night we'd left the Porsche behind and taken a taxi to dinner. John lives in Miami Shores, and he said the police hit on the idea of barricading the streets so on any residential block there's only one way in and one way out. Because of mobile crime, Miami Shores is now essentially a gated community, with 96th Street the only east-west thoroughfare open from one end of the village to the other. Other communities in Greater Miami are picking up on the same idea.

I drove up to 103rd Street to show Beth my old house. It was a very strange house, at least to someone who'd spent his life in Mississippi. I remember the day I landed. My parents met me at the airport in our baby-blue 1955 Ford. When we turned into the driveway of my new home, I didn't know whether to laugh or cry. My brother, Phil, and I called the place The Alamo. It was a small white stucco house with a flat roof surrounded by a notched parapet, which looked like a row of bottom teeth with every other tooth missing. The house had belonged to an opera singer, and Dad had bought the place with all her possessions in it. Nearly forty years later, Mother told me that the woman had died in the house and no one had found her for several days. When they did, her dogs had gotten to her. To my father's credit, he didn't know this when he bought the house. Mother learned the story ten years later when a neighbor's daughter blurted out, "Oooo, I don't know *how* you can live in that house." The girl's mother quickly dispatched her from the room, but the deed was done.

I told Beth to get ready, that we were almost there—and then I drove right past it. The house looked very different from the way it had when we'd lived there. We had a double lot, so the yard was huge. But 103rd Street had been widened since I'd been back, and several feet of the lawn I used to mow was now a thoroughfare. Also, the people living there now have created a forest of tropical plants obscuring the house itself. Only the curved driveway seemed familiar. Dad and I had built it ourselves, though it was gravel then and is paved now.

There was a time when that driveway was my open road. After I got my learner's permit but before I was a licensed driver, I would often ask my father for his keys after supper, and if it suited his mood I would go out to the driveway and slip into the driver's seat of the blue Ford. In the days before padded steering wheels, the grip was thin and hard. Holding in the "ten" position with my left hand (though my dad had taught me that "eight" and "two" gives more turning flexibility), I would reach over with my right and insert the key into the ignition. With my left foot hard on the clutch and my right foot heel down and poised over the accelerator, I would turn the key and press on the gas. The power was instant, and addicting. For the next hour or so I would back the car as far as possible, then pull it forward, then back, then forward, all the while dreaming of the day I could actually drive on the street.

When that moment came, it was life-changing, like having sex for the first time. Much more than the simple act itself, it's a passage. We're transformed by it, even if people can't read the change on the outside. On the afternoon I passed my driver's test, I drove my father back to our house and let him out of the car. Then I backed the blue Ford out of the driveway and onto 103rd Street, my left arm straight and wheeling clockwise as I aimed the back of the car squarely into the lane. At the apex of the arc I braked and clutched, shifting into first, then second. Half a block away, stopped at the light at 103rd and Miami Avenue, I searched the faces of the motorists who came toward me, the pedestrians who walked in front of me, the mirrored reflection of the driver at my rear. Nobody seemed to notice a thing. And yet I was no longer the boy I had been just minutes before. I was driving to my girlfriend's house, and I would never be that boy again.

Being on the road is by definition a transitory experience, a float through space and time. Leaving one locale bound for another, we're in a sense suspended from the world. And yet that time in the car may be the most *real* part of any given day. For us, the beauty of a road trip is the travel that takes place inside ourselves. It doesn't even require a long trip—the drive to and from work can be enough. Freed from the chain of snarling families and mounting bills and overflowing in-boxes and back-stabbing colleagues, we narrow our panorama of worry to the road ahead. Watching it, we can drift to a place where we're finally the person we might have been, could be, maybe still will become if things work out right. We can hold this image for minutes or days, as long as we don't have to stop the car.

I suspect you can't truly be On The Road like that if you're traveling with anyone else.

On the afternoon of our first day in Miami, I said something to Beth that brought our reality down on us like a meteor. I'm not going to tell you what I said—even if I did, you wouldn't understand it without my writing a chapter of background. All husbands and wives have their smoldering issues, and I just opened my mouth and breathed lighter fluid on one of ours.

I had received some good business news that day, and I was happy to be showing Beth Miami. We were sitting by the water in Key Biscayne having a rum drink and admiring the beautiful, sexy Boxster in the lot just yards away. Maybe I started thinking I was somebody else. Suddenly the words slipped out, mean and cruel. I saw them take physical form and connect with her jugular. By then, I couldn't do anything to change what had just occurred.

We discussed it for a few minutes, and then silence settled over us. "I can't trust you," she had said to me, and she meant emotionally. I paid our check and we left, driving back across the blue-green water to our darkening hotel room above the crowd.

That night we took the cab ride to the Delano, the hotel now owned by Ian Schrager. I watched us step out on the glamorous avenue, and the image took me to a time long past when a carful of boys cruised the Beach looking for just such a well-dressed and stylish couple. The night that lingers was a New Year's Eve, late fifties or early sixties, at a hotel just up Collins. The unsuspecting couple alighted from a limo, she in a glittering white gown and he in a crisp tuxedo. They were laughing. Suddenly, as in a movie, the scene turned to slow motion. They were touching, she reaching for his arm, when the egg looped into the frame from above. It was a direct hit, perhaps on his shoulder, exploding soft yellow shrapnel over both of them. It had been one of those shameful moments I carried deep inside into manhood.

Then one night in Chicago two decades later, I was on my way to meet my wife at a restaurant, driving in my creamy Fiat Spider on a top-down night in late October. The movie didn't look the same from that side—because there was no expectation, there was no slow motion. The egg slammed into my forehead, splattering all over me, my clothes, the upholstery, the dash. I almost lost control of the car but managed to guide it to the curb. When I realized what had happened, I sat there laughing. If the drive-by eggers were watching, they must have been baffled. I laughed and laughed, at long last relieved of the guilt, and I wheeled the car around and went home to change.

At the Delano we sat on one side of a huge round table and watched the people. The Delano is like a dream. Thin curtains rustle in the ocean breeze. Tall, tan young men with glistening hair drift to and fro as though on moving sidewalks. Tawny waitresses in hip-huggers dip to reveal a fetching edge of pelvic bone. Trying to make up for the afternoon's transgression, I ordered a bottle of champagne—$99. I put it on Visa. The Porsche was doing something to my brain.

While sipping that champagne and watching the beautiful people, I began to consider the connection between shoes and cars. Miami is a sexy town. It was sexy even back in the 1950s, but it's become more sophisticatedly so in the ensuing years. I suspect that's due to the increased Latin influence. At the Delano, I spied a mocha-colored young woman with a profile straight from a Roman frieze. Her hair was short and dark with echoes of sunshine, and it was parted on one side. Sometimes when she stood in front of a lamp, the highlights on her hair made a nimbus. Her nose was strong and elegant, her eyes dark and moist, her lips full and painted bright red. She wore a black see-through blouse and black slacks, but what I couldn't take my eyes off were her feet. They were beautiful, with toenails to match her lips. She wore strappy black high-heeled sandals of the sort that gives bondage a good name.

I started studying the shoes of the other women, and even of the men. They were sleek, sultry, made more to be seen than walked in. They were cruising shoes. Mostly Italian, I guessed, like the Ferraris and Lamborghinis that slunk along Ocean Drive before the admiring eyes of the masses. I was reminded of something someone had said the night before. We'd been at the China Grill for drinks, and a handsome black man sitting on the other side of Beth at the bar began talking to us. When he heard what I was doing, traveling across the country in a Porsche, he said that what he loved were fancy *Italian* cars. "I may not be able to afford them," he said, "but I can wear Ferragamo shoes." He held out his foot to show us a shapely loafer.

I wasn't surprised. Miami is a place where style reigns—always has and always will. No wonder Gianni Versace made it his home away from home. Style is style whether you're talking clothes or shoes or cars. At some level, it's all the same.

The shoes I most loved in the late fifties were two-toned black-and-white loafers with a jelly-roll strap. I remember a neighbor's new Plymouth, which had almost exactly the same look. When I moved to Miami a dozen years after World War II, the country was bursting with wild style and fashion. Miami was "America's playground," and after the selfless years of Depression and war, there must have been a bone-deep feeling that we were due a little play time. It was a wonderfully excessive era, and I feel fortunate to have experienced it in a place that took such pleasure in celebrating excess. My mother, a second-grade teacher in Miami Shores, taught the daughter of Zorita the Snake Woman. Zorita was a legend in Miami exotic-dance circles. I went to school with Cricket Shapiro, daughter of the man who played piano for Sophie Tucker. My friend Richard's girlfriend—a senior at our high school—was a June Taylor dancer on "The Jackie Gleason Show." This was not a culture that valued sensible cars.

During Miami's heyday tourist seasons in the 1950s, Frank or Dean or Sammy or Tony would always be playing the Beach hotels. My friends and I shook hands with Tennessee Williams during intermission at a Harry Belafonte concert at the Fountainbleu. Outside in the gauzy night, black limos would be lined up like dominoes along Collins Avenue, while flashy roadsters zipped nimbly in and out of traffic. The Beach was a parade, and expensive cars were always prominent among the attractions. The 1950s also happened to be the heyday of the automobile industry. To a boy discovering Miami and life at the same time, it was as though American cars and that shiny city had been made from the same mold. A silver gullwing Mercedes 300 SL forever parked on the 79th Street causeway echoed the drawbridges that lifted to let tall masts pass. A Chrysler New Yorker (with continental kit) on North Beach was the exact pink of the plastic flamingo in the manicured yard. The air-slicing fins on a green Bal Harbor Caddy were as sharp as palmetto fronds.

I have a 1956 copy of *Printer's Ink,* an advertising trade journal, in which appears an article about cars called "Ad Theme for '57 Autos: MORE." That word could have been the theme for the decade itself. People didn't want to hear about practicality or prudence. "Safety as an advertising theme will not be emphasized in '57 as it was in '56," says the *Printer's Ink* piece. "Ford Motor Co. lost $800,000 in promoting the use of seat belts and crash padding on its 1956 models. . . ."

The man who translated the mood of the times into automobiles was one Harley Earl. Beginning with the 1927 LaSalle, which bore his stamp from gear shift to grille, Earl revolutionized auto design. Not so coincidentally, he hailed from Hollywood. His father had been a wagon builder in Michigan but had migrated to California to make coaches for the movies. Young Harley worked with his dad, building chariots and stagecoaches for Hollywood spectacles, and also designing and building splashy automobiles for movie stars. Harley understood very early that cars weren't just to get you from here to there. Before he was lured to Detroit to work for General Motors, he even lived next door to Cecil B. DeMille. He was the first to see that Detroit's product was as evocative of the American dream as was Hollywood's, and he created cars the way his former neighbor created movies. "Now, guys," one of his men recalled Earl telling the designers of the 1958 Buick, "I want you to do a sweep sphere, and I want you to do some hoop scoops, bubble bombs, Dagmars, portholes, and rockers, and chrome wheels. . . ."

I don't know what hoop scoops, bubble bombs, and rockers are, but I do know about Dagmars. That was the name of a blond bombshell of the era who was known for her enormous breasts. They were quintessential late-1950s breasts, breasts of a shape and firmness best captured by the term "knockers." By ordering Dagmars, Earl, I assume, was talking about those cone-shaped protrusions on the front bumpers of most of the GM cars of the era.

I looked up the 1958 Buick in my *Encyclopedia of American Cars*. The one pictured is a convertible, with a young woman who appears to be a beauty queen perched high in the backseat. Even by 1950s Miami standards, the car is over the top. "Sales were far worse for 1958, notable for the gaudiest Buicks ever," reads the accompanying copy. "From contrived chrome-draped fins to a monster grille holding 160 shiny little squares, Flint's 'B-58' models looked overly ornate. . . ."

A professor I know, David Gartman of the University of South Alabama, believes that 1958 was the year *more* finally became not enough. It wasn't just the year of the gaudy Buick; it was the year of the Edsel. It was also the year after the Soviet orbiter Sputnik launched a national wail of second-guessing in America—and a search for someone to blame. A late-fifties article on cars and culture in *Fortune* magazine says, "The words 'tail fin' came to stand as a symbol for whatever any critic considered materialistic, tasteless, or misguided in American life." Detroit, says Gartman, was trying so hard to be different each year that car buyers began to see through the Harley Earls of the world. Earl, by the way, is generally credited with creating the concept of planned obsolescence. You had to sell something fresh and innovative every year so the guy who still owned last year's model would feel like he wasn't keeping up. "People, in cars just like in Broadway shows, want to see something new and exciting," Earl said. For thirty years, he gave it to them.

Looking back, I'm amazed that for a moment it even seemed to work with my father, who one day brought home that used 1958 Ford, red and white, with its outrageously tacky strip of gold anodized aluminum side trim separating the red from the white. My mother was out of town, and in retrospect I wonder if that wasn't part of the chemistry of the gesture. Dad was beaming when I came out to see the "new" car. My initial response, which I tried to keep to myself but may have betrayed by my demeanor, was that this was possibly (I wasn't sure) an uncool car trying to be cool, and that it was totally antithetical to any value I'd ever known my dad to hold dear. I wonder now if he wasn't reaching out to me by buying this car. We'd had our conflicts, and I felt he thought I was a frivolous kid who would rather spend Saturday mornings lying on the beach than working in the yard with him. Of course, he was right. Cars can be a strong bond between fathers and sons—at least they often were back then. My friend Olin's dad bought him a 1932 Pontiac with a rumble seat. My friend Teddy's dad bought him a candy-apple red 1956 Chevy. My friend Danny's dad, a man named Mort whom we referred to as "Sporty Morty," drove a constantly changing array of fine automobiles, including Ferraris, Jaguars, Aston-Martins, and Lotuses.

I like to think now that my dad knew I was embarrassed by the old blue stripped-down Ford, and did what he could to fix it. I wish I had loved that red-and-white car more.

Beth was to fly home at 6:45 A.M., Sunday. I would then be on my own, on the road.

I was a little uneasy about my feelings about that. I loved being in Miami with her, but I also felt the real trip hadn't started yet. I was getting restless. The familiarity of Collins Avenue began to make me feel like I was marking time. Cruising needs to be a short-term activity. Stretch it out too much and you have to face the fact that you're headed nowhere.

On Saturday afternoon, we went to the Taste of the Beach on the Lincoln Road Mall. Most of the restaurants on South Beach pitched tented booths and served up spicy shrimp, Cuban sandwiches, crab fritters, black beans with pork and onions, and plenty of rum and cold beer. It's a testament to the vitality of the city that the Taste brought out both the old and the new Miami Beach. Among the whizzing, half-naked Rollerbladers, a little old Jewish man and his wife doddered along from booth to booth, picking at the food in that we-expect-to-be-disappointed way of the yearly snowbirds. The man, about five foot five, wore tan slacks and matching loafers, and a sleeveless tan crocheted sweater topped with a tan cap. He had obviously seen it all. He hardly noticed when one prissy young man called out to a passing Rollerblader: "Ricardo! I'll kiss your tootsies!"

At the Taste we met a man named Dano, who worked as a waiter at Pacific Time restaurant. Beth had found several people to tell me stories about cars, and one of them had pointed us in the direction of Dano. He was represented to be a bona fide "car nut," though that turned out to be not entirely the case. He was a car *philosopher*. Dano, whose name is Daniel Howard, owns a 1963 Mercury Comet. That car seemed symbolic to him. It represented growth, maturity, a return to a kind of grounding. His father had a 1962 Ford Falcon when Dano was young, and if you know anything about cars you know that the Comet and the Falcon shared the same body style. Dano had progressed through the wheel cycle, from skateboards to bikes to motorcycles to cars, and had discovered that he liked to drive very fast. He was partial to Alfa Romeos and Thunderbirds, and almost killed himself in a T-Bird on an S-curve in mid-Beach. He swore off driving for a while, and when he went back to it he bought the old Comet. It felt right, like going home. We made a date for him to show me the car at the beginning of the week.

That night at dinner, Beth said she didn't want to leave with this thing hanging over us. She was hurt by what I'd said, but she was trying to forgive me and let it go. We had a nightcap at the News Cafe and then went to bed. At 5:30 in the morning, I carried her bags down and handed them to the cab driver. We kissed, and she was gone.

I woke up at nine o'clock feeling anxious. I wanted to get out of South Beach, out of its cloying trendiness. I wanted to get out of Miami, but I couldn't yet. I still needed to talk to Olin and Teddy, and other old friends if I could find them. I still needed to know if Jack was dead or alive.

I didn't know where I would stay that night, but my criteria were simple: less expensive and less active than the Colony. When the valet brought the Boxster, I headed up the Beach and decided to drive until someplace spoke to me. It happened just past Haulover Bridge, from which I once had jumped (sixty-five feet high) to impress a girl. The Ocean Palm Motel is north of Haulover Beach and Marina, on the Atlantic side. It looked friendly, old-fashioned. I liked the strip of blue neon waves dancing across the front.

I checked in, for a third of what the Colony had cost, and decided to take a walk on the beach. Beth and I hadn't even stuck our toes in the ocean. In my Miami days, Haulover had been one of our favorite beaches. My girlfriends and I had made out under its scrubby trees and in the parking lot across the street. I remembered one soft summer night sitting hidden in the lifeguard's stand while translucent waves washed in and sparkled all around us. I hadn't walked this beach in thirty-two years.

My first inkling of Haulover's change was a quick glimpse of a man's butt disappearing into the bushes. I wasn't sure I had seen it at all—but then he came back out, totally, frontally nude, carrying his towel over his shoulder. I looked around me. People were naked *every-where*. Over there was a guy wearing nothing but a gold chain. To his left was a grizzled old Cuban man with bongos that hung to mid-thigh. Together on a blanket were a young thin woman with small firm breasts and an older woman whose bosoms rested on her ample belly. Coming toward me were an older man and woman wearing matching caps. They could've been one of those couples you see in RVs with a sign on the back: "There go the Olsons!" Except they weren't wearing a stitch.

As soon as I could manage without looking startled, I headed back to the Ocean Palm to begin making my phone calls.

Dano met me on Monday near Lincoln Road. His Comet was parked around the corner. It was white, with a red dashboard and steering wheel, and the red-and-black upholstery was covered in a plastic bubble material bought at one of those places that sells plastic covering for furniture. It was a fine car, spotless, with what Dano proudly pointed out was an original Aloha surfboard rack on top.

We went for a drive, again up Collins Avenue. I mentioned that morning's TV traffic report, which had been full of ominous news: *I-95—Backed up. Highway 826—Slow. I-75—Jammed.* "I live two blocks from work," Dano said, "and I don't *ever* want a job where I have to get on I-95. I'm not living that way. I only need a car to get off the Beach occasionally; I only need a car for dates. I don't need a car to get to work. Fashion your life so it works."

As he talked, I gathered his life hadn't always been so fashioned. A car with a "Sick of It All" bumper sticker drove through an intersection ahead of us. "Get inspired, there's a lot around you," groused Dano, taking a corner. "Like everybody else, I hit some dead ends. And it came down to this: You do want to be here, or you don't want to be here. I decided being here ain't bad."

Someone had knocked off the Comet's antenna, so we couldn't listen to music. The car has only the original AM radio, and though Dano's friends tell him he ought to slide a CD player under the dash, he steadfastly refuses. "I *want* AM radio in here," he said: "That's what this car comes with. When I get in this car and shut the door, it's

1963." That was a good year, before he got out of control with cars. "I used to crash 'em and fix 'em and break 'em," he said. "I had an addiction, and it hurt my life. I was always pouring out money to fix my Alfas and pay speeding tickets. You know, if you have a certain amount of money and you put it all here, then you're watering one part of your life and that's growing, but everything else is shrinking. I realized you got to spread it around. You got to eat a healthy diet— your meat, your vegetables, your grains. I had to go back to before the Alfas, when my life was more balanced. This Comet is my car in recovery. I drive it slowly, like an old guy. The speed limit here says thirty-five, and I'm *going* thirty-five. Anybody who wants to argue with that can just go on by. I'm not sorry, and I ain't changing."

I thought of Dano that night as I sped south on I-95 to Olin's house. All around me, cars were zooming. I was doing 80, 85, even 90 at times. Why was everybody going so fast? As I caught my reflection in the rearview, I remembered something else Dano had said: "Too many people try to live up to their cars. They need to choose a car that's right for who they *are*."

When my family was in Miami, nobody I knew lived far south. Now Olin could have given me directions to his house by saying, "Turn north at Cuba." It was twenty-five miles from my motel. Olin's name is Olin McKenzie, and like his late father before him, he's a dentist. We met in the eighth grade, when the only important things in life were girls and getting our learner's permits. Since then, there have been marriages, divorces (mine), children, college, and the deaths of fathers. But over dinner at an Italian place, we returned to the basics. He told me about seeing another school friend of ours recently, and how whenever they get together they inevitably drift to the subject of cars.

"Of *course* it's about nostalgia," he said. "It's about getting older. It's about getting your feet back onto more predictable ground."

Speaking of which, what about Jack? "Oh," Olin said, completely without emotion, "he's dead. Got killed coming home from a car race. Must have been twenty years ago. Teddy had to identify the body." Even hearing it for the first time, I wasn't shocked. This wasn't news, it was confirmation. We all had known where Jack's road was heading.

Olin remembers more than I do. He reminded me about a boy we'd known who loved getting his hot Ford up to 50 miles an hour on rainy nights and seeing how many times he could spin it on Biscayne Boulevard. The same boy unbolted his stick shift from the column and switched it around to the left, so when he was street racing he could pull *down* from first to second instead of pushing up. He always got the edge in second gear. He went on to make millions on the American Stock Exchange.

"Today's kids don't care about cars that way," Olin said. "They *can't*." He told the story of his family's visit to another family's lake house in upstate New York. "When we landed, I saw a sign about this big hot-rod show. I told my sons and their friends about it, but nobody wanted to go except my older boy. There were ninety-two hundred pre-fifties hot rods there. At the motel, instead of the backs of Lexuses, you saw these gorgeous old cars. It was an art show—functional art."

But most of the people at those art shows are our age, drawn inexorably to a time of "character cars," as Olin calls them, when they could tell one car from another. When folks could pop the hood and understand what they were seeing. There was even *daylight* shining through around the engine—the ground was clearly visible. That was both a fact and a symbol. Of course many of the people who go to those shows searching for the good old days are also the ones who now overprotect their children. It's part of the culture of fear we've all come to live in. They'd feel like bad parents letting their teens drive off in older, fixed-up cars like the ones *they* drove. Instead they hand over keys to safe, solid, dual-airbag machines, preferably leased so the car is always new and presumably reliable. You can't be too careful in these uncertain times. Under the hoods, the mechanisms are undecipherable. No wonder today's kids put more stock in hot stereos than hot engines—it's something they can understand.

This doesn't mean that the coming generation won't care about automobiles. "We live just blocks from school," Olin said, "and yet our kids, and most others we know, were driven to school every day. Our sons grew up in the Adam Walsh years—the little boy who was kidnapped and murdered. For that and other reasons, they've been driven around all their lives. They're more addicted to cars than we were. It's just that the joy is gone."

Teddy Neuweiler goes by Ted now, as befits his silver hair. He survived his fast-car and fast-boat days to become a manufacturer's representative like his father, before the discount giants made such people extinct. Now Ted has his own marketing firm.

Nobody I ever knew loved cars as sunnily as Teddy did. Others were drawn to the darker sides of the machine—the life-threatening speed, the salacious thrust, the portentous rumble. Teddy seemed to laugh at life, and his candy-apple red '56 Chevy was part of his laughter. He liked all of the above, the speed, the sexiness, the sound. But somehow with him it was upbeat and positive.

Teddy and I were friends, but there was always a distance between us that wasn't present in my other friendships. Teddy taught me what little bit I know about driving. There were no formal lessons, just things he would say: *Accelerate into a curve. Let off the gas when you're in a spin.* When my dad brought home that red-and-white '58 Ford, I drove it first to Teddy's house. His driveway was a mecca for car guys. Good boys and bad boys alike would pull up there, brought together by something more elemental than parents' income or address or social station. Car hoods were always open, and metal chests of ratchet wrenches littered the pavement. Radios played Buddy Holly and The Coasters. I remember a guy who used to hang around, an older boy I knew only from Teddy's driveway. He drove a chalky-gray primered car, maybe a Mercury, and he always had a skinny necktie draped over his rearview mirror. He claimed to be James Dean's half brother.

I doubt that Teddy thought my red-and-white Ford was a hot car, but because it was new to the group, we had to race. The Friday-night drags were held on a lonely stretch of U.S. 1 north of the city, on the way to Hallandale. A quarter mile was measured off, and cars parked with their headlights on to mark the start and finish. Someone took off his shirt and waved it as a starting flag. I never knew how to race. I never felt the urge. But I do remember my adrenaline surging as I glanced over at Teddy at the starting line. He was grinning at me and revving his engine like it was his own heart pumping. My car was automatic, so I revved it in neutral. When the start was called, I dropped into gear and got off the line, but Teddy's Chevy was squealing and fishtailing and already becoming a pair of red embers in the night. My car didn't sound hot, like other cars did. When I accelerated, my engine emitted a wheezy sucking sound, like a man with emphysema.

Having run my race, though, I was able to enjoy the rest of the night. I stood around wisecracking on the sidelines, smoking Marlboros—Donkeys, we called them, because of the "boro"—and looking over T-shirted shoulders at gleaming carburetors I didn't try to fathom. Unlike the others, I didn't care about carburetors and engines in and of themselves. But I cared deeply about the nights they brought—dangerous pounding nights like this one, as well as quieter nights parked with girls at 105th Street, overlooking the bay. When I drove to meet Ted for breakfast on my last morning in Miami, I noticed that everybody's favorite make-out spot had long since been turned into condominiums.

By the time Ted and I connected at a cafe on Biscayne Boulevard, I was itching to leave Miami. He'd been out of town, so I'd delayed my departure an extra day. My Porsche was packed and ready. Over coffee and bagels we talked about the cars and the nights and the kids we were then. Then I asked him to tell me about Jack.

"He wasn't driving," Ted said. "He owned a race car that he would run on weekends. On this particular weekend, he and his crew had been to Atlanta. Jack had a wholesale distribution business and he was trying to get back in time to open on Monday morning. Jack was asleep in the backseat, and one of the other guys was driving. On the turnpike around West Palm there's a jog in the road, and there used to be trees dead ahead. The driver must have fallen asleep at the wheel. He went straight and slammed into the trees. Of course, the race car they were towing smashed into the back of the car they were in. Everybody was killed."

After breakfast I showed Ted the Porsche. There was a time when he would have been wild about it, climbing in and starting it up and listening to its roar. Not now. He still laughs, and he says he still likes to drive fast, but I can't help reading an underlying seriousness. Something about his eyes behind his glasses. Maybe I'm seeing myself in them. Like all of us, Ted has a wife and kids and business pressures. Like all of us, he's found the real race tougher than a quick quarter mile on Friday night. "I spend most of my time in airplanes now," he said.

Ted spread my map across the Porsche's hood and pointed out the road we all used to take through the center of the state, before the turnpikes. Then we shook hands and said so long. I watched as he walked back to his sedan.

TWO

Fatal Attractions

There is a time for departure," wrote Tennessee Williams, "even when there's no certain place to go." I had no idea where I would spend the night, and I loved that feeling. Back in Little Rock, I'd told a friend my plan was to drive to the end of every day and see what happened. Now I was finally about to do that. The TV weatherman this morning had predicted "another beautiful day in Miami." He was dead-on, of course, and it was making me crazy. I had enjoyed seeing the city again, but I remembered anew why I couldn't possibly live there. Palm fronds never change colors. The present would always be perfect, and insufferable in its perfection. The past would soon fade into oblivion, taking with it a certain richness of life. Memory requires benchmarks.

The Boxster wraps around you like a pact. The interior of my silver bullet had gray leather seats that curved to my back. Behind them rose a mesh-covered roll bar. The dash was black, and the instrument panel featured an old-fashioned round analog tachometer that slightly eclipsed two flanking smaller moons showing speed and fuel status. There wasn't much cockpit storage space: a small compartment between the seats, a zippered slip behind, a cubbyhole for glasses or cell phone beneath the radio. On the doors under the armrests were covered scoops where I kept maps, cassettes, and suntan oil. The interior of the car had a distinctive scent—leather, yes, but somehow more than that. "Ah," said my neighbor John when he stuck his head in for the first time. He inhaled deeply, like a man getting high. "It's the *Porsche smell*."

The black canvas top rose or dropped at the click of a latch and the press of a button. The Porsche had to be in park, with the emergency brake on, before the top would go up or down. Whenever I started to lower it, the windows automatically dropped slightly to keep the top from catching. That happened too when I unlocked the car, so the window wouldn't snag the top when I opened the door.

When the Porsche people described the car's transmission, I was worried that using it would be tricky. They said it was both automatic and manual; I couldn't imagine that. Just glancing at the floor shift, I didn't notice anything unusual. It looked like a normal automatic transmission—except that in drive you could jog the shift lever over to the letter "M." That took the transmission from automatic to manual—but where was the clutch? There *wasn't* one. You shifted with your thumbs by pressing buttons on the steering wheel. This "Tiptronic" transmission, Porsche told me, was technology adapted from race cars.

On the interstates and in city traffic, I had kept the Boxster in automatic. It was easier. Now I was aimed for open spaces. Ted had advised me to head up I-95 to West Palm and then cut left onto 710 to Lake Okeechobee, a distance of about a hundred miles. I'd said I wanted to revisit the little roads for this first leg of the trip. I remembered my family traveling to and from Mississippi on U.S. 27 before the interstates were completed. My friends and I also went to the Sebring races that way. I wanted to go to Sebring today, too. I wanted to see that little highway one more time.

"It's not there," Ted had told me. He meant it wasn't little anymore. It was four lanes now, a swollen channel pumping inflated heartland traffic into larger arteries such as I-4 and I-75. The road I recalled was a thin hot slash in the flat Florida midsection. I didn't remember specifics necessarily, but essences: advertisements for alligator wrestling, signs to a Passion Play, snake farms, Key lime–pie places, a speed trap called Leesburg where my father always got a ticket. I also remembered a game our family played on car trips in those days. Mother or Dad would say, "Brothers and sisters I have none. But this man's father is my father's son. Who is it?" Sorting out the connections drove us crazy and passed the time. Somewhere along that route I once took a wrong turn and drove my mother and brother into an orange grove. Mother was furious with me, but my brother, Phil, and I sat there amid the trees, laughing till we cried.

The *joy,* Olin had said. *The joy is gone.* I thought about that as I raced the I-95 traffic toward my turn into the heart of Florida. *My* joy was suddenly palpable, though it was laced, I noticed, with a curious low-level uneasiness. The top was down, the sun was hot, the sky was blue, and I was speeding alone in a beautiful automobile. Nobody in the other cars knew me, so I became the man they saw. I adjusted the seat so that my arms were straight as I gripped the steering wheel. I seemed to recall—another subterranean lesson from Teddy, perhaps?—that race drivers held the wheel that way, no crook in the arm, the better to control the car with split-second accuracy. The traffic hurtled north at the standard 85 m.p.h., and I settled into the pace. I've been in some cars that felt reckless at that speed, as though they might vibrate loose and fall apart, but the Boxster was just cruising, its whine strong, not stretched. I slowly bent my big toe inside my sneaker and instantly felt the car respond—87, 90, 92. Then just as quickly I let off the gas and dropped back into the crowd.

I've never been a fast driver. Once, on a country straightaway, I pushed my first Fiat Spider up to 105 before my fear got the better of me. That was fast for that car, but this Boxster was another story. Maybe that was the source of my anxiety, I decided. We so seldom experience unrestrained freedom that it scares us, and with good reason. Most of us are reared to fear the dangers of immoderation. We know in our hearts that there's a reason God invented gravity.

But in spite of my butterflies, on that May day I also felt the soaring thrill of independence. It was my first day on the road alone, and the whole country lay before me, from sea to shining sea. This must have been the way travel felt in the 1950s, I thought. The American road trip takes on the tone of its purpose, and in the mid-fifties that purpose was freedom, celebration, expectation, adventure. "See the U.S.A. In your Chevrolet!" sang perky Dinah Shore. "America is asking you to call." There was joy in the journey then, a going-toward instead of a running-from.

I have a vague image in my head: My father and I are standing outside an automobile showroom as the first bite of fall nips the air. It is early evening; the showroom is closed. But the lights inside are on, and in the center of the room, a new car sparkles like a jewel in a case. We stand silently outside. For a minute my nose is pressed to the glass. We say nothing, each of us lost in hopes, dreams, perhaps regrets.

For a quarter century after World War II, the joy my friend Olin remembered was institutionalized in a yearly event called the Announcement. Like baseball, cars had their own season then. Every fall, amid great hoopla and orchestrated secrecy, the new cars for the following year would be unveiled—sometimes literally. For days before Announcement Day, the cars might be in showrooms but covered, like sculptures about to be revealed. Young boys and their fathers, and even whole families, would make the rounds of the showrooms. They would wonder what surprises waited under the cloths. They would speculate about more streamlined taillights, a cool scoop on the side, maybe twin strips of chrome running down the hood like the open road itself. Everyone knew cars then. We knew the differences between them. Catching only a glimpse of colored steel disappearing around a corner, we could name that car as easily as we could name the current tune from its first four notes.

In the earliest of those joyful days, a handsome, square-jawed young World War II veteran, a Navy fighter pilot named Thomas Adams, landed a job with an advertising agency in Detroit. The agency was called Campbell-Ewald, and among its accounts were several products for General Motors. Though he didn't know it then, Tom Adams would stay with Campbell-Ewald forty years, eventually becoming its president and, finally, its chairman. Adams was assigned to the Chevrolet account, which was, even before television, a $1.4 million piece of business for Campbell-Ewald. By the early to mid-1950s, as people like my parents splurged for TV sets, the Chevrolet account had become the top advertising account in the world. The packaging of Chevy was tantamount to the packaging of America, and that was obviously a very rewarding experience for Adams. Today he splits his time between Detroit and California. "You're a lucky man," I told him the first time we spoke by phone.

"I know that," he said.

Some of Adams's fondest memories involve Announcement time. "We had about fourteen dealer groups in the big cities back then," he says. "Chevrolet found out that the dealers were willing to spend some of their own money putting together glitzy advertisements, and so we would have two or three million dollars in extra advertising that the division wouldn't have to pay for. A very active group was the Chicago Chevrolet dealers. They were aggressive and loud and tough, and they would have such things as a city-wide drawing. If you came into the dealership during the first five days of the Announcement period, they would put your name in a barrel and you'd have a chance to win a new car. They had lots of affairs at the dealerships—special nights for special viewers, such as their truck customers. They would have everything short of hard liquor and peanut butter sandwiches. I think they should still do something like that. Today the cars just sort of drift out."

From 1947 to 1960, William G. Power was the advertising manager for Chevy. In the automotive section of the Detroit Public Library, I ran across a photo of him, a sturdy confident man in a double-breasted suit, a white handkerchief jutting jauntily from his coat pocket. In the picture he displays a strong chin, sparkling eyes, winning smile. He looks like an Army general, or a baseball manager. In the file on Power was a typed sheet of paper with the heading: COPY FROM CARDS USED IN BILL POWER SPEECHES. Here's a sampling:

PROSPERITY GROWS ON SALESMEN'S ORDER BOOKS

LET'S GO AMERICA

SALES PRODUCTION JOBS PROSPERITY

WHEN YOU CAN'T MAKE A SALE—MAKE A FRIEND

PEP WITHOUT PURPOSE—PIFFLE

HOW HIGH IS YOUR CEILING

$^2/_3$ OF PRO-MOTION IS MOTION

GO FORWARD TO THE GOOD NEW DAYS

I've been in the business world. I've heard salesmen speak. I know that a certain invincible optimism is a necessary part of a successful salesman's makeup. But if you read between Bill Powers's lines, you can sense an America still receptive to that optimism—still cheering, still celebrating, still working from the lighter palette.

Adams and Powers and their counterparts at the other car companies promoted automobiles through glamor and excitement and family. In Detroit, I found pictures of Roy Rogers in a 1947 Cadillac, Rita Hayworth and her '47 Lincoln, Art Linkletter and a '48 Studebaker, Jane Wyman in a '50 Mercury, the Duke and Duchess of Windsor in a '50 Buick Super Model 59 Estate Wagon, Gene Autry in a '52 Caddy Sixty Special, Lawrence Welk and His Orchestra in a '59 Dodge Custom Royal convertible. The car ads themselves packed positive images of a country having fun together. "Pride of the Family Reunion" was the headline of a Chevy ad from 1950. It showed a Chevrolet pulling up into a yard full of aunts and uncles and cousins. Another ad showed a Chevy family approaching the ski slopes, with a sleigh in the background. The copy sang a veritable song of holiday happiness.

> Chevrolet, Chevrolet,
> Smarter all the way;
> Oh, what fun it is to ride
> In a brand-new Chevrolet!

But as early as 1956, a new message had crept into the mix: "More people named Jones* own Chevrolets than any other car." The tagline at the bottom inserted the shiv: "(*Are you keeping up with the Joneses?)."

I wonder if this was my father's thought as we stood, my breath fogging the dealership's window, outside the sparkling American theater of dreams.

Lost in thought, I missed my turnoff from I-95, so I picked up Highway 706 and jogged over to catch 710 a few miles away. Almost immediately I was stuck in traffic. The speed limit was 55, and I had approached the last car doing 75. Now we all were lumbering along at 40. The culprit was an eighteen-wheeler rumbling toward some discount chain in the heart of nowhere.

Right away I wished I had washed my windshield before getting off the interstate. I had forgotten about the love bugs, which became a Florida nuisance sometime in the mid-1960s. You don't see them much north of, say, Tallahassee, and on the coasts the Gulf and ocean breezes make their aerial copulation too hit-or-miss for evolutionary purposes. The center of Florida is perfect for them, however. Flat, wet, hot, and still, it allows them to breed and hatch and grow until, each May and June, the vast tropical sky becomes a black cloud of sex-crazed insects. It's only later, when you stop the car, that you can tell what they are—two black bugs in a coital lock. They crawl as one, they fly as one, and whenever an automobile zooms along a strip of central Florida highway, they die as one.

I pulled over and put up the top. In a car, you experience love bugs first as a rat-a-tat of tiny explosions against the windshield. Then, squinting for better vision, you see them coming toward you ten or fifteen yards away, like tracers in the negative of a night skirmish. There's no way to duck them, drive around them, avoid them. They are everywhere. I thought of Lewis and Clark's men trying to repel mosquitoes with a mixture of tallow and hog's lard applied to the skin, and when that didn't work they would simply stand in the smoke of their campfires. By God, I was finally out of the settled city. I was in the wild, fighting the elements. *See the U.S.A.* I aimed the Boxster west and floored the accelerator.

The love bugs were dying magnificently just inches from my nose, but now when I used the windshield washer, all it did was smear their remains. I scrunched low and watched the traffic through a clear spot just above the steering wheel. The road was straight for miles, there being no hills to skirt in these parts. On either side, scraggly trees rose from anemic dirt. The heat turned to steam and smoked up from the blinding highway. I passed a mobile home with a Jaguar XJS out in front, and then, just off the shoulder, a spray of fresh flowers propped against a crude wooden cross. You see several of those memorials a day if you drive at all in this country. I understand their poignant purpose—to elevate the mundane spot where a loved one perished. Death comes in such unholy places.

When I stopped for gas in Okeechobee, the nose of the Porsche was an oozing sore. "Shit," said a guy pumping regular gas into an old pickup at the next island, "if I'da paid as much as you paid for that car, I'd take it back to the dealer and tell him to *lick* them love bugs off." This was a bit of a twist on the thumbs-up I was becoming used to, and I didn't quite grasp the logic. I decided not to try.

"Yeah, it's bad, isn't it," I said, watching the gas gauge tote up the tank of premium. When I had opened the door to get out, several love bugs crawled into the cockpit with me. I flicked a humping pair off my sleeve as I pumped the gasoline.

"You got three hours to get them bugs off," the other man said. "Elsewise, they'll flat eat your paint." He had a look of laconic glee in his eye. As he drove off, I noticed the bumper sticker on the back of his truck: "Redneck Town Car."

Okeechobee, Florida, is on the northern tip of the big lake of the same name in the lower central part of the state. Look at your U.S. map, and Lake Okeechobee is that big knothole poked out of the peninsula. I have no idea how big the lake is, but when you stand on its shore, you can't see the other side. My family used to drive along the southern edge of it in the fifties and sixties, on our way up Highway 27. My only personal experience with the lake was bathing in it one morning after several hygienically challenged days with my friends at the races at Sebring. We had spent the night in an abandoned house on the lakeshore, wisely having elected to pull over and rest instead of pushing on through the perilous dark toward Miami. Back then, Florida's roads at night were like tightwires—one misstep and you were off in a swamp, 'gators splashing all around you.

My brother ran into an alligator once. Phil lives in Tampa, and he had been visiting a buddy whose house is in the country. The road home was narrow and curvy, snaking between several lakes. Near midnight, Phil was barreling along in his blue Dodge Colt when he suddenly saw a six-foot alligator lying in the road. You don't get much warning in that kind of darkness, and in the curves you quickly outrun your headlights. So he couldn't stop, and he couldn't swerve either, or else he'd plunge into the lake. Before he knew it he was *on* the thing. The Dodge Colt bounced into the air, as though it had hit a brick wall. Then Phil was rumbling over the 'gator, hearing it vibrate against the bottom of his car. Afterward, he stopped to look at the damage. There was blood everywhere, and the 'gator's top jaw and skull were missing. The car still ran, though, and as Phil drove on he got scared that he had just *convinced* himself he had run over an alligator. What if it was really a person? When he got home, he asked his wife, Joyce, to come out to the driveway with him. They shined a flashlight on the front of the car, and there was the alligator's decapitated skull and jaw around the front bumper. "No," Joyce assured him, "that's not human." The next morning, Phil called his insurance company and stammered out the story. The woman who answered the phone put her hand over the receiver and yelled to her office staff: "Hey, this guy hit an *alligator!*" She was in Springfield, Illinois, where alligators are near-mythical creatures. Phil's insurance agent told him they now use that story as a selling tool: acts of God or 'gator, they'll take good care of you.

The little town of Okeechobee has fewer than 5,000 residents, and I wondered what would have become of the local economy if the automobile had never been invented. Cruising down the main drag, Parrot Avenue, in my bug-stained Boxster, I could read the story of the twentieth century in the kinds of businesses lining the road in this small town—car rentals (huge, all brands), Chevron, Shell, Ford-Mercury, Radiator and Air Conditioning Repairs, Napa Auto and Truck Parts, Willard-Mays Auto Sales, Marcus Motor Company Used Cars, Car Circus ("Buy here, pay here"), John's Auto Sales, a go-cart track. I once read a quote from a business-school professor to the effect that one-sixth of the businesses in America are somehow related to cars—either manufacturing or sales or servicing or washing or repairing or towing or stacking in junkyards. It's another whole cycle of life that happens all around us, and we're as much a part of it as we are of the palms and pines that never change color. Maybe more so.

I saw a cute barefooted girl washing love bugs off a red Camaro that had one of those black leather "auto bras" on the front of it. I'd rather let my paint peel than drive a car that wore one of those, but this Boxster wasn't mine—yet. I wheeled into the service station where the girl was concentrating on the wheel wells. She was about nineteen, brunette, very tan, red toenails. It had been a couple hours since I'd left Miami. There was some part of me that needed a thumbs-up.

"Hi," I said through the window. The top was up because I didn't want love bugs slamming into my forehead.

She glanced over long enough to take in the mess on my hood. "Hello," she said. Then she turned back to what she was doing.

"Listen, do you know where I could get one of those, uh, leather things for this car? Can I buy one at a hardware store?"

"I think you've got to order them."

"Oh, really?"

"Really."

"Um, okay."

"You want me to wash it?"

"No, thanks," I said, "I've got fifty more miles to drive. I'll wash it in Sebring." I suddenly felt foolish saying such a thing—and then I felt foolish about feeling foolish. I told myself that most men would've paid good money just to watch this girl hose down the side-walk. They would've talked with her, joked with her, flirted with her. Why didn't I? And now, why was I asking myself that question? Somehow, this car was putting pressure on me to be someone I wasn't.

The girl shrugged and turned back to the pristine Camaro, whose owner, a young man in jeans and a T-shirt, came over to inspect the wash job. As I pulled away, I watched them laughing together in my rearview mirror.

At the next stoplight I was still thinking about the barefoot girl when I heard an engine rev in the lane next to me. I looked to my right and into the eyes of a pimple-faced boy of about seventeen, driving an old red Mustang. He was grinning, as was his shotgun-seat com-panion, a boy of similar age with his baseball cap on backward. *Vroom vrooommm,* went the Mustang. The pimply boy's grin got bigger.

I pressed the button to lower my window. "Nice car," I said, ges-turing toward the Mustang with a magnanimous thumbs-up. I felt like a king blessing a peasant's mule. "What year is it?"

"Sixty-seven," said Pimple Face. "What year's yours?"

"Ninety-seven," I said—not too smugly, I hoped.

Both boys admired the Porsche. Then Pimple Face cut his eyes at me and smiled slyly. "How much horsepower's it got?" he said. He gave the Mustang's gas pedal the slightest hint of a feathery goose.

I froze inside. I hadn't a clue about the horsepower. The Porsche people had admonished me not to do two things: look under the hood or leave the country. Not that I would have known what I was seeing had I opened the hood. (Come to think of it, where *was* the hood? This car had front and rear trunks and an engine in the middle.)

But I had to say something. The Mustang driver was waiting. The light was about to change. I met Pimple Face's gaze. "Enough," I said, and he and his friend laughed. It was a good answer. As the green light flashed on, the Mustang lurched and slowed, lurched and slowed. I smiled and shook my head at his invitation. He waved as he roared his Mustang up the main street toward his own distant moon.

On the radio, Paula Cole was singing a song that was suddenly everywhere: *Where Have All the Cowboys Gone?* I was ready to leave Okeechobee. From triumph in Miami, I had come to the bug-infested heartland and met humiliation. "The trouble with America today," I remembered Click and Clack saying on NPR's "Car Talk," "is that guys don't know anything about cars anymore."

Sebring, to me, was more about ambiance than competition. When I used to go there in the late 1950s and early 1960s, I felt I was visiting a foreign country. I became someone else there. I loved the romantic language we spoke during that race weekend — Grand Prix, Le Mans, Monza, Pininfarina, Ferrari, Por-sha. The drivers' names evoked worldly sophistication — Juan Manuel Fangio, Stirling Moss, Jackie Stewart, Phil Hill. We didn't pay much attention to the race it-self. Sebring was a twelve-hour endurance event, and it was most fun to watch at the beginning and the end. When the starting gun was fired, the drivers ran across the track to their cars, like fighter pilots scrambling to their planes. Then the engines began to bark and roar, filling the air with a surprisingly hollow sound, the way real gunfire pops instead of bangs like it does on TV. By this time, my friends and I would have staked out our campsite and pitched our tents, built our fire, and begun to consume the first of many beers we had brought with us. As night fell, we sang songs and told jokes and got happily drunk, while all around us the race cars whined their way toward morning.

My plan was to drive the Boxster around the Sebring track, but when I got to the race course and pitched the idea to the man in charge, he told me it couldn't happen. The track was torn up for much-needed repairs. Disappointed, I got back in my bug-splattered car and headed toward town in search of a car wash. While I was scrubbing the Porsche back to respectability, a lady noted the license plate and said, "I bet you don't have too many love bugs in Nevada, do you?"

It had been a grim day. I was tired, hot, and discouraged. The day got worse when I checked into my motel room and caught a glimpse of myself in the dresser mirror. I had taken off my sweaty shirt in preparation for searching out a much-needed gin and tonic, but as I walked past the mirror, I saw my father there. I sucked in my stomach, flexed my pecs, and studied the image before me. No matter how hard I squinted, the picture that came inexorably to mind was from August 1957—my father and mother in swimsuits at a beach in Delaware.

I've always found that snapshot troubling. My parents seemed so out of place there. Beaches are for fun and relaxation, two words my dad equated with work. A month shy of forty-seven, he was pale and thick, and his chest had begun to sag. Mother, who had turned forty-seven the month before, couldn't swim and felt self-conscious about revealing her body. She looked vulnerable against the wild gray sea. And yet they both wore smiles that break my heart. Why couldn't this have been their life?

Inevitably, that picture also reminds me of how we got to that beach that summer. We borrowed my aunt May's 1955 Oldsmobile 98 and drove from Hazlehurst, Mississippi, to Bethesda, Maryland, to visit my mother's brother Oliver and his family. They had relatives who owned a beach house, so we all went over for a Saturday night. I remember how I hated our borrowing May's car. It was threatening to me. I would rather have gone up in our own Ford, but I suppose my aunt graciously offered her Olds because it was more comfortable on a long trip. It had cushy seats, carpeting, automatic transmission, a radio. I liked it too much.

Instead of going straight for a drink, I dropped to the carpet and huffed out twenty-five laborious push-ups. Then I went for a run. There was a golf course across the street from my motel, and I jogged on its paved cart trail. I couldn't get the image of my father out of my head. A psychologist I know once told me that when you dream about cars, you're dreaming about how you're progressing in the world. As I ran that day, I daydreamed about my father and his cars.

When he and Mother met, in 1939, he owned an old blue Plymouth coupe with a rumble seat. He'd named it Daphne, and Mother said he loved that car. He was twenty-nine at the time. When Mother told me about it years later, I couldn't imagine the man I knew as my father caring so for an automobile—though I certainly could understand how, to him, the road might literally have meant escape. At age sixteen he'd run away from his parents' farm and the remainder of his fifteen siblings, hitchhiked to another town, and paid room and board to a family named the Tyrones while putting himself through high school, then college and graduate school. Most of this had happened during the years of the Great Depression. Daphne was his first car, a pale blue declaration of independence. Mother said that when the streets of Vicksburg, Mississippi, turned icy during that first harsh winter they were together, Dad and Daphne pulled everyone out of the ditches. He was proud of that car.

He owned Daphne until 1942, when he joined the Navy. After the war, he bought a used gray Ford, probably 1946 vintage. One night he, Mother, and my aunt Augusta went to the movies in Tupelo,

Mississippi. Dad parked the car behind the Lyric Theater, with the keys left in the ignition. I guess he hadn't noticed that the world had changed. When they came out after the movie, the Ford was gone. It was found weeks later, stripped to a shell. Dad then bought a used Chevrolet, a tan sedan. It was the first car I remember. I was three, and I liked to lie in the space above the backseat and look out the rear window at the trees we passed under and the cars rushing up behind us. At night I liked to study the stars. This was long before seat belts and baby seats would lock us into a life of caution. When my brother was born and we moved to Jackson, Mississippi, he and I fought for that special spot. We wanted to see where we were and what temptations we were passing. Dad played a trick on us that worked every time. "Okay, boys," he would say, "shut your eyes." We shut them tight, expecting a surprise. The surprise was that we had just passed a drive-in theater.

In 1955—at age forty-five—my father bought his first new car, a baby-blue 1955 Ford. Then came the used red-and-white 1958 Ford, and finally—finally for me, anyway, before I left home for college— he bought only the second new car of his life. He was fifty-two years old. The car was a 1962 American Motors Rambler in a scintillating shade of beige. More than any other car we owned, that Rambler expressed the difference between my father and me—and perhaps between our generations. Advertisements for the Rambler pitched it as a safe, sane, smart-value car—"built to last longer, not look longer." In diagrams, the Rambler was compared to the Chevy, the Ford, the Plymouth, and was shown to be both shorter and narrower: "That's why Rambler fits any garage . . . parks where others can't . . . eliminates mere bulk for economy, comfort, and performance."

My family's post–World War II history, like that of many Americans, was characterized by movement. If you didn't come from a family dynasty, you had to make your own way in the world. After the war, young men like my father moved to where the opportunities were. I lived in six different towns before I was in the third grade. But I think "the road" meant something different to my dad than it has to me. Even though it was his means of escape, his definition of the highway seemed marked by practicality, much like the cars he bought. For him, the road was simply what it was: a dirt ribbon covered by so many inches of crushed rock topped by a certain number of inches of asphalt or concrete, producing a smooth surface that allows practical drivers to guide their safe sedans comfortably from one place to another—to find jobs, if need be.

By the time he bought the Rambler, I and others of my generation had come to view the road as a more magical concoction. I had devoured the exuberance of Jack Kerouac's *On the Road* ("Whither goest thou, America, in thy shiny car in the night?"). I had snaked through hill-country blacktops with Robert Mitchum in *Thunder Road*. I had bopped to Charlie Ryan's hard-driving "Hot Rod Lincoln." To me, the road had become an accessory integral to my personal mythology. Too old now for my former favorite personas—the cowboy or army roles that I'd seen in the movies—I picked up *On the Road* and wanted to play Sal Paradise.

It was my fortune, for good or ill, to be a member of the choosy generation. I have a *Business Week* article from August 14, 1954, in which the new field of motivational research (MR) is explored in depth. MR refers to the application of the behavioral sciences to understand consumer attitudes. The *Business Week* article points out that the American society had changed over the previous two or three decades.

Choice has become a new, mysterious chaotic element in twentieth-century American society. Through most of history, people have had to lead fairly circumscribed lives. Economic, political, and technical conditions just about dictated what they had to do to survive. What they had to do, they did—and a businessman who understood those conditions could deal with people fairly successfully. Today's business-man has begun to realize that he is operating in a society so rich, fluid, and skillful that few people in it are completely gov-erned by necessity. Most people, a good deal of the time, do what they want to do, not just what they have to do.

Time and again during my growing-up years, my father told me that I had to "stop that wanting, wanting, wanting." I can't even re-member what I yearned for so eagerly—probably toys at the begin-ning, then a coonskin cap, then a Schwinn bike, then Elvis records, then the latest cool clothes. Stuff I saw on TV or in the movies. Part of me understood and accepted my dad's admonition, but another part rebelled. I was too incomplete to resist having my head turned. Kids are always incomplete, but I sense that my incompleteness was directly related to my new freedom to choose. Only later would I understand that the more choices you have, the more incomplete you're likely to feel. Tocqueville had known that 165 years earlier, when he wrote that Americans, with their classless society, had so much opportunity that it produced in them "anxiety, fear, and regret." Imagine if he had seen our time.

In the fifties, marketers began co-opting our restlessness and turn-ing it against us. Advertisements in general took on a more internal direction. Vance Packard wrote the book on MR in 1957—*The Hid-den Persuaders*. In it, he quoted a pamphlet called "Automobiles, What They Mean to America," which was the report of a study prepared for the *Chicago Tribune*'s advertising department.

The investigators found that only a minority of the popula-tion, mostly men in the lower class, have any real interest in the technical aspect of cars. And the major finding that stands out in the survey is that automobiles are heavily laden with social meanings and are highly esteemed because they "provide avenues for the expression . . . of the character, temperament and self concept of the owner and driver. . . . The buying process is an interaction between the personality of the car and the personality of the individual."

The report stated that "people buy the cars they think are especially appropriate for them" and then made these points:

People who want to seem conservative, to tell the world they are very serious and responsible, tend to buy Plymouth, Dodge, DeSoto, Packard, four-door sedans, dark colors, minimum accessories and gadgets.

People who want to seem sociable and up-to-date but in a middle-of-the-road sort of way tend to favor Chevrolet, Pontiac, Buick, Chrysler, two-door coupes, light colors, moderate accessories and gadgets.

People who want to express some showiness, to assert their individualism and modernity, tend to buy Ford, Mercury, Oldsmobile, Lincoln, hardtops, two-tones, bright shades and hues, a range of extras, gadgets, fads.

People who need to express unusual status on individual needs favor Cadillac (ostentation, high status), Studebaker, Hudson, Nash, Willys, convertibles (impulsiveness), very bright colors, red, yellow, white, latest gadgets and accessories.

Ironically, the report listed the Nash Rambler as one of the handful of cars people buy when they want to show "a sophisticated flair." But the Rambler produced by Nash was an automobile very different from the one later manufactured by American Motors. My father was obviously impressed with the practicality of his new car—the impervious-to-stains black rubber floor mats and gray cloth seats, the clashes-with-nothing beige exterior, the ever-reliable manual transmission. The jutting fins of the 1950s had given way to a more sedate style. My brother recalls that the Rambler "looked like a Kleenex box."

When I first saw the car—at the beginning of my senior-year in high school—I had two distinct thoughts about it: one, appearing at the latest hot drive-in restaurant in such a vehicle was a truly daunting prospect; and two, luring a date into that car was a concept almost beyond imagination. Fortunately, I managed, using what today would be known as spin—the "Beige Bed"—to diffuse what I knew secretly, in my teenage heart, was a tragic situation.

After my run on the Sebring golf course, I went back to the motel and showered. Then I dressed quickly and repaired to the bar, where I worked on my notes and drank more than I had in days. The road is hard on fitness. At home, I work out at a gym several mornings a week. Now I was enjoying the suspended reality of travel, in which nothing sticks—not bills, nor booze, nor burritos, nor even mortality itself—as long as you keep moving and avoid mirrors.

THREE

Running with the Elk

The Cat House Restaurant is where Sebring eats breakfast. Not the worldly Sebring of Grand Prix racers, but the stolid Sebring of pickup trucks and John Deere caps and Skoal cans in hip pockets. I had spent the night at a motel on the highway called Inn of the Lake, and though it was perfectly nice—its bar even featured photos of all the Sebring winners— I wanted to see the little town square that I vaguely remembered from one of my trips to the races thirty-five years before.

I was also looking for a drugstore where I could buy Sebring race postcards, but the corner druggist told me there were no such cards to be found. He thought it was crazy that the town didn't promote its most famous event, and I agreed with him. "Go complain to the Chamber of Commerce," he said, and directed me to a storefront a couple of doors away. I did go and tell the woman in charge that I was looking for Sebring Grand Prix postcards and that it seemed strange not to be able to find them in downtown Sebring. She said the

Chamber was thinking of producing some, but I left with the distinct feeling that there was a conflict of some kind between the world-famous racetrack and the town from which it derived its name.

That's when I went across the street to the Cat House. I sat at a booth and ordered coffee, orange juice, and an omelet, and set about reading more of *Undaunted Courage*. In the nine days I had been away, I had given up newspapers. Part of the joy of being on the road is creating your own reality, and anything that interferes with that undermines the trip. My nightly phone calls to Beth, for example, reminded me not only of how angry she still was over what I'd said in Miami, but also how absolutely selfish I was to be driving around in a sports car while life at home progressed along its predictable course. She didn't actually *say* that, of course—years earlier, we had agreed that whenever either of us was away, we wouldn't pass on bad news that the traveling party couldn't do anything about. But I could hear in her voice that the lawn needed mowing, the children needed disciplining, the roof needed fixing, my marriage needed tending, and all the stresses of holding down the home front rested squarely on her shoulders. This trip was costing me plenty, I knew, and I wasn't thinking of the American Express bills I was running up.

I did carry a cellular telephone in the car—more a nod to safety than constant communication. But occasionally the phone would ring (almost scaring me off the road) and it would be Beth or, more likely, my agent passing along some message that served merely to take my head out of whatever cloud I was in. I remembered reading how out of touch travelers could be in Lewis and Clark's time. Once, early on in the expedition, Lewis wrote to President Jefferson that he intended to spend that winter of 1803 to 1804 on horseback exploring the Kansas River toward Santa Fe, instead of sitting tight in a military camp up the Missouri River near St. Louis. Jefferson was adamantly against the idea—if anything happened to Lewis, his expedition was done—and began worrying about Lewis's judgment, but letters took months to be delivered. Fortunately, by the time Lewis received Jefferson's strict order to abandon that excursion, he had already decided against it. In my own situation, my cell phone liberated my family from the kind of anxiety Jefferson felt during the three months he waited to hear if Lewis had heeded his order, even as it linked me to the world I'd left behind. Today, it's very hard to leave home. Considering all of that, I elected at least to avoid newspapers.

While I thumbed through my book to find my place, my antennae picked up a snippet of conversation between two older men sitting at a table in the middle of the room. They were drinking coffee and smoking cigarettes and talking about a mutual acquaintance named Jimmy. I started listening:

"You know, he bought a ranch over yonder near Ona," one said.

"He did?" said the other. This was obviously news.

"Yeah, he did. Big place."

"Man."

"You know, his brother died. The one down in Miami."

"He did?"

"Yeah, he did. Now *he* was the brains in the family. Old Jimmy, he's got brains, but he's also dumb as a box of rocks. You know, he didn't know how to change a tire."

"Naw."

"Yeah. I was with him. He got a flat, and I had to change it for him."

"*Naw.*"

"Yeah. He couldn't even find the spare. You know, it's under the car. Now that's dumb."

"Yeah—*that's* dumb."

I thought about that conversation as I headed toward Orlando that morning. It stung a little. One night when I was in high school, I was parked with a girlfriend in the dark lot of the Greyhound dog-racing track, only to find that when we were ready to leave, the old red '58 Ford had a flat tire. I panicked because though I knew *in theory* how to change a tire, I had never actually done it. I liked that girl and didn't want to disappoint her, so of course I lied to her. I told her there was no jack in the car. She suggested we walk to the house of a boy we knew, a couple of blocks away. He came over and changed the tire, though I have no idea how I (a) managed to open the trunk to get the spare without revealing the jack, or (b) finessed it so *he* would change the tire. I wonder if they knew what a fraud I was. You never know when, or where, a moment of reckoning will happen by. They seem to come most frequently in cars, because cars by their very nature take you into unfamiliar territory. Cars challenge a hothouse competence. Driver's tests ought to include changing a tire. They should probably go even further than that. Driver's tests *ought* to include probing to see if you have the slightest idea of who you are before you take keys in hand and head out into the volatile night. But that wouldn't work, I suppose—most of us wouldn't be able to get a license until we were well into our forties, and some of us never.

I drove north on clogged Highway 27, a stretch of road that today never quite breaks from settlement into countryside. So much for the road less traveled. At I-4, I turned northeast toward Orlando. Traffic was slow because the interstate was being widened, from four lanes to eight. That afternoon I hoped to connect with a man named Terry Spear, who I had been told was "a GTO nut." His father, my uncle by marriage, was the one who told me that. Meanwhile, I made a note into my tape recorder: "Here I am doing the thing I most wanted to be doing—driving my dream car across America—and I'm homesick. After only nine days, I'm *homesick*."

In Sebring the night before, I had awoken in the middle of the night and tried to fall back to sleep by reading another of the books I had packed for the trip—Bruce Chatwin's *The Anatomy of Restlessness*. The Englishman Chatwin argued that while the human animal has an emotional, if not biological, need for a home base, his real nature is to wander. "Evolution intended for us to be travellers," Chatwin wrote. "Settlement for any length of time, in cave or castle, has at best been a sporadic condition in the history of man." I didn't know whether to take Chatwin literally, though he probably expected me to. It occurred to me that there were many ways to wander from the safe home base—alcohol, food, work, shopping, Net surfing, love affairs. I was eating and drinking too much on this trip—a way of wandering from my wanderings, I suppose. If Chatwin meant that no matter what we do we want to be doing something *else,* then maybe he had a point.

But I don't think that's what he meant. He extolled the life of literal nomads, those rootless tribes who squat for a week or two and then move on. I read a piece about nomads in the *New York Times* a few months back. The particular tribe I read about lives in the Sahara desert, north of Timbuktu. The father of the clan likes his life, which was the life of his ancestors, even though it dooms his family to poverty and a certain level of ignorance—he "has never used a television, toilet or telephone," the reporter wrote of the nomad father. "He has never read a newspaper. He has never heard of a facsimile machine. He has never seen an American dollar." Except for toilets and dollars, I felt a tinge of envy. The nomad's fifteen-year-old son, however, seems restless to move beyond that time-honored existence, though only in form, not in substance. "I would like to see if driving a car is different from riding a camel," the young man said.

There is a delicious simplicity to life on the road—even the life *I* was living, on the roads I was traveling. I ate, drank, slept, and drove.

I ran up bills and left them in my wake, escaping to the next town like a desperado. It's when you quit moving that life gets complicated. But the trade-off is that life also can grow richer. Stop the stirring and the mixture has a chance to gel. "Show me a man who cares no more for one place than another," wrote Robert Southey, "and I will show you in that same person one who loves nothing but himself. Beware of those who are homeless by choice."

Thinking about Chatwin, I recalled a conversation I'd had the winter before with Alfred Dupont Chandler, Jr., a Pulitzer Prize–winning historian now retired from Harvard Business School. I had asked Chandler to tell me if he believed restlessness was a particularly American trait, as I had so often heard, or whether the whole of the human race were Chatwinesque nomads.

Chandler doesn't put much stock in Chatwin's theory. Of necessity, people were nomads until they settled down with agriculture, he said, but after that they created entire economic, social, and governmental infrastructures to support their livelihoods. Once in place, most Europeans didn't venture far from home. "The British and the French, those people don't move. The Irish move, because otherwise they couldn't eat. The people from the maritime regions moved around some." But generally, Europeans have stayed put for hundreds of years—except for those antsy upstarts who were compelled to cross the Atlantic Ocean looking for a life not lived under a king's thumb.

Once in America, they settled down until after the revolution. And then they began, gradually, exploring the unknown continent whose eastern edge they had landed on. Chandler's family had established itself in Andover, Massachusetts, but they also had property in Maine. "In the summers they went, by canoe, to Maine to settle the new land, but they always came back by winter." Other families were doing the same thing—moving here and there, pushing the frontier forward, then returning home. Eventually, when the new land was ready to be inhabited, a second or third son (the first son would inherit the family's original land) would move his family permanently to the new ground, creating another toehold from which future generations would travel.

"That was the way America was settled," Chandler said. "Westward to New York, farther westward to Michigan. You didn't just go out and start up. You moved back and forth, and eventually the family settled farther west. After the Louisiana Purchase and especially the War of 1812, people began moving all the way from Alabama to the Mississippi delta, and then to the new states on the western side of the river. Just as my family had moved from Massachusetts to Maine, people moved, gradually, from Ohio to Kansas and so on. The assumption in America—unlike in Europe—was that you wouldn't live in the place you were born. There was too much rich land out there."

And then, by the 1890s, Frederick Jackson Turner delivered his epic pronouncement: *The frontier is closed.* . . . Turner was alarmed. From the very beginning, American society had been based on the notion of a frontier.

"What Turner couldn't see," said Chandler, "was that there were huge opportunities coming not from agriculture but from the industrial revolution." The railroad and the telegraph were just being finished in the 1890s. Americans now could indulge their restlessness on a larger scale. Distribution of goods created the creature known as the traveling salesman. In the 1890s, the railroads and electricity—not the automobile—brought about the suburbs. When the automobile came along, the country was ready for it. "It's inherent in Americans," Chandler said. "In almost every decade, Americans have moved around."

During the Great Depression, when jobs were scarce and money was tight, Americans took to the road in record numbers. In a 1934 issue of *Fortune*, James Agee wrote a piece called "The Great American Roadside." It touched on what was even then a $3 billion industry of tourist courts and service stations and restaurants shaped like ice cream containers. Hard times had slowed new-car purchases between 1930 and 1934, but the car culture was putting down roots in subtle ways. The first drive-in theater opened in Camden, New Jersey, in 1933. The first parking meter was installed in Oklahoma City in 1935. By mid-decade the traffic was flowing again. Chevrolet made 620,726 cars in 1934; the next year the number was 793,437. Ford's numbers were 563,921 in 1934 and close to a million the following year. Agee concluded that such feverishness was founded upon a solid rock.

> God and the conjunction of confused bloods, history, and the bullying of this tough continent to heel did something to the American people—worked up in their blood a species of restiveness unlike any that any race before has known, a restiveness describable only in negatives. Not to eat, not for love, nor even for money, nor for fear, nor really for adventure, nor truly out of any known necessity is this desire to move upon even the most docile of us. We are restive entirely for the sake of restiveness. Whatever we may think, we move for no better reason than for the plain unvarnished hell of it. And there is no better reason.

In Orlando, I got a red-nailed thumbs-up from a big-haired blond in an Acura. At a stoplight, a kid ran out and handed me a business card. "If you ever want to get this badass car window-tinted, call me," he said. I pulled into a car wash, where three teens on bicycles came over to watch me hose off the love bugs. "You must have been rich when you bought this," one of them said, and I told them no, I had *stolen* this car. As I drove away I watched them in my rearview mirror. Their mouths were gaping. I hoped they knew I was kidding.

That afternoon, I visited Terry Spear and heard about some of the 300 automobiles he had owned in his life. That's a misleading statistic, probably, since Spear has spent much of the past fifteen or so years buying old cars, fixing them up, and selling them at a profit. Mostly they were "muscle cars" from the early to late sixties, the years when Spear was in high school. "It was the time," he said, "when they took a family sedan and put a big motor in it, and big tires, and they turned it into a weekend race car." Meeting Terry Spear made me think of the magic of first cars: They may not be the best cars we'll ever own, or we may not own them at all, but we can never quite let them go. Many of us spend lifetimes trying to re-create that extraordinary blip in time when the world was a frontier and the rivers weren't yet dammed.

It's searchers like that who have afforded Terry Spear the chance to live his version of the perfect life. He's always loved cars, since he was fourteen and his uncle John bought a brand-new 1967 GTO. "My parents bought a new car as well," Terry said, "but it was an Oldsmobile Delta Eighty-eight four-door." Terry got to wash and wax both cars each weekend ("I got paid for my uncle's car"), and one day he found a hide-a-key under the bumper of Uncle John's 1967 GTO. "I used to sneak out in that, and it was so *fast*, it beat all my friends' cars. GTOs will turn heads like no tomorrow—especially if they're really loud."

As a grown-up, Spear is tall and thin, with long wisps of blondish-brown hair twisting down from beneath his baseball cap. He's in his forties now. For fifteen years he worked as an electrician, fixing up cars in his spare time. Then in 1991, he and his wife, Aimeé, bought a house with a big two-car garage, and soon the garage was littered with cars and parts. Finally he decided to take the plunge. "I bought a compressor on my Sears credit card," he said, and he used that to open his own restoration shop, specializing in Pontiacs. It's called

Terry's GTO, and many of his restored cars have won awards and been pictured in magazines. "People come to me with a car they've bought, and they want us to change everything so it's exactly the way their old car was back in the sixties—or else they want it how they would've done it back then if they could've fixed it up the way they wanted. *Now* they can afford it. And it warms their hearts to go back there again."

For Terry and Aimeé, GTOs are a family thing. "My wife and I started a Pontiac club that now has eighty or ninety members. We have meetings every month and a big show once a year. And see that gold wagon over there? We're going to take it to the GTO Nationals in Atlanta in July." The car he pointed to—one of a couple dozen sitting outside his garage in Orlando—was a 1964 Tempest station wagon in a color I would've called "champagne." The GTO Nationals are a drag race. Both Terry and Aimeé will drive in various classes of the event. "This gold wagon has won its class in the Muscle Car Nationals two years running. The big mentor of Pontiac drag racing is a guy named Arnie 'The Farmer' Beswick," said Terry, getting revved up now. "He's sixty-six and has been drag racing since he was about twenty. I met him at a national meet, and we became friends. He used to race a station wagon in the early sixties. The thing that makes this wagon so fast is the weight distribution. It'll travel sixty feet in 1.58 seconds, both wheels off the ground. It's phenomenal."

I drove away thinking of Terry Spear as a kind of catcher in the rye. "I've seen so many great cars go to the crusher," he told me. "It makes me feel good to save them from that—to fix them up the way they were or better, and get them back on the street."

That night I stayed with my aunt Polly and uncle Paul—Terry's dad—who told me about the Orlando they remembered from just thirty years ago, the sleepy little town that existed before Disney came and turned the area into a fantasyland. Disney's representatives told the city fathers that their development was going to have a huge impact on the community, but since nothing big had ever happened in Orlando, no one could imagine the kind of change the Disney people were talking about. My uncle Paul even had a chance to buy some land at $300 an acre, but the property was so swampy that he didn't see the point. Now it's the site of one of the lakes at Disney World.

The old Orlando must have been nice—homey, slow, sweet with the scent of orange blossoms. But that place is long gone now, buried beneath a Hollywood set. I don't mean just the various Disney parks. To me, Orlando is the city that escapism built. In that sense it is a quintessentially American postwar city, the first in this country to be created by the movies. Even Hollywood developed organically, but the Orlando of today exists to support our love of, and need for, illusion—for fanciful worlds of fierce pirates and frontier heroes, of handsome knights and fairy princesses. One of Disney World's dearest illusions is Main Street U.S.A. Thinking about it reminded me of what a new urbanist named James Howard Kunstler said about EuroDisney—that the reason it didn't do well in France was because the French, the Europeans, have never lost the quaint cozy quality of their old-world villages, so they don't *need* to gather in ersatz town squares and soak themselves in pretend good-old-days simplicity. Much of the reason Europe retained that charm, of course, is that the old villages were built before cars, when transportation was by foot or horse or cart. America's villages, especially since World War II, were built to accommodate the automobile. Wide streets encourage speed. And speed begets its own myriad forms of fallout.

Friday morning I made the seventy-two-mile drive from Orlando to Tampa at a leisurely pace. For one reason, the roads were so congested with repair crews that nobody could go much faster than 60.

The other reason was that I had discovered that speeding on these roads made me tired. It required too much concentration. Instead of filling me with adrenaline, it sapped my energy. The novelist Milan Kundera says that people speed in order to forget their lives, in order to achieve that exquisite moment when there is no past and no future, only the rushing present. "Speed is the form of ecstasy the technical revolution has bestowed on man," Kundera says. I remembered something I had read in *Undaunted Courage* about speed in Thomas Jefferson's era: "A critical fact in the world of 1801 was that nothing moved faster than the speed of a horse. No human being, no manufactured item, no bushel of wheat, no side of beef . . . no letter, no information, no idea, order, or instruction of any kind moved faster. . . . And except on a racetrack, no horse moved very fast." And yet, merely sixty years later, when Abraham Lincoln became president, goods moved faster by a factor of twenty or more, and information—via telegraph—moved "all but instantaneously." Now, 140 years after Lincoln, the fastest plane moves how much faster than a horse? By a factor of nearly 1,000. With such a benchmark, no wonder life has become a blur.

Halfway to Tampa, a Ford Explorer zipped around me. The driver was talking frantically into his cell phone. On the back of his vehicle was a bumper sticker that said, "So many pedestrians, so little time."

I spent two comfortable nights at my brother's house, catching up on sleep and touching base with family—not necessarily in that order. While Phil's wife, Joyce, and daughter, Anne, went about their normal business, Phil and I sat by his pool and laughed about Dad and the Beige Bed. After I had left for college, Phil began driving it. I wished Dad were there to hear the stories—I'm sure I could've gotten him to admit that Phil was even harder on the car than I was. One Saturday night in the sixties, Phil and a bunch of buddies were cruising when one of the boys tried to buttonhook an egg at an oncoming car from the right rear seat through the left rear window. The egg hit the bar between the front and rear windows and splattered all over the inside of the Rambler. This was the vehicle my parents were going to drive to church in a matter of hours. The only thing Phil had to clean it up with was a brand new-Gant shirt he was wearing for the first time.

But the real damage came from Phil's newspaper route. He had been delivering *Miami Herald*s for years, at first by bicycle. It took an hour and a half to drop off his papers on a bike, but when he turned sixteen, he began using the Rambler. Phil's friend Dwight, who also had a paper route, went along with him, and in the car they could deliver 300 papers in forty minutes. They would meet at about 4:00 A.M. to fold the papers. Then they would stack them like a cord of firewood in the Rambler's backseat, where the still-damp ink would bleed into the gray cloth of the car. Phil drove, and Dwight reclined the front passenger seat so that he had the perfect angle for backhanding the papers out the passenger window. Phil drove the old Rambler through the dark streets of Miami Shores at about 30 miles per hour, while Dwight peppered papers out of the right front window like they were balls popping from a tennis machine.

By the time they finished their routes, it was only 5:30 A.M.—too late to go back to sleep before school, but clearly too early to go home. So Phil disconnected the speedometer (he said it was easy in those days, just unscrewing a nut and pulling a little pin out from under the dash), which also stopped the odometer. They were then free to drive to Miami Beach for bagels or to their girlfriends' houses for predawn groping (while the parents slept, they hoped). Then Phil would drop Dwight off and come home and reconnect the speedometer cable.

They got caught the day Dad backed out of our gravel driveway to go to work and the speedometer registered 60 miles an hour—

going *backward*. He had it checked, and the man said, "Somebody's been fooling with your speedometer." Dad was angry and gave Phil a lecture, but he didn't bother to ground him. "I think," Phil said, "he had given up by then."

My brother is an interesting touchstone on the subject of cars. For one thing, he drives to work (unlike me now—I simply walk upstairs) in a city of more than a million people. For another thing, he's smart and incisive. And for a third thing, he's got a flash temper. He admits to having screamed—twice—at other drivers (he suspects he said, "You fucking *idiot!*" or maybe, "You want to fuck with *me!?*"). Neither time did he and the other driver actually get out and fight, but one day in a fast-food-store parking lot, they came close. Phil was ready, and that scared him. "I now curse only under my breath," he says. "I'm fifty years old with a bad shoulder, and I'm probably the only guy on the road without a gun in the glove compartment."

I was curious to know what he thought of the reckless speed I had seen on south Florida's highways. "We humans are herd animals," he said, "and we haven't evolved fast enough to handle the car. We are elk, out there in cars, and the cars are our horns. We bump each other, we cut each other off, we scare each other, we threaten each other. Cars give us the means to take out our aggressions on strangers. Nobody has any time anymore, and nobody has any patience anymore. The stream of rush-hour traffic going bumper-to-bumper at seventy miles per hour shows a horrendous lack of appreciation for physics. Florida is insane."

On Saturday night, Phil's friends John and Colette Bancroft came over to see the Porsche and to tell me car stories. When you drive an automobile like the Boxster, you become a lightning rod for such tales. It happened time and again, all across the country. I came to understand that car stories, no matter how temporal and anecdotal, serve as a kind of common mythology in America. In ways that we all can identify with, they tell of our coming of age, our youth, our aspirations and expectations, our middle years, our successes and failures, our winding down. There's nothing else in the culture that speaks to us quite so universally of life and death, ego and yearning, comedy and tragedy, love and loss.

John Bancroft, who is my brother's age, grew up in the all-American town of Speedway, Indiana, a suburb of Indianapolis. It is close enough to "the Brickyard," the Indy 500 track, that for him every Memorial Day was filled with the sound of droning engines, as though a swarm of giant insects had swooped down from the heavens to invade the nearby cornfields. This was still a time when the 500-mile race lasted almost all day—as opposed to now, when the whole thing is wrapped up in a couple of hours. "Today, there's hardly time for the people in the infield to get drunk before it's over," John said.

In 1964, when he was sixteen, John spotted a beautiful 1957 Chevrolet on a used-car lot. He had some extra money (among other jobs, he sold newspapers in the Indy infield), and he was suddenly siezed with an overwhelming urge to *own* that car. It was pristine, a sparkling white streak with chrome in that little sideways Y that characterized the styling of '57 Chevys. The interior was red and black, with flecks of silver. The dash and steering wheel were bright red. John's mother went with him to buy the car, and though the salesman pretended to engage her in such motherly matters as safety and practicality, he also communicated to John in the timeless tongues of the hot to trot: "This car has *great pickup power,* heh-heh."

The Chevy changed John's life. "It did indeed have great pickup power," John said. "As a result, every male in my high school hated my guts, and would've cheerfully ripped them out, steaming, if given the opportunity. On the other hand, I had many lovely, and quite delicious, senior girls chatting me up, calling me pet names in the cafeteria." His first serious sweetheart was a girl I'll call Carolee, and she was from the south side of Indianapolis, which John described as "a serious redneck stronghold. They had moved up from the rural South, and not moved up very much." Carolee loved John's Chevy. "When I picked her up in it the first time, I could see that it was a transforming event in her life. And it was in mine, too, because Carolee was an older woman with a certain reputation. The backseat in that car was enormous. You could easily live in the backseat of a 1957 Chevy. Leg room? You could put a *bathroom* back there." One moonlit night in that capacious sanctuary, while parked among stalks of heartland corn, John lost his virginity to the lovely Carolee. You can't tell a more American story than that.

John and Carolee went steady for a period that teens consider a long time, until one night when Carolee's drunk younger brother stole John's car and went joyriding. John and Carolee were in her house listening to Johnny Rivers records on the stereo system she was buying from Zayres on the installment plan, when suddenly they heard the unmistakable throaty sound of the Chevy roaring away into the darkness. It was being driven by "a little rat bastard," as John recalls him, of about fourteen. John wanted to call the police, but Carolee talked him out of it. "I'll be very stern with him," she said. Hoping to assuage John's anger, Carolee changed the music to "Johnny Angel."

But John was not assuaged. "Her brother drove my '57 Chevy at very high speeds, very recklessly, as a matter of fact, and ran the oil out of the crankcase," he remembered. "The car stalled out and he just left it there, defenseless, on the streets of the south side of Indianapolis."

When the kid brother came home without it, John began screaming at him, threatening him with lawsuits and hit men (everything except physical violence—the fourteen-year-old outweighed John by about a hundred pounds), while Carolee tried to quiet him down. The brother showed no remorse, and John screamed louder. Then Carolee began defending her brother. Feeling betrayed, John stormed out.

Did he ever speak to Carolee again? "Yes, but it wasn't pleasant."

Today, John and his wife, Colette, drive a Nissan Stanza, with which they do have "a relationship," John said, "though it isn't passionate." Occasionally he sees a car that quickens his pulse. He still yearns for a '57 Chevy or a '67 Mustang. He once owned one of the latter but had to give it to his ex-wife in their divorce. Divorces being wars of aggression, that was the one piece of property she wanted most. The Mustang had those chrome pins on the hood, which John loved. He said they were great for helping you "steer true" even if you'd had a couple of beers. But his ex-wife's new husband shaved off the hood pins, saying they detracted from the lines of the hood.

"Well, but see," Colette said, "this was a guy who collected"—and here she paused disdainfully—"Saabs."

"*Saabs?*" I said.

"Saabs," sneered John. "Old Saabs. He had pieces of them—"

"He had four or five old *Saabs,* in various stages of dismantlement, all over the garage and the backyard," added Colette.

John had to change the subject. The memory was too painful.

Sunday, May 11, the twelfth day of my trip. Mother's Day. Before leaving Phil's, I called my mother and then my wife, wishing each a happy day. Beth seemed angrier than the last time we'd spoken. I took solace in hitting the road again.

In early afternoon I crossed over to Clearwater and turned right on U.S. 19 toward Tallahassee. Total mileage on the Boxster—since I'd picked it up in Dallas two weeks before—was 3,150, and I had barely begun my journey. Florida seemed endless. It always had, but now with all the traffic it seemed more so—and especially the way I was driving it. Tampa was only 273 miles from Miami, which I had left four days before. I was eager to pick up the pace.

But it wasn't going to happen on U.S. 19. That venerable highway hugs the Gulf shore until the peninsula begins to curve westward. The road continued north into the scrubby shoulder of the state, an area that has more in common with Georgia and Alabama than with the flashy tip of Miami. In north Florida, both the shoes and the cars I was encountering seemed clunkier—more wavy-soled Nikes accelerating more Camaros and Firebirds and Mustangs, all with sculptured excess around the hips and spoilers poised high like scorpions' tails.

Anybody who does more driving than flying knows that America's Main Street is now a strip of fast-food joints and franchise retailers, everywhere the same. This is what James Howard Kunstler and other new urbanists refer to as the "architecture of nowhere." I hadn't driven on U.S. 19 for two decades, and in my memory it was still a drive lined with quaint non–chain motel signs and mom-and-pop cafes. My mother recalls that when she and Dad and Phil made their first drive to Miami from Hazlehurst in 1957, while I stayed with Aunt May to finish the fall semester, they spent a night in a tourist court on the shores of the Suwannee River, which crosses 19 just outside a little burg called Old Town. Driving in those days meant seeking out the unfamiliar. You were traveling to see the U.S.A., driving toward the horizon, and you trusted your inner compass to find the most promising restaurants ("go where the most cars are") and the cleanest, most comfortable motels (we usually stayed in the Bambi, whose cuddly fawn hinted at wholesome, Disneyesque quarters, or the Skylark, whose very name conjured images of flocks heading home to roost against the purple dusk). From the backseat, my brother and I begged for a place with a swimming pool, and it didn't matter that the pool was the size of a coffee table and was plopped in the middle of the parking lot. There was something cozy about motels then. Most of them were single-story, arranged in a horseshoe around a central courtyard. I could squeeze every nuance of nostalgia out of these memories, but the amazing thing to remember now is that there was a time in America, and not more than forty years ago, when we not only searched for but reveled in—even *trusted*—the unknown.

So how did U.S. 19 become the tedious stretch of predictability that it is today? As I drove, I read the names of the businesses into my tape recorder: Water Bed Sensations, Cash Loans on Car Titles, Cox Car Care, Chiropractic, Papa John's Pizza, Used Car Sales, Thai Palace, Pest Control, Call of the Wild, Pelican Marine Center, Publix Supermarket, Holiday 24-Hour Self-Serve Car Wash, Community United Methodist Church, Pinella's Rent-A-Car, Sav-A-Lot Food Store, Video Rental, Burger King, Mr. Wok Chinese Restaurant, Computer Store, National Auto Supermarket, Highland Auto Sales, Tire Sales, Pawn Shop. I could have been anywhere. By indulging our urge to go, and our need for familiarity, we've created a country not worth going to.

A Volvo pulled beside me, and the family inside gawked and pointed at the Boxster. The driver honked at another car, full of women, and pointed at my Porsche. I assumed they were traveling together, but they had different license plates. The carload of thirty-something women looked and smiled and giggled. It made me slightly uncomfortable. When the light changed, I sped off a little faster than normal. At the next light, a young woman in a red Eagle (whose license-plate frame said "Whatever") motioned for me to lower the window. "What is that?" she said. When I told her it was the new Porsche, she said, "*Veerrry* nice."

I once wrote an essay about anonymity. When I was a magazine editor in Chicago, I loved riding to work on the train in the mornings and peering into the windows along the tracks. From my tenth-floor office on Michigan Avenue, I often stared into the windows of the building across the street. One of the businesses was a dance studio, and on late winter afternoons I watched the dancers moving gracefully in their leotards to a ballet scored in my head. Early one morning when it was still dark, from the backseat of a taxi on my way to O'Hare, I saw a woman standing naked in her bathroom. All these scenes reminded me of the slice-of-life views in Edward Hopper's paintings. I enjoyed being anonymous in the big city. I liked the freedom it gave me to sit in restaurants and listen to the conversations around me. I liked looking into windows and imagining the lives I saw there, but I also liked not really knowing about them. I could make up my own stories. The life of the imagination is often more rewarding than the life of everyday reality.

I was thinking about all that at a Taco Bell where I stopped for lunch, I don't remember where. After ordering, I sat at a table and read my road atlas while I ate my burritos. Suddenly I felt the presence of people. I looked up to see several customers lined up waiting for service, but nobody was behind the counter. Then I glanced out to the parking lot. About six young men and women in Taco Bell uniforms were milling around the Boxster, shading their eyes to look in the windows. When they finally came back into the restaurant, one of them smiled broadly and gave me a big thumbs-up. All the people in the place craned their necks my way. That's when it occurred to me that if you're serious about maintaining your anonymity, the last thing you want to drive is a Porsche Boxster. On the other hand, I had to admit that a body could start to find this sort of attention addictive.

It took me all afternoon to get to Tallahassee. The traffic was heavy with shoppers, every other one in a minivan or sport utility vehicle. Somewhere along the way I approached a bridge that seemed strangely familiar. It was a high bridge over a river. I pulled to the shoulder and studied it until a scene from long ago came back to me. When I was fourteen, having just gotten my learner's permit, I was driving my family on this leg of a trip to Mississippi. My father was in the front seat next to me, my mother and Phil in the back. Mother, who didn't drive, was the worst kind of backseat driver. At lights she jammed her feet to the floorboard as if slamming on the brakes. If another car turned in front of us at an intersection, she put her hands over her eyes, as though she couldn't bear to face the inevitable— which, of course, was imminent violent death. She sometimes made a sucking sound with her mouth, the way people do when they've suffered a burn and are trying to endure the excruciating pain. Dad and I were used to her reactions and often shared in a little fun-making at her expense. When Mother saw this formidable bridge looming, she panicked. "Leger," she said to my father, "you can't let Jim drive across this bridge." Dad and I laughed, but she persisted. Finally, to keep the peace, I pulled over and let my father take the wheel. I was furious, and I'm sure I sulked all the way to the Alabama line.

By the time the Boxster rolled into Tallahassee, I had long since felt the pull of cocktail hour. The evening was hot, and I wanted gin. I rationalized my unseemly craving by noting that whiskey was one of the essentials that Lewis and Clark carried west with them. Ambrose estimates that they packed 120 gallons of the stuff. On one level, you could say that that was a poor use of their precious cargo space. But if you believed that, you would be denying something basic in human nature. Booze and restlessness are connected somehow—at the very least, they both have to do with escape. Meriwether Lewis and William Clark both were heavy drinkers, and in fact you could say it was whiskey that first brought them together, in 1795. In November of that year, a young Ensign Lewis, having gotten drunk and challenged a superior officer to a duel, was brought up on charges of disturbing the peace. Lewis was acquitted in Court Martial but was transferred to Captain Clark's unit, where he promptly recognized a kindred spirit.

So both leaders well understood the importance of spirits to the spirit of their expedition. Every night, each member of the party was allotted one gill—about four ounces—of whiskey, which meant their supply would last just over 100 days. The strategy seemed to be, Carry at *least* enough alcohol to get the men past the point of no return. Every man guarded his ration jealously, and raids on the whiskey supply brought appropriately severe punishment—100 lashes.

I am not a clubby fellow, but I was starting to find my own solitary company a mite tedious. After driving by myself all day, and listening to myself speak my brilliant observations into my tape recorder, the last thing I felt like doing was checking into a motel and sitting in my room alone reading or writing. I didn't necessarily want to talk to people, but I wanted to be where people were. I looked for a motel with a lounge attached or nearby, so I wouldn't have to drive the Boxster after having drinks. My plan was to stay where America stays, which meant chain motels. A part of me abhorred the idea, but another part welcomed it—the part that realized we *don't* live in 1957 anymore.

I spotted a Days Inn near I-10, across the street from Julie's Restaurant and Lounge. We have a Julie's in Little Rock, and it's a place I would never go to at home. It's too packaged, too Benniganesque. In my own town I know the good places and the dives, and even the good dives from the bad ones. But on the road, I had become hesitant to park the Porsche (or even my van) in front of some roadhouse and walk through the door. The unknown has taken on a different quality since we were urged to search out the new and the unusual in the fifties and sixties. We've heard too many stories now. We've *seen* the U.S.A.—on the evening news (not to mention in *Psycho*). And so, just as small road inns like the Bates Motel once welcomed the weary traveler, today signs promising familiarity and homogeneity along the interstates now comfort the wary traveler.

I checked into the Days Inn and walked across to the bar, where I ordered a straight-up Bombay Sapphire martini, very dry with extra olives, and worked on my day's notes. This would become my M.O. for the duration of the trip: I would seek out a place where the locals gathered, and I would catch up on my notes, sometimes talking with people and sometimes not. The TV in Julie's Lounge was tuned to the Chicago Bulls–Atlanta Hawks NBA playoff game, which I watched with one eye while taking in the scene around me. I could see the entrance to the restaurant from my lounge table, and the place was packed with mostly fresh-faced young mothers being taken out to Mother's Day dinners by their fuzzy-cheeked husbands. Some were dressed up, others not. One young man in shorts came into the bar and lit up a cigarette, which he puffed on purposefully while watching the ball game and glancing nervously over his shoulder at the restaurant he had just left. "Looks bad for Atlanta," he said, and I agreed. Then he stubbed out his half-finished smoke and returned to the restaurant.

After a second martini, I went to the dining room. The young man in shorts was sitting in the booth next to mine with his wife, their baby, and someone I took to be his mother-in-law. There are many kinds of journeys, I thought, and he was just starting on one with which I was oh-so-familiar.

The summer before I went off to college, I stayed with my aunt May in Hazlehurst. My father and I had had a falling-out, and my mother wanted me out of Miami—out of his sight. After being away for a couple of months, in late August I drove back to Miami to pick up my clothes and my trunk for college at Ole Miss. The car I drove down in was the maroon 1960 Thunderbird belonging to Aunt May's son, Alex, the hospitalized schizophrenic. I had never driven the T-Bird so far before, and I relished every minute of the trip. I loved the way I looked in that car.

I stayed in Miami about a week. By the time I was due to head back to Mississippi, most of my closest friends had already gone off to school. So the night before I left, I ended up driving aimlessly around town in the T-Bird with a buddy. We looked like a couple of lost characters out of *American Graffiti*. We'd been in school clubs together and had run with the same general crowd. The year before, I had lent him my formal studs and cufflinks to wear to a prom, and he had lost one of the cufflinks. I kidded him about that that night, about how I was really going to need that cufflink in college. At some point in the evening we hooked up with another former classmate at a drive-in restaurant. She was a pretty girl I'd known since junior high but with whom I'd probably exchanged, at the most, 200 words. Even in the moment I knew it was a bittersweet end to my Miami years. Though I would be back in the summers for the next four years, it would never be the same.

The three of us drove over the causeway to the Beach that night, then up a few miles and back over another causeway to the mainland again. Finally we got bored and parked the car in front of a motel on Biscayne Boulevard. We sat talking on the motel lawn, and eventually we all lay back in the soft fragrant grass and stared at the moon and stars while we wondered what the future held for us. Pam Whitman was the girl, and Rusty Calley was the boy. I don't know what happened to her. As for Rusty, in a few short years I would open a newspaper and see that he'd been charged with wiping out a village of civilians in Vietnam. My Lai, the village was called. By the time I read that, everything had changed everywhere. I remember looking at Rusty's picture in that paper, and then at that lone cufflink in my jewelry box, and trying my hardest to recall the way he had been—the way we *all* had been—back in Miami in the early years, back under those billion stars before the moon shifted and the tide turned.

After dinner at Julie's, heading back across the street to the Days Inn, I noticed that the entrance ramp to I-10 was just a block away. It reminded me again of that last Miami cruise in the T-Bird. On the morning after I had ridden around with Rusty and Pam, I awoke early and drove north as far as Tallahassee. In those days, I then headed west on U.S. 90 across the Florida panhandle, where road crews sweated in the August sun to etch parallel grooves in the face of the earth. They told us this was the sign of the future—the new interstate highway system.

Thirty-five years later, some people would probably argue that the moment we started building the interstates was the moment we began to lose our way. In any case, I was glad to see that familiar red, white, and blue sign pointing the way to I-10. The next morning, I would guide the Boxster to that very on-ramp and from there would run west toward the opposite coast. I went to sleep dreaming of speed.

FOUR

Blue Highways

Monday, May 12, brought a welcome crispness to the air. Finally I had left the tropics. The day was clear, and I put the top down right from the start. As I slipped my parka over my T-shirt and shorts and turned the heat up on my bare legs, I remembered a time years before in Minnesota, when I had driven my first Fiat Spider with the top down even on cold fall mornings. There was a stretch of open country between my house and my office, and I loved taking the curves around frigid ponds with clouds of steam rising from them. There's nothing like that for clearing the morning haze from your head, but you have to have the heat on high. I suppose that's why convertibles are the vehicles of choice for the midlife crisis. After being weighted down with responsibility and propriety, a person finds a convertible wonderfully impractical. You lower the top to get cool, but you blast the heat to stay warm. It's somehow freeing to be so profligate.

My garment bag broke as I was hauling it into the Days Inn the night before. The shoulder strap came off—pulled right out of the socket. Once I wrestled it to the bed, I noticed that the seam around the main zipper was ripping, too. I had packed too much, especially considering that I'd worn T-shirts, shorts, and tennis shoes the whole time I'd been on the road. Yet each night I tugged the huge bag from its tight nest in the front compartment and lugged it inside only to change underwear, shirt, and socks. I thought again of Lewis and Clark. In June 1805, when they decided they were carrying too many provisions for a particular portion of the expedition, they simply buried the excess, planning to dig it up on the return journey. But I wasn't passing this way again. At this rate, my bag wouldn't survive the trip.

Interstate 10 connects the coasts of the country, from Jacksonville, Florida, on the east to Los Angeles on the west. Running some 2,500 miles along the southern edge of the central United States, it cuts through a cross section of scenery, from marshland to mountains, from rich farmland to arid desert. I-10 echoes the shape of the continent, rolling flat across Florida, Alabama, Mississippi, and Louisiana, then dipping down to San Antonio, evoking the steep plunge of the vast state of Texas itself. From there it curves gently west-northwesterly with the national border, skirting the southern edges of New Mexico and Arizona before crossing the Mojave Desert to Palm Springs, and on into L.A.

Today we take such fine roads for granted, and for Americans of a certain age it's almost impossible to imagine life without the interstates. William Least Heat Moon took to the back roads—the "blue highways" on his map—in search of the real America. In my new road atlas, interstates are shown as blue highways. There is a profound irony in that. With so many of the smaller highways now simply access roads for strip malls, it's up to the interstates to give us what remains of the experience we envision when we dream of being on the road. The interstates wind through some of the most beautiful country in America. And yet a trip on those blue highways isn't the same trip that Sal Paradise and Dean Moriarity made, or William Least Heat Moon.

There is an insular loneliness to interstate travel. Life is confined to prepackaged pods placed at predictable intervals, signified by bold symbols perched atop tall poles. Otherwise, you rock along in your personal capsule, ebbing and flowing in the eternal rhythm of the road. You pass cars and drive in front for a while. Then they pass you. Soon you pass again. Nothing stays constant except your mutual movement. You get to know certain cars, certain bumper stickers, certain quirks of the drivers in your loose caravan. Sometimes you see a car you recognize stopped at the same Flying J travel plaza, and maybe you nod to the driver or maybe you don't. Later you see him on the road again, and perhaps he's turning onto a different interstate, to join a different caravan. You almost feel a sense of abandonment.

The interstate system began with such high hopes. It was the culmination of more than sixty years of efforts to create good roads in America—efforts that, like early car travel itself, often ran into dead ends or became mired in place. Since the middle of the nineteenth century, roads had been the responsibility of states and municipalities. They were usually awful, but most travelers didn't care. They did their traveling by rail.

It was the popularity of the bicycle, in the 1890s, that first drew public attention to the poor state of the roads. In 1893, the federal government created an Office of Road Inquiry to help state and local officials improve their thoroughfares. Various bills were introduced to Congress advocating federal aid to states for road building (with the states picking up half the cost), but most ended up shelved in some committee. Then as now, money was the sticking problem. Roads were a never-ending drain on finances. You couldn't just build them and let them be. You had to keep repairing them. Also, farmers resented being taxed "so wealthy city peacocks could ride their bicycles." In fact, the nation's first documented auto accident happened in New York City on May 30, 1896, when a bicyclist was struck by an out-of-town driver.

Country folk and city folk have always had their simmering mutual resentments. I suspect I was the target of some of that back in Okeechobee, when the pickup-truck driver at the gas station hoo-hawed about the love bugs on my expensive foreign car. Until roads and cars came along, city and country people didn't have much interaction. Unfortunately, the very first drivers were the sons of the wealthy, who were the only ones able to afford cars. These hotheaded scions tore through whatever roads there were, upsetting farmers and city fathers alike. Their early conflicts were hilarious: City people, resenting the scaring of horses and the danger to pedestrians, passed ridiculous ordinances, such as one in Michigan requiring "every self-propelled vehicle moving on the highway to be preceded by 'a man of mature age,' walking not less than ten rods or not more than twenty rods in advance. When the machine approached a cow, horse or other domestic animal, either from front or rear, the driver was required to stop and 'gently' lead the beast to a place of safety." Farmers joined forces to stop the drivers from invading their sanctity. They buried rusty nails, broken bottles, barbed wire, and crosscut saw blades in the dusty roads. Eventually, the farmers began to see that there was money to be made from the hapless automobile drivers—by towing (behind a team of horses) their disabled vehicles to the nearest blacksmith shop, or hauling them from the muddy ruts of a country road.

The standoff began to change form when good roads promised to give farmers something they wanted and needed—free mail delivery. Then, in 1908, when Henry Ford introduced his low-priced Model T for the masses, everybody became interested in good roads. The problem was that they weren't interested in the *same* good roads. Farmers wanted good farm-to-market roads, while motorists wanted good interstate roads. Like me back in Miami, American drivers were ready to roll. They'd been pent up too long.

The debate raged for the next three decades, but the farmers won the first round. In July 1916, President Woodrow Wilson—himself a bit of a car nut, reportedly spending two hours or more daily in his White House Pierce-Arrow to "loosen his mind entirely upon the problems before him"—signed into law the Federal Aid Road Act of 1916. It established state highway agencies manned by professional engineers, and also gave the feds project approval so they could ensure certain standards. The act focused mostly on rural post roads. The very first center line on a rural highway was painted in 1917, between Marquette and Ishpeming, Michigan.

Entering I-10 from Tallahassee, I spotted a young blond woman hitchhiking at the entrance ramp. She looked like a student. I stopped before I even considered what I was doing. "Where you headed?" I said.

Up close she looked harder than I had detected from a distance. Her blond hair wasn't clean, and there was a weariness in her eyes. She had a nice smile, though, and she flashed me her homemade cardboard "Mobile" sign. My initial plan had been to take I-10 across the Florida panhandle to Pensacola, then over Mobile Bay, and from there along the Mississippi Gulf Coast into Louisiana, where I would turn north on I-55 and reenter Mississippi. That was a distance of some 400 miles. But in Tallahassee I changed my route. Instead of staying on I-10, I decided I needed to make a couple of detours. So I told the blond girl that I was indeed headed toward Mobile, with various side trips along the way. As soon as I said that, I realized it sounded like a line. I offered to take her as far as the Chattahoochee exit, which wasn't but a few miles west. She decided she'd be better off hitching from Tallahassee than from the much smaller ramp where I would have to drop her.

I hit the gas hard when I curled out of the cloverleaf onto the interstate. I noticed that I was shaking. It was a stupid thing to do, stopping for a hitchhiker. Even though she was a young woman, you just never know. Hadn't blond serial killer Aileen Wuornos preyed on hapless male drivers very near here?

When my brother and I were young, our father used to tell a story about picking up a hitchhiker on one of his travels. The event had taken place in the late 1940s or early 1950s, before our national paranoia about strangers had taken hold. Dad traveled throughout Mississippi a lot in those days, mostly on rural roads between Tupelo and Jackson. One day toward dusk he picked up a fellow who said he was bound for Jackson, which was exactly where my father was heading. The man got into the car, and they talked for a few minutes, and then they lapsed into silence. As darkness fell, Dad kept his eyes on the road, though he couldn't escape the uncomfortable feeling that his passenger was staring at him. He glanced over, and sure enough, the man was studying him. Maybe Dad said the man had a "goofy grin" on his face. After many miles of that, Dad pulled into a well-lighted service station. "This is as far as you go," he said to the hitchhiker.

"I thought you were going to Jackson," the man said.

"I am, but I'm not taking you."

The next day, Dad opened the newspaper and saw the hitchhiker's face staring out at him. He was wanted for murdering his wife, whose body he had hacked into tiny pieces. He killed her because he didn't like the way she had fixed her hair.

I loved that story and asked Dad to tell it again and again. My mother says it really happened, and I believe it did. But truth or not, it was my first urban legend. It was a cautionary tale about life on the road—which is to say, life itself. The journey. You don't hear urban legends about houses. Houses are supposed to be safe places. Urban legends are part of our coming-of-age, and they almost always have to do with cars. Just as I was about to learn to drive, I heard the tale—sworn, as all of them are, to be true—of the couple who were making out in their backseat in a dark, secluded place. Hearing sounds, they decided to leave. There had been reports of a madman with an artificial arm on the loose. When they got home and the young man walked around to open the door for his girlfriend, he found a hook—a prosthetic hand—on the door handle of the car.

That story had a big impact on me. When I started dating, I always kept one eye out for predators. Implicit in such stories was the titillating danger of being on your own, of venturing from the warm safety of your family's four walls. Strange things waited for you in the dark of night. A car could take you there.

Driving toward Chattahoochee, I thought back to my own hitchhiking experience on this very interstate. The year was 1965, and I was heading home from college for the summer. But it wasn't to be just any summer. Before August was out, I would be a married man. I was twenty-one years old.

I was a fool, of course. That goes without saying. I can't explain now how I got to be that way. There was—is—something inside me that makes me ignore possible consequences. I do this, I suppose, in exchange for not being bored. I'm not talking about putting myself in physical danger—I don't climb mountains or do whitewater rafting or even ski. The danger I gravitate toward is emotional and financial. I can think of many metaphors for how this risk-taking feels—stepping off base, getting out on a limb. It's thrilling in its chaotic way. At its heart, it is leaving home.

I had spent a couple of days with friends in Biloxi, on the Mississippi Gulf coast, before I was to leave for my final single summer in Miami. On the appointed day, I hauled my guitar and suitcase to U.S. 90 and stuck out my thumb. It was a drizzly May morning. Almost immediately, I saw a car slow down, make a left turn, and double back to pick me up. I knew what that meant. Who but a lonely gay guy would go around the block to pick up a wet college student and his luggage? He was a clean-cut young man with tortoiseshell glasses and a friendly smile. He looked like somebody's big brother on one of the fifties family sitcoms. I got in, and we went through the usual preliminaries. Then, just before we reached Mobile Bay, he began talking about Dauphin Island, a barrier island resort community on the Gulf. He said it was a beautiful place, lush and fragrant, and he wondered if I would go there with him.

I had him put me out at a turn in the road where the comforting image of a mom-and-pop store seemed to promise warmth and safety. The rain had stopped, and I hitched up my guitar case and bag and headed toward a cigarette and a cup of hot coffee. At that moment, another car slammed on its brakes and skidded to the shoulder. Then it backed up. An older man, cherubic in a porkpie hat, was ducking slightly to look at me through the passenger window. "Need a lift?" he said.

In the 1960s and even into the 1970s, you could never be sure whether the interstates shown on your map were actually complete. There was a lot of getting on and getting off. As I recall, Cherub and I headed along U.S. 90, connecting with whatever parts of I-10 were finished. I looked straight ahead as he talked with great fervor about his church work, a topic that triggered a certain uneasiness in me. Having grown up a Baptist, I knew something about the hypocrisy of those who protest too much. All across Mobile Bay and into western Florida, he recounted his good deeds and engaged me in telling him about my years in Sunday School and Baptist Training Union and Wednesday-night prayer meeting. Finally it seemed that we had exhausted that subject. He was silent for a long moment. "Do you like sex?" he said.

I got out at the fork of two highways. No sooner had I lit my Marlboro than another car pulled to a halt about twenty yards away. I stomped out the cigarette and jogged up to the open passenger window. Thank God it was daylight. At first, all I saw was a gnarled leather-clad hand stretched across the seat. Black leather. I ducked to look at the driver, who was smiling what could only be called a ghoulish smile. He reminded me of Frankenstein. His hair, which started in a definite line just above his eyebrows, was swept back in a single wave across his squarish skull. "Where you headed?" he said. There was something the matter with his voice.

"Oh," I said tentatively, "Tallahassee."

"I'm going all the way to Jacksonville."

Had I not been brought up in a home where we were taught not to hurt people's feelings, I would've said, "No way I'm getting in this car with *you*." Instead, I thought, *How can I say no? He'll know it's just because he looks like a monster.*

"Great," I said, and I opened the door and threw my bags into the backseat. As he pulled away, I cut my eyes to try to catch a glimpse of his strange right hand. The left one looked normal (though unusually large and powerful), and was not hidden inside a leather glove. The gloved hand was capable of pulling down the gear shift lever, but after that it rested between us on the front seat.

We rode together across the Florida panhandle that day, with only occasional attempts at conversation. Once, we stopped at a cafe for a cup of coffee. Through his speech impediment I gathered that he was on his way to Jacksonville to murder his ex-business partner, who had screwed him out of money. It was dark when we got to Tallahassee. When he dropped me off, I went straight to a phone booth and called my mother. I told her I was taking the bus the rest of the way home.

After some twenty miles on I-10, I eased the Boxster down the off-ramp and onto the small country road to Chattahoochee. I had never been there but had heard about the place since the day I moved to Florida. Chattahoochee is where the state hospital is. People are crazy there.

Chattahoochee wasn't my destination—I was headed toward Sneads, population 1,746, a hamlet that once held out the promise of great wealth to me. In the late 1960s, after I was married but still in graduate school, my father wrote letters to my brother and me suggesting that we buy land in Sneads, Florida. He had bought some from a friend, and the word was that when I-10 was finished, one of the exit ramps was going to be at Sneads. "Do you know what that means?" Dad said when I phoned him to talk about his letter. "Property values will skyrocket."

He made the purchase easy, selling Phil and me five acres apiece and allowing us to make incredibly small monthly payments for an incredibly long time. It was the only way I could've done it—I was living in a $67-a-month apartment, earning $1,200 a year in assistantship money and being otherwise supported by my secretary wife. But I remember feeling proud that I was suddenly a "landowner." I often worked into conversations the phrase "my property in Florida." It was a delusion almost as great as the one I had experienced when I married into my first car and began to think of myself as an "automobile owner."

My first wife—a high-school girlfriend—had opted for a job

instead of college, a decision that probably haunts her to this day. But while her friends were struggling to get through school, the career girl treated herself to monthly payments on a brand-new 1962 Chevrolet Super Sport coupe in a cunning shade of icy blue, like Aqua Velva. I loved driving that flashy car when we were dating (it was a time when the male always drove, no matter who owned the vehicle), and once we were married and living in Oxford, Mississippi, I would drop her off at work and have it all to myself. Circling the famous town square where Faulkner trod, I cruised in and out of a fictional world of my own. There was an easy glamor about that Chevy Super Sport that had appealed to my callow grasp of reality. I wouldn't go so far as to say I married my wife for her car, but its existence as part of the package undeniably presented a comfortingly skewed image of grown-up life. If neither of us had had an automobile, I wonder if we would have been as quick to tie the knot.

To my moral credit, after the wedding I quickly felt like a fraud driving my wife's sporty Chevrolet. I felt like a fraud because I *was* a fraud: Trying to handle the household bills on our meager income, I had taken to making only the minimum payment on our gasoline credit-card statements. Within mere months we had run up a staggering balance. I consider my first adult decision not the momentous one of taking a wife but the much harder one of coming to terms with trading that beautiful car for one we could actually afford. One night in the spring of 1966, paying bills at the dining room table my parents had given to us, I broke it to my wife: *We can't go on this way*. The next weekend we drove the fifty miles to Tupelo, where we left the ice-blue Super Sport on the used-car lot of a Volkswagen dealership and drove back to Oxford in our new beige ("Sea Sand") 1965 VW beetle. That drive could well have marked the beginning of the end of our marriage.

So when my father called about the land in Sneads, perhaps I saw more to the opportunity than even he did. It was a chance to redeem myself, to show that, yes, even an immature English major can make money in this world. I can't remember the exact amount I paid him monthly—something like twenty-five dollars. By the time I had paid off the note, my dad was dead, my wife and I had divorced, and I'd had to reimburse her for half the total amount so I could keep the land. Some fifteen years after all this began, my sons and I drove to Sneads to see "my property." We couldn't find it, even with a map from the tax collector. All the land looked alike—scrubby and undeveloped. Nothing much had happened in Sneads, because in fact the I-10 exit *hadn't* gone there. Instead it had been placed a dozen or so miles to the west, near Marianna.

Such was the power of the interstate highway system: It had about it the magic to spark dreams. The country's most ambitious public-works project ever, the interstate was, at long last, the truly open road, open meaning unpredictable, full of promise, pregnant with possibility for all—for the Kerouac manqués who yearned to crisscross America (burning in the night!), for the urban merchants who saw that the road to the heartland was paved with gold, for the small-town Babbitts determined to land a piece of the action for their own dear burgs. Like rumors of a map to buried treasure, whispers of the interstate's supposed path intoxicated the senses of everyone who heard them. It was no less than the reopening of the American West.

Even those crusty, pragmatic engineers in charge of building the road system felt its power. "It was a great time to go to work," says Francis C. "Frank" Turner, one of the acknowledged forces behind the interstate highway system. I first heard about Turner when I phoned the Federal Highway Administration for background on the interstates. Highway historian Richard Weingroff immediately sent me a packet of research material, including a special issue of the department's publication, *Public Roads,* this one commemorating the fortieth anniversary of the interstate highway. On the cover were pho-tos of President Dwight Eisenhower and four other men, over the cover line "Founding Fathers of the Interstate System." One of the men pictured was Frank Turner.

He's an old man now, but his memories of building the interstate haven't dimmed. At the time I phoned him, he was living in Arling-ton, Virginia, but was about to move in with his son in West Virginia. In Arlington, he lived "on the heaviest-traveled street in town. Sixteen thousand vehicles pass in front of my driveway every day." We had a good laugh at the irony, since it's pretty clear that the interstates added cars to the roadways of America rather than simply solving problems of congestion. "I can't complain about traffic," Turner said. "I put triple windows on my house. The noise doesn't bother me anymore."

Turner got his civil engineering degree from Texas A & M in 1929. "I graduated on a Friday, and on Tuesday I went to work for the Bu-reau of Public Roads." He worked his way from Texas to Little Rock and from there to Washington. In the 1940s he spent four years in Alaska supervising construction of the Alaska Highway. When he got home in 1945, his boss, chuckling, told him he had a plan to help Frank get "thawed out." He was soon dispatched to the Philippines for four more years, rebuilding all the roads that were destroyed during the war. By the time Dwight Eisenhower was elected, Frank Turner was in a position to become part of the president's hand-picked brain trust for figuring out how to give our country the kinds of roads Ike had seen in Germany during the war.

In a way, Frank Turner's story is the story of this country in the twentieth century. His father was a railroad man, first a fireman and then a locomotive engineer. The elder Turner used to come home from his trips and talk about the roads that paralleled the railroads al-most everywhere. The railroads had pointed the way for the roads. Tracks had been laid along the most advantageous routes, snaking around the sloping grades, streaking through the flatlands. Frank's father loved his job on the railroad, but by the early part of this century he saw more and more automobiles dusting along on the parallel path. He immediately grasped the compelling power of the automobile: no rails; total freedom.

"He told me," Frank says, "that if he had his life to live over again, he would get into the road business." Frank's grandfather had told him the same thing. Young Frank spent his summers at his grandfather's farm in Lawton, Oklahoma, where his grandfather was the first man in the community to own an automobile—a Maxwell. "He would let me sit in the driver's seat and pretend I was driving the car. At nights in those days we didn't have TV or even radio, so I would receive lectures about the world from my grandfather. He told me, too, that if he were a young man, he would get into the highway business. 'Roads,' he said, 'are going to be the big thing in this country.' "

News of the Indy 500 time trials crackled across the airwaves, an American countdown to summer. I didn't linger long in Chattahoochee, though the hospital, with its campus of early-twentieth-century white buildings shaded by live oaks, looked like a perfectly nice place to be insane. Sneads lies a few miles to the west, across the Apalachicola River in the Central Time Zone. On this May day the town was prettier—more rolling, more farmy—than I had remembered it from my one and only visit fifteen years earlier. The only flaw in the bucolic canvas was a shotgun-toting guard eyeing young field workers at a correctional facility on U.S. 90.

My vague plan was to poke around and see to what effect the failure to land the I-10 interchange had doomed this town so many years before. A sign from Lions International welcomed me to Sneads proper, which consisted of a strip mall with, on the north side, a

Family Dollar store, a Movie Max, a McDaniel's ("your superior food store"), and on the south a Dyno-Max, a discount muffler shop, a Faith Baptist Church, Tatum's Hardware and Feed store, and a barbecue place called Shoestrangs. I stopped at the tax collector's office, to which I had sent yearly checks for so long, but found it closed on Mondays. One wrong turn later and I was out in the country again, on a winding two-lane road that would have been fun to drive on had it not been for the ominous pickup truck suddenly following me bumper to bumper. In Jackson County, Florida, Nevada Porsches make poor hiding places.

I neither sped up nor slowed down, but silently cursed James Dickey for instilling in me the ever-present fear of off-road deliverance. Dickey probably owned stock in Holiday Inns, or another of those clean, well-lighted places. After an eternity of silent harrassment, the truck driver veered off into the rural ether. He was there in my rearview, and then he wasn't. For a second I wondered if he had been there at all. I made a U-turn back toward Sneads, pulling up in the loose dry gravel in front of Shoestrangs. It looked like a place to meet people.

Toting tape recorder and notebook, I weathered the blank stares of the locals, including a table of four men wearing camouflage caps. At another table near the front, a pretty blond woman smiled and said hello, and gestured to a free spot near the window, where—thankfully it wasn't said—I could keep an eye on my fancy sports car. Soon a big friendly boy brought water and a menu. I made a big deal of not being hungry enough for their special barbecue—which I knew was excellent, next time, maybe—but instead ordered iced tea and a plate of black-eyed peas. With pepper sauce. The camo stares palpably softened.

Before long the big friendly boy came over and asked me what kind of car I was driving. "Dang," he said when I told him, "it doesn't look like a Porsche. I thought it was a Ferrari or something." His name was Rick Kyle, and I asked him to sit down and tell me about life in Sneads. It didn't seem to be a subject he had thought much about. He knew that many people lived in Sneads and worked in other towns. They drive fourteen miles to Marianna to buy their groceries, he said. His real insight was that a lot of them spend their personal time, their dreaming time, restoring old cars. They're getting up an antique car club. Rick has his eye on a 1948 Mercury coupe over near Marianna. He's been trying to talk the owner out of it for a year now, but the boy really doesn't want to sell it because it belonged to his grandfather. "I'm gonna keep on till I get it from him," Rick said.

Old cars appeal to Rick and his friends because they can work on them. Rick, who took a small motors course out at the Vo-Tech, said he loves anything to do with motors. He even has a three-wheeled cycle that he's building a motor for. Right now he drives an old Camaro he's worked on. "But it isn't street legal," Rick said, grinning. He told me he once fixed up a Ford Galaxie with so much horsepower that it required two batteries even to start the thing. A policeman pulled him over and didn't give him a ticket. "All he said was, 'What you got in here?' " and the two of them popped the hood and stood together silently admiring the power of America, as echoed in the husky throbbing of Rick's gleaming carburetors. It was a power you could understand. Throughout the country, away from the precious capitals of fashion and commerce, I got the feeling that we invest in our cars a reflection of our nation's successes and failures. They're how *we're* doing in the world. Today something real seems to have been lost. Bill Gates may be the richest man in America, but it's not the same as when Henry Ford and John D. Rockefeller ruled the world.

As I was paying my check, I complimented the blond woman on the peas. Her name was Sue. Then I told her what I was doing in

Sneads—that I had come to see the town where I had once bought property in the vain hope that I-10 would make me a rich man. Sue seemed slightly offended at my implication. She told me about having bought property there herself for $2,500 an acre that was now selling for $7,500. "But you'd really make a killing if you'd bought in Marianna," she said. My point exactly. As I was leaving, Sue gave me a parting message: "Sneads is a nice town. There are good people here."

When I drive through places like Sneads, I often play a game in my mind. I wonder if everyone else does the same. What I do is imagine hiding out. Say I wanted to escape from my life and disappear. Where can you hide in America? Towns like Sneads, off the beaten path, with their crazy quilt of fine old houses and next-door trailers, their warrens of work sheds and auto garages and outbuildings and tin lean-tos—is there a room for me there, in a garage apartment, maybe, beneath the bare rafters and behind the dusty panes of glass? But of course that would be the worst place to try to hide. Little towns turn inward—they know everything that happens in them, even if they can't fathom what's happening *to* them.

No, you have to hide where the world is moving. What had happened to Sneads—and to thousands of other perfectly nice little towns like it—was that the coming of the interstate highway system finally confirmed and codified its irrevocable status as a backwater. Frank Turner says that the 1916 highway act that laid the foundation for a national highway program required each state to devise a system of connected routes based on various criteria, such as traffic volume, economic impact, and other national effects, that would allow the state highway people to identify the routes to be given top priority. Entrances and exits were kept to a minimum, and were placed where "joiners" had a reasonable need to get on the main line at some point.

"In almost every case," says Turner, "they were obvious."

FIVE

The Man with the Car

My other detour from the straight shot across I-10 was to lead me to the new town of Seaside, which rises like a mirage from the white sands of the Florida Gulf coast a few miles west of Panama City. Built in the early 1980s, Seaside presented not just a new kind of resort but an object lesson in how the best of the past could be incorporated into new suburbs. Seaside, designed by the Miami husband-wife team of architects Andres Duany and Elizabeth Plater-Zyberk, had quickly become the Lourdes of new urbanism. Architects from around the country have flocked there to behold the wonder and to take its healing lessons back to their respective communities. I decided that since I was this close, I had to make my own pilgrimage.

I had come to that decision the previous night in Tallahassee, while settling in to my usual bedtime reading. The book in hand was new urbanist Philip Langdon's *A Better Place to Live: Reshaping the American Suburb,* and I was particularly struck by the evocative message on its cover. It features a photograph of a beach community like the one that lives in everyone's rose-tinted memory. In fact, there *is* a rose-tinted quality to Langdon's book jacket. The picture was taken late on a summer's day, and the sun's waning light gives the pastel houses and picket fences a homey glow. In the middle of the narrow street—only one parked car is in sight—a young mother in shorts strolls home with three children, all holding hands, all returning to hearth and home after a happy day at the beach. The street is lavender in the slanted light, and the mother and children are preceeded by their own long rosy shadows. The whole scene—including the tan young mother in short shorts—reminds me of the movie *The Summer of '42,* a story of innocence lovingly lost and the exquisite thrill of human touch. But the photo on the cover of Langdon's book isn't of a beach town from the forties. It is instead a picture of Seaside.

Rick Kyle had told me that Panama City was only twenty-five miles from Sneads, that he sometimes rides his bike there. In small out-of-the-way towns where it's nothing to drive fourteen miles for groceries, maybe space and time aren't as important as in the cities. Maybe you lose perspective. Following his directions ("Turn left where the IGA store used to be . . ."), I soon saw a sign that put Panama City an hour and a half away. I really didn't mind. The interior of Florida's panhandle is refreshingly open, untrafficked, and the roads are flat and straight, with the occasional winding curve. I hadn't driven the Porsche above 75 m.p.h. in days. On the empty Highway 167, I floored the accelerator, hitting 95 before I had to brake for a turn, which I took at 80. My skin tingled as I fought to keep from sailing into a stand of pines. Back on the straight and narrow, I imagined myself in a movie scene in which the camera follows me from above, gradually pulling up, higher and higher, until the Boxster is just a silver speck flashing through the sun-dappled green.

Just after I connected with Highway 231, I caught a glimpse of something that caused me to hit the brakes and make a U-turn. On the east side of the road, in the middle of a fenced pasture in front of what looked like a barn, except for the big round Coca-Cola sign over the door, stood a stunning row of antique automobiles. I wheeled into the corral and pulled up in front of the cars. Soon a fortyish man in jeans emerged from a nearby trailer. He had a mustache, a small goatee, and graying blond hair that didn't want to lie down. I introduced myself. His name was John Sullivan, and he was a transplanted Michigander who couldn't outrun his passion for cars. "I grew up loving them," he said. "My dad got me into it. We especially love the cars from the 1930s—I turn on at 1932 and turn off at 1935." He reeled off the names of designers from that era, people like Gordon Buehrig and Ray Dietrich, who had created images of impossible elegance against the bleak background of the Great Depression—Dietrich's Packards and Cadillacs, Buehrig's Duesenbergs and coffin-nosed Cords.

The cars in John's pasture weren't of that elegant era, but they were old and sweet by today's standards. On the left was a black 1968 Lincoln Continental, "one of the last years for the suicide doors," John said, pointing out the rear doors that opened from the center of the car. Next to that was a black 1955 Ford four-door, a mustard-colored 1969 Pontiac Firebird, a 1947 black-and-cream two-door Ford sedan, a white 1963 Cadillac Fleetwood, a green 1966 Rambler station wagon, and a white 1977 Mercury Marauder. He invited me into the building, where three other cars were stored: a red 1932 Buick with white sidewalls that looked to be at least a yard wide; a tight gray 1965 Buick Skylark convertible; and a rare open wicker body for a 1909 Sears high-wheeler car, for which John is building a chassis. He showed me the rear post where a parasol went. This treasure he found twenty years ago at a car show in Hershey, Pennsylvania, where he bought it from the great-grandson of the man who originally owned it.

In the building with John's cars was also an amazing collection of bicycles, including some made by Pierce-Arrow, Cadillac, Peerless, Columbia, J. C. Higgins, and Schwinn. They hung on the wall, from floor to ceiling. The most valuable of them, John said, was the Schwinn Black Phantom ("We couldn't afford one of these when I was a kid—it was the rich man's bike. Now I have two of them"). I recognized it—in about 1951, my neighbor in Tupelo, Mississippi, got one just like it for Christmas. It had fat white sidewalls and a thick sloping straddle bar with a button you pushed to toot the horn. I envied (wanted, wanted, wanted) it the way John Sullivan must have envied the ones from his childhood.

With the bikes were also a few jukeboxes. John's father had started his career delivering Cadillacs from the production line to the shipping yard, and after that he had gotten into the vending machine business, which led him into jukeboxes. John grew up loving not only cars but also the gurgle and glow of the music machines, as well as the big-band tunes that emanated from them.

He invited me next door to his house to see his prize jukebox, a 1939 Rock-Ola Luxury Light-up. It sat in his bedroom by a window, under a border of album covers that encircled the room. The jukebox was huge, like a robot from the comics, with amber translucent shoulders and a head that was a speaker. Or maybe it looked more like the world's largest lava lamp, except that this one combined its mesmerizing burble with the soothing embrace of sound.

As I was leaving, John told me a story about when he was a hippie back in the 1970s, "when my hair was down to here," he said, chopping at a spot on his back about three inches above his belt. "I was going through a place in Michigan where people didn't much like long hair. But I was driving a 1931 Chrysler Imperial. I blew the engine, and suddenly people were coming out of the woodwork. 'What kind of car is it?' they said. It was a time when people in this country weren't relating to one another much, but that car brought us together. They helped me tow it to a garage, took me into town, and one guy even invited me back to his house to have dinner with his family. It was like they didn't even notice my hair. But without that car, they wouldn't have given me the time of day."

I remember when Seaside was new, how magazine editors loved it. It was cozy then, a tin-roofed fantasy world all alone in the scrubby wilderness. Now as I approached from the east, the fantasy appeared to have produced its own quaint sprawl. Whatever happened to plain old beach houses? On U.S. 98 between Panama City and Destin, the waterfront is being overtaken by "beach communities." I passed a sign for "Rosemary Beach: A New Traditional Town on the Gulf. Established 1995."

Rosemary is one of Seaside's many babies, the love child of late-century Boomerish nostalgia. No matter how hard I try to suspend disbelief, I can't seem to let places like Seaside push the buttons they're supposed to push in me. Even though they're bold and brave attempts to re-create life the way it was before we screwed it up, I can't help feeling more sadness in their midst than joy. Or hope. We are who we are, and there's no going back from that. I thought of what my friend David Sanders, whose family *likes* Seaside, told me about the place: "It's like trying to create an egg by analyzing its constituent parts and getting all the necessary chemicals and compounds together rather than just having a chicken. A chicken does it much better."

Unfortunately, as the new urbanists will tell you, the chickens all have moved to the suburbs. Now when they cross the road, it's to feed on wistfulness. Cars from all over were parked in front of Seaside's community center. Michigan, Tennessee, Alabama, North Carolina, Indiana, and now, with me, even Nevada. It's too easy to note the irony in all these people's driving such distances so they can then leave their automobiles and stroll along Seaside's tree-lined, picket-fenced streets or meander through the narrow back alleys. Our search always leads us in a circle.

I parked my Porsche near the cute dollhouse post office and conducted my own foot tour. Seaside is like a designer room open to the sky. There are studied vistas everywhere—here a tiny balcony with a single rocker; there an old blue Ford against a periwinkle cottage; and over there a pot of pink geraniums peeking through a pure-white fence. The place was designed as the antisuburb.

It didn't take long to get the point, and I soon decided to move on. By then it was mid-afternoon of a day that felt interminable. I had begun to lose my sense of what I was supposed to be doing, driving across this vast country (this vast *state*) in this Porsche. As I lowered the Boxster top to leave, a fortyish woman alighting from a Suburban smiled meaningfully, and a tad too long. I laughed at the absurdity. Even at Seaside, you are what you drive.

I passed through Destin, rebuilt bigger after a recent hurricane, and turned up toward Pensacola, where I planned to reconnect with I-10 and get the hell out of Florida. Heading west from Pensacola, I soon realized that I had missed my best opportunity for lodging unless I wanted to drive many miles farther, which I didn't. There was a man I wanted to see in Mobile—David Gartman, the sociology professor who had written a book and articles about the automobile and might be able to tell me more about this bigger subject I was pursuing. Academicians come up with the strangest studies. In my initial research for this book, I ran across several of them: "Bright Cars and Speeding Tickets" (drivers of red/orange, gray, and brown cars are more likely to receive speeding tickets); "Effect of Car Status on Helping Behavior in the Parking Lot" (comparing reactions to a 1986 BMW and a 1982 Mazda, researchers found no significant difference in the helpful behavior of others); "Changing Rates of Suicide by Car Exhaust in Men and Women in the United States After Car Exhaust Was Detoxified" (the male rate dropped immediately after emission controls were imposed, but the female rate continued to rise).

Back at I-10 exit five—Pensacola—I had a choice of a Red Roof Inn ($49), a Hampton Inn ($69), or Motel 6 ($31). Had I been on somebody's expense account, I would have hied straight to the Hampton Inn, but since I was paying I checked into Motel 6. "What kind of car is that?" asked the woman behind the desk.

"Porsche. The new Boxster."

"My daughter's graduating from high school this month. She wants a Lexus."

The directory I picked up in the lobby billed the Motel 6 chain as "The Road Warrior's View of the World," and noted that 33 million people—"like yourself"—stayed in Motel 6 in the past year. I noticed they accepted the AARP card, which I carry but prefer not to admit to. They start sending you the thing once you turn fifty, along with a subscription to *Modern Maturity*. I console myself with the thought that if Mick Jagger were an American, he'd be eligible for an AARP card, too. With my discount the Motel 6 came to $28 plus tax— $32 total. The room was clean but spartan—no shampoo, no remote control, a shorted-out light that blinked off and on to its own internal drummer.

For drinks and dinner I walked next door to a "restaurant and bar" (as they're called in the suburbs, instead of the other way around). This was a place named Darryl's, which I recognized because Beth and I once took our daughter to one just like it in Knoxville. I selected a table beneath a giant photograph of a silver Ferrari. Over other tables were portraits of a 300 SL Gullwing Mercedes and a white Caddy from 1957. Why is it that so many bars and restaurants use automobiles as a decorative motif? Why don't they adorn their walls with pictures of homey Craftsman cottages or cozy backyards with swing sets? A stupid question. Cars go hand in hand with bars, with being *away* from home, with being out in the uncertain, restless night.

As I sipped my gin and tonic and worked on my day's notes, I began listening to three people talking at the bar. Two men and one woman, the woman married to one of the men. Her husband used a lot of swaggering profanity, but when he went to the restroom the wife flirted shamelessly with the other man, her husband's coworker. "You can push *him* around," she said, talking about her husband and smiling, "but I'm tougher than he is. He's a wuss." They began having a chugging contest, and the man clearly let her win. The husband came back, and the other two kept it up right under his nose, but he didn't seem to notice. He just cursed a lot. The husband's colleague put his hand on the wife's back and shoulder, rubbing softly. He started talking about his new Camaro. She had long tan legs that tapered to black sexy sandals. Her crossed leg pumped with the heat of his gaze.

After a good night's sleep and a short run through an industrial park, I packed the Porsche and went to the Waffle House by the interstate. Waffle House restaurants have their place, which is usually very late at night after you've drunk too much and you have a craving for grease. My brother-in-law calls that craving the "big lie." In the daylight, though, the Waffle House isn't so enticing. This particular one was filled with a rough-looking clientele, people with tattooed biceps and keys dangling from their belts, people with ladders in their pickups surrounding my Porsche. I was glad I had changed caps, from the "Merrimack College" one to the "Terps" one. Both represented colleges, but at least the Maryland Terrapins had a ranked basketball team. I ordered the lightest thing on the menu—scrambled eggs, three pieces of bacon, raisin toast, orange juice, hold the grits. When I finally squeezed into the cockpit of the Boxster for the trip to Mobile, I was uncomfortably aware of my burgeoning second chin and the inflated spare tire around my middle. I'm not usually a big breakfast eater. So why was I compelled to stop so frequently and load up so much on this trip? Are interstate highways and the increasing chunkiness of the average American somehow connected?

I reached the Florida-Alabama line at 10:05 A.M. on Tuesday, May 13, the first state line I had crossed in almost two weeks. *Finally,* I thought, *I'm about to* really *get on the road.* Then the car phone rang. It was my agent in New York, calling with bad business news. That just topped off my day, and it was only mid-morning. Before breakfast I had spoken with Beth, who was also in New York on a project. She said nothing specific about our ongoing cold spell, but I gauged the chill factor in her voice at about ten below. Among my wife's most admirable qualities is her refusal to ever—*ever*—give up on anything. And while I believe I apologize readily—Beth disagrees—I confess to a troublesome disinclination to groveling, even when groveling is clearly the best policy. I told her that since I had overpacked and my suitcase was broken, I might swing by Little Rock on my way west. I was going to go through Memphis anyway, which was just two hours from home. Fine, she said. But unlike Motel 6, she didn't seem to be leaving a light on for me.

I slouched on toward Mobile feeling like a man without a country. This particular Boxster didn't have a CD player, just a tape deck. I had rounded up a bag of old cassettes from the corner of a closet at home, but they weren't much comfort. Neither jazz nor classical makes good road music. I fiddled with the radio. Everybody's road has its own soundtrack. Mine is early rock and roll—Jerry Lee Lewis, Little Richard, Buddy Holly, and of course mid- to late-fifties Elvis, who hit the big time the year Ike launched the interstates. No wonder John Sullivan collected both cars and jukeboxes.

But with modern prepackaged radio, the music is the same for all of us. Paula Cole had virtually made this trip with me. I could look into other cars and watch the drivers tapping on the steering wheel to the exact beat of her cowboys lament. Back when I started driving, one of the joys of a long trip was the noirish mood created by the green dash light of the radio, the red ash of a cigarette, and the stalking beams on the road ahead. Even on the radio you could *go* someplace. You could hear Chicago stations, Texas stations, even Mexican stations. Now if we don't listen to CDs from home, we all listen together to Leeza's Top 25 Countdown.

More than once on this trip I had been duped into listening to Christian music on the radio. That was new to me. Not that I don't consider myself a Christian, but I'd much rather hear a good-old rousing truth-in-advertising Baptist spiritual than some sneaky Michael Bolton or Roseanne Cash soundalike making me believe I'm hearing a love song when it's suddenly obvious that I'm hearing a Love song. "You're listening to Right Turn Radio," the unctuous announcer will finally say. "Christian country music." Travelers just can't trust radio anymore.

In Mobile, I phoned Professor Gartman at the University of South Alabama. I had never met him, never even talked with him. I had just read an article in which he was quoted. I got his answering machine, and in the middle of my rushed spiel about a book and a Boxster, the professor picked up. He said he couldn't see me until the next morning, and I reluctantly agreed to stay over. That meant that my total distance for this day would be forty miles. The day before, I had made more than 200. I consoled myself by thinking about Lewis and Clark in June and July of 1805, when they were portaging—carrying their supplies overland—around the Great Falls of the Missouri River and worked like dogs to make twenty-five miles in a month, when by water they had sometimes traveled that far in a single day.

As I was scouting around for a motel in the area where I would be meeting Gartman, I decided I deserved a balm for all the bad news I had received that day. A Motel 6 beckoned, but I didn't feel like a Road Warrior. I wanted to be taken care of, so I opted for the Best Western–owned Bradbury Suites Hotel over the Motel 6. The Bradbury had a pool, a gym, complimentary cocktails, and a free breakfast.

While parking at the rear of the hotel, I noticed a group of young guys drinking long-neck beers around the swimming pool. One of them raised his head above the brick wall of the pool area and watched me unload the Boxster. He wore his baseball cap backward. Soon he ducked his head down and said something to the others, who raised up too and looked my way. I pretended not to see any of them.

With an afternoon to kill, I decided to read, relax, and concentrate on the questions I needed to ask Gartman the next day. I slipped on my swimming trunks and carried my towel, book, and writing pad out to the sad little pool. No sooner had I opened the gate than one of the men who'd been watching me piped up from across the pool area. "*Well*," he said, and there was a sneering turn to that simple word, "there's the *man*. The man with the *car*." I glanced over and saw three guys and a girl staring at me. They all appeared to be in their early twenties. They had tattoos and beer, and curls of cigarette smoke snaking around their long greasy hair. Peeking out from behind the backward caps of two of them were those little hair tails that rednecks persist in thinking are cool. The woman was a dumpy brunette who flicked her ash on the patio and took a long pull of her long-neck. Then they all just glared.

I nodded and waved and laughed good-naturedly while I spread my towel on one of the chaise lounges. "Is that the new *Boxer?*" said another of the men. Suddenly I was *The Boxer Guy*. "Yeah," I said, and hoped to leave it at that.

"That's the first one I've seen," said the first man.

"Yeah, they're new and backlogged. I've driven from Miami to here and only seen a couple." As Beth would say, Too much information.

"Ooooh, *Miami*. You from there?"

"No, I live in Arkansas. I just picked up the car there." I decided to cut my story as short as possible.

"What kind of engine they got in that thing?" the second man said.

I was now in extremely dangerous territory. Ever since Okeechobee I'd meant to dig out the manual and study up on the engine, but I hadn't done it yet.

"Hell, *I* don't know," I heard myself say. "I just bought it anyway." I cringed inside. That was the worst thing I could have said to those particular people, with the exception of expressing how rhapsodic I was over the color of the interior. I lay down on the chaise, hoping they would let it go.

But no. The first and second guys looked at each other like they had just encountered a Martian. "*Shiiiitt,*" they said in unison, and I could tell they weren't impressed with my insouciance.

"Nah," I said, backpedaling. "It's not my car. I'm, uh—I'm working on a *project* and Porsche let me use it. They made me promise two things: not to look at the engine, and not to take it out of the country. I'm not so sure I can stick with the second one." One last desperate joke to see if I could avoid the fate of Ned Beatty in *Deliverance*.

The men seemed happy suddenly, relieved to know that the hottest car in the parking lot wasn't really mine. The dismal little wall around the pool area contained only equals. They left me alone after that.

For the next hour I tried to work on my questions, but I couldn't help listening to their conversation. They were pipe fitters there on a job (which they had to leave for in mid-afternoon). At one point the second guy dove into the pool and said it was "as cold as a well digger's ass in winter."

"What?" said the first guy. "Cold as *what?*"

"A well digger's ass in winter."

"Shit. What do you know about a well digger's ass?"

"You're a mental giant," the swimmer said, and pulled himself out of the pool so he could sun his back.

The other two people were apparently a couple. When the man left to get more beer, the woman told one of the other men, "We've been married nine months, but we been separated a lot. He cheated on me. I know I'm no beauty, but I saw *her* and she looked like a catfish."

That evening, after spending the rest of the afternoon reading and dozing, I attended the Manager's Complimentary Cocktail Party in the hotel lobby. Against the mauve-and-green decor, a middle-aged woman in a waiter uniform stood behind a bar and fixed whatever drinks people wanted. In the corner, the TV was on to a game show. A platter of popcorn was set up on a coffee table. I waited my turn at the bar behind a heavyset man in a knit shirt who ordered Evan Williams and Coke.

I have been lonely in my life, but that evening at the Mobile Best Western was one of those moments when I yearned so deeply for home that I thought I was going to have to pack up the Porsche and forget the rest of my trip. The way Americans travel today is terribly dispiriting. I ordered a gin and tonic and sat down on a sofa next to a salesman from Montgomery, who told me he always stays at this hotel just because of perks like this.

When I got a refill, I told the barmaid that I had to take it back to my room because I was expecting a phone call. The truth was, I just couldn't stand being a part of that party in the lobby. Forty-five minutes later, when I went for one last drink, five or six men were sitting around drinking and smoking and laughing like the best of friends. The popcorn was all gone.

"Americans have always made that connection between geographic mobility and social mobility," David Gartman was saying. "Ever since we landed on this big, unexplored continent, the common way to deal with a problem was to get up and move. To go somewhere else."

I found Professor Gartman cordial, accommodating, and very smart on the subject at hand. He had written a book called *Auto Opium,* which I hadn't read but which I gathered treated the automobile as the escapist instrument that the professor calls "*the* epitome, *the* symbol of twentieth-century life."

"Did you know," he said, "that in 1923, half the cars in the world were Model T's? All black, every one exactly alike. But Americans quickly became disenchanted with black. Anyone with any respect and a little money soon traded to something more distinctive. I think the Model T carried too many reminders of what people wanted to forget in that era—the drab plain monotony of their work lives. If people couldn't find individuality and release in their work lives, certainly they wanted to drive a car that distinguished them a little bit. That was the genius of Albert Sloan, head of General Motors—to figure out that Americans wanted more from cars than mass-produced transportation to get them from here to there. Very quickly they wanted style and distinction and an escape machine. Sloan hired Harley Earl to give it to them."

We talked for more than an hour, ranging over decades of stories about cars and what they mean to us ("During the Depression, cars were the last things people would give up. They would sell their houses before they would their cars"), how designers push our emotional buttons ("After the war, the new things were jet aircraft and the buzz about space. Fins are part of the euphoric freedom that people felt then"), and the life cycle of this intense romance ("By the mid-sixties, this thing, this explosion of automobility, was shown to be self-limiting. When *everyone* gets in their cars and tries to escape, it pretty much means *no one* will be able to escape").

After leaving Gartman I decided to stop for lunch. On Airport Boulevard, one of Mobile's main suburban drags, I felt viscerally the professor's words about the inability to escape in today's herds of cars. Airport Boulevard consists of several lanes going in each direction, flanked on either side by a frontage road lined with the usual commercial clutter. But what makes Airport Boulevard so crazy are the access lanes, cut in at regular intervals, connecting the main boulevard to the frontage roads. So in addition to the regular stop-and-speed-and-stop traffic, you have to keep your eyes peeled for the merging minivan or the exiting Explorer.

Gartman had told me that his newest focus was going to be on the architecture that's sprung up because of automobiles. He won't have to leave Airport Boulevard. Before cars, store signs were small and discreet. Now they scream and flash and wave and point, trying to catch the attention of the harried motorist traveling along at 50 miles an hour. There's no time for subtlety, much less serenity.

And they all look alike. For anyone driving across this country at century's end, one of the questions that continually comes to mind is, "What is real?" Why is it that everything has a *virtual* feel to it these days? I understand why Disney World and Seaside feel that way— they *are* virtual. But what about Taco Bell and Burger King and Wal-Mart and Best Buy? Why do they feel less "real" than the old plate-lunch place or the five-and-dime store I grew up with in the era of mom-and-pop stores on Main Street? For one thing, they feel thrown together, plopped down whole, instead of organic. It used to take time to build a building. Now you can have trees in January and a strip mall by June. We have a chain restaurant in Little Rock called The Macaroni Grill, which is supposed to look like the American image of a big old friendly Italian eatery. Stone walls, wooden beams, tile roof. Except if you tap on the walls, you find that they're not stone—they're some kind of lightweight stone-looking material, like one of those fake doors in the movies that cowboys used to knock the bad guys through. Those are the doors we all walk through now, all the time, everywhere. The illusion industry has seeped out of our dark movie houses and into our streets.

Finally I escaped Mobile and headed toward Mississippi, a place where I had a past—where at every turn, car stories intertwined with all the other stories of my life. But I didn't think about all that. I just enjoyed the drive. The trip from Mobile to Biloxi presents subtle delights, such as marshland, which I suppose is an acquired taste. It was for me. For the past few summers, our family has been going to the beach at Pawleys Island, South Carolina (the thing Seaside aspires to be). It was at Pawleys that I finally began to appreciate the beauty of the marsh. I like it best at red sunset, when the shadowy grass and curving mirrored creeks evoke some cosmic ice cream flavor—black raspberry rainbow swirl, perhaps. For the first score of miles on westbound I-10 in Mississippi, the highway is basically a bridge, though not over a river or creek but over marshland. Herons dot the landscape. In the absence of conspicuous vistas, I found myself noticing the interstate itself, which looked wide, reflecting the horizon, and impossibly white in the midday sun. The interstate, any stretch of it, is really an amazing feat. Now that it's all complete, it's hard to remember how it was in the fifties, sixties, and seventies when the interstate highway system was on everyone's mind—if for no other reason than that it was hard to ignore the dust and noise. Night and day, cranes and bulldozers moved the earth, rearranging it, putting a new face on the country that long had been.

I thought of old Frank Turner and his stories about road building. In the early days, from the mid-fifties to the mid-sixties, America's engineers ruled the country. The Federal Aid Highway Act of 1956 had given them authority to accommodate the nation's innate restlessness. The mission, as the engineers saw it, was simply to move America's traffic faster. No more, no less. Frank Turner was both the heart and the head of this massive project. From 1957 to 1972, he served what eventually became the Federal Highway Administration as deputy commissioner, chief engineer, and then administrator—the only head who rose through the ranks. I asked him what he and his men did right and what they did wrong. "I think the interstate was a tremendous force for economic betterment," he said. "I don't know how we would operate America without it." Turner is a proud man, as well he should be. He devoted a lifetime to helping the rest of us achieve the American dream.

"But displacement of people was the hardest thing for us to do. We were touching people's lives. We didn't realize how bad it was going to be." Not even after Turner's own parents, in the 1940s, were forced from their home in Fort Worth when a new road cut right through their driveway.

It's funny—when I started this book, I made a note to myself to "find out what the people who built the cars and the roads knew about the human heart." It turns out they knew nothing—no more, at least, than the rest of us. The early car men were convinced that people wanted practicality and durability, and it took Harley Earl years of internal combat to show them that they were wrong. As for the road people, they just loved the dust and roar of building roads. In their minds' eyes they were Paul Bunyanesque heroes, putting their heads and shoulders to the massive task of easing a nation's traffic congestion.

The first piece of the interstate to get underway—on August 13, 1956—was a section of I-70 just west of St. Louis, near where Lewis and Clark had begun their momentous journey 150 years before. Soon, sections of pavement were going down along the eastern seaboard, over and through the mountains, across the Great Plains, and crisscrossing the cornfields of America's heartland. As with the baseball diamond in *Field of Dreams,* the builders of roads had tapped into something deep and basic and very, very American: *If you build it, they will come.*

SIX

Cross the River at Memphis

It didn't take long in Mississippi for me to feel that I was too close to home. It isn't where I live, but it's where I'm from, where my parents were from, where their parents were from. People know me there. Being in Mississippi wasn't like being *on the road*. Stopping for gas in Alabama, I had found myself feeling sorry for a poor black man at the next pump because his car was old and run-down, and because it wasn't a Porsche. Then I caught myself—*Hey, wait a minute, I don't own a Porsche, either.* In Alabama I could forget who I was. Now I had entered the no-bluff zone.

On the other hand, I was just a river's crossing from where I *do* live, where Beth was, where I had made my home. I wanted to see her, to know that I was forgiven. I determined to make fast work of Mississippi.

In Biloxi, I happened to catch my old friend Mendum Dees Briscoe in his office at Dees Chevrolet. It had been fifteen years since we'd seen each other, which I wish weren't the case. Mendy is one of those people I feel a kinship with, but after college we went our separate ways. He comes from a long line of car people. His family's dealership was founded in 1925 by his maternal grandfather and great-uncle. When Mendy and I met in Oxford in 1963, it was a good time to be in that particular end of the business. While Mendy's dad was running the store, and while Frank Turner and his engineers were paving the way for more and more automobiles, Tom Adams and his team at Campbell-Ewald in Detroit were continuing, as Adams says, "to make Chevy America's car." By that year Chevrolet was selling more than any other car on the road, some two million automobiles annually. "From the late fifties into the sixties was a pretty ebullient time for the economy," Adams recalls. "Our strategy was to spring off from the basic idea that there must be something good about Chevy, because everybody was buying it."

Mendy took time to tell me what he knows about the tortured heart of the American car buyer. He's acutely aware that selling cars isn't like selling prefab sheds from Sears. Instead, he's selling dreams and image. We potential buyers may put on our serious car-shopping faces and *say* we're looking for reliability and gas mileage, but a good car salesman can read us like an Ayn Rand novel. "A lot of the time it's who the buyer is with. If a man comes in with his wife and children, that's a very good sign. At least the buyer is with you—you may not know at first which one it is, but at least the buyer isn't at *home*."

He told me a story about a man who came into the dealership years ago saying he wanted to buy a used car. "The man had only one arm— the left one," Mendy said, "and the car he had his eye on was a full-size Impala convertible, red, with a manual floor shift." He paused to make sure I gathered the significance of that last detail.

"The salesman showed him the car, but he did so reluctantly. 'You do realize, sir,' he said, 'that this is a standard shift.'

" 'You let me worry about that,' the man said.

"He paid for the car, told the salesman, 'Stick her in first,' and then he slung gravel. We never saw him again. And I learned something crucial from that episode. I've missed many sales by trying to direct people to what they needed instead of what they wanted. Did that one-armed man *need* that stick-shift convertible? It's the last thing on this *earth* he needed. But he *wanted* that car."

Listening to Mendy talk, I gathered that the car business bears little resemblance to the way it was in the heady days of the fifties and sixties, and even into the seventies. In those days, cars seemed like the future instead of the past. People were so infatuated with automobiles that they would place an order for the exact model with the exact options they wanted and wait *months* for it to come in. Today, Mendy said, it's a spontaneous sale. No savoring, no sweet appreciation. As the century rushes to its conclusion, we're all in a race against time.

One of the casualties has been brand loyalty. Just as there used to be die-hard loyalty to baseball teams (until owners began moving their franchises because of money), there was a time in this country when people, even families, were identified by the cars they drove. My dad was a Ford man. Our Miami neighbors were Buick people. "But sometime in the mid-eighties," said Mendy, "a revolutionary new thought dawned on people who'd been General Motors customers for generations: 'I guess I really don't *have* to buy a GM product.' " Restlessness turned to ruthlessness. The momentum now, in the nineties, has moved to the huge superstores—conglomerations of dealerships transformed into one stunning high-volume entity—which threaten to make the smaller dealerships, especially in the urban areas, as outdated as Wal-Mart made the mom-and-pop stores downtown. Mendy urged me to look up a mutual friend of ours, Erich Braun, a former car dealer who now lives in California and knows a lot about what's happening in the auto industry. "Boy, has *he* got stories to tell."

From the moment Erich's name was mentioned, even though I was paying attention to Mendy's tales, some part of my mind was scrolling back to a rainy night in the summer of 1967 when our mutual friend Bill Ballentine was killed at the wheel of his maroon Mustang. Unlike Jack in Miami, Bill didn't have the scent of inevitable violent death about him. His energy and his laughter were like charms, protective charms. He seemed too happy to attract tragedy. Mendy introduced me to Bill, and Bill introduced me to Erich. Bill and I became fast friends. His mother, Audelle, and I corresponded at Christmas for nearly twenty years after his death, but in the late eighties I let that slip away. I jettisoned Christmas cards at about the same time I simplified my wardrobe. My mornings are easier now, but I miss some old friends. I planned to see Audelle Ballentine if she still lived in the same town. By my estimate, she would be in her seventies now. Mendy said he'd lost touch with her, too, much longer ago than I had. He asked me to give her his regards. We didn't talk about Bill.

After leaving Dees, I pulled into a service station for directions through Louisiana to I-55. Just as I was opening my door to get out, I heard a voice say, *"Niice caaarr."* I looked up to see a fortyish man in running shorts bent over the Boxster's sloping hood, like a jeweler inspecting a precious gem. I held my breath.

After exclaiming over the beauty of my car, he said, "There's my heap over there." He pointed to a pristine white 1967 Corvette at the gas pump. "I have five thousand man-hours in it," he said, and he did all the work on it himself but the mirrors and the interior. "I have two—this is the one I drive. The other one I take to shows. It's insured for $165,000." The mechanic had cranked it up to 400-something horsepower, he said. "But *this* car—I would *never* go up against this."

I smiled magnanimously and thanked whichever saint watches over fraudulent travelers, and I made a silent vow—*this* time I really meant it—to study up on the engine specs of the Boxster. Otherwise, I said to myself—literally out loud—I'm going to disappoint a lot of men in this country. They don't want to hear precious theories about the American dream. The American dream is power.

I spent that night in Hazlehurst at my cousin Augusta's house, the same house where I'd raked leaves while counting '55 Chevys on a fall more than forty years before. We lived in that house for a couple of years while my father worked for my uncle in Hazlehurst. It was there, in the paneled back bedroom, that I kept photographs of James Dean's totaled Porsche taped to my wall. That night I made the mistake of telling Augusta I had done that, which was incredibly insensitive of me. She was appalled. The words not spoken were that her youngest son, Clayton, was killed in an automobile accident in the spring of 1989. He was in his late teens. His bedroom was the one where I'd displayed the James Dean pictures.

I was restless in Hazlehurst. It's a town that's meant a lot to me, but most of the reasons no longer exist. My aunt May died in 1993, leaving a hole where the center of a bustling extended family used to be. My friend David Sanders, whom I met in the sixth grade, has long since moved to Jackson. The town itself seems to reflect my sense of loss. A couple of years ago I went to Hazlehurst to hide out and try to finish my house book, but I left Little Rock without enough underwear for two weeks. It's okay, I told myself—when I get to Hazlehurst, I'll just go downtown to Sherman's department store. But when I drove into town, Sherman's was no longer there. Nor were any of the other stores or cafes I had known. Many windows on the main commercial street were boarded up. I remembered Saturday afternoons in the fifties, the sidewalks jammed with country people in town for their weekly shopping and socializing trip, every parking space filled with cars and trucks and many others circling. Obviously, the Hazlehurst in my mind had become an anachronism.

I decided to spend only the one night at Augusta's. But the next morning, before leaving for Jackson, I gave the Boxster a much-needed washing. It was nice to take time to do it right, instead of rushing to beat a coin-operated clock. In the driveway I lined up my sponge, chamois, tar remover, and chrome polish. After hosing down the Porsche, I spent nearly an hour wiping the grit and grime from the car's crevices. Then I sprayed the body clean and buffed the pearly finish until it gleamed. The Boxster is breathtakingly beautiful when it's clean. As I worked on it, the neighbor's son, a sixteen-year-old, came over to salivate. "You know," he said in front of his mother and my cousin, "you can get *any woman in the world* in that car."

"You think so?" I said.

"Aw, yeah."

He was too young and cocky for me to explain the dangers of underestimating women. Still, the car made an interesting prism for considering the genders. My neighbor John once told me something he had observed about women and cars: "Most of the time, the fastest driver in town, and also on the highway, will be a woman under forty in a Honda." That's not scientific, but knowing John, it's probably close. I thought about some of the women I know.

Augusta later told me she was amazed at how much attention the Boxster attracted. She said she'd never thought much about cars before. She didn't come from a flashy-car family (though her grandmother did own a black Rolls Royce, and her brother and male cousin drove T-Birds). Gusta's mother, my aunt May, owned Oldsmobiles and Chrysler New Yorkers. Her father, my uncle Alex, once drove a beautiful 1955 Mercury Montclair, cream-colored with soft leather upholstery. I remember riding in that car with him as he surveyed the construction area of the interstate around Hazlehurst in the late fifties. He paid no attention to the signs warning motorists away. Instead, he drove right up on the graded dirt. The Mercury had electric window controls, one of the first cars I had ridden in that was equipped with them. I placed my finger on the button, and the glass pane hummed shut. It was so smooth and easy. I sat back and smiled as my uncle hit the gas and a billowing cloud of red dust churned up behind us.

Beth has never cared much about cars, except for transportation and convenience—though if you were to dig deeply into her psyche, I imagine you might find some automobile imprinting from her father. When she was a little girl her family had a station wagon, in which they took long car trips every other year. The Arnolds were the quintessential "See the U.S.A." family—father, mother, and three adorable children. But they didn't stop at the border. In the early sixties, the family drove from Batesville, Arkansas, all the way to Mexico City. They were planning a summer-long trip to Alaska for the summer of 1970, but Beth's father died in a diving accident in 1969, when Beth was fifteen. After that, she drove her father's light-blue Bronco, until her mother sold it. In college, Beth, a budding hippie, used some of her inheritance to buy a Chevy Vega in a shade of yellow that I think of as Seventies Happy Face.

I will say, however, that in spite of Porsche's admonitions against my letting anyone else behind the wheel, Beth drove the Boxster some on the way to Miami. She took to it instantly, with almost frightening self-confidence. It was while driving the Boxster that she told me women do *indeed* dream of driving to the grocery store and never coming back.

Our friend Lisa could probably afford just about any car she wanted, but until recently she drove a Honda station wagon. For years she mused about "buying a statement car—a car that makes a statement about me," but she didn't seem to know what statement she wanted to make. She likes her privacy, so I can't imagine her buying a fancy sports car or even a convertible. But she also likes her irony. Three years ago, she went to great effort to locate and recondition a

1962 Corvair, which she promptly had painted the exact pink of her Barbie car from girlhood. As far as I know, she's driven it a couple of times, but mostly it languishes under a car cover at the end of her driveway. Last summer she splurged for a silver Lexus RX 300, the sport-utility model, which I can see makes a statement that fits Lisa—elegant but active, refined but unfussy.

I'm sure it's a dangerous generalization to say that men respond to cars differently than women do, but I believe it to be true. To men, cars seem more likely to be mistresses—trophy wheels. To women, they seem to be pals. I read an essay by a writer named Ana Veciana-Suarez, who was dismayed to find herself at the point in life of hauling children in a minivan—"transportation's answer to Levi's loose-fit jeans." She yearned, instead, "for a pink pickup, with a Great Dane in back." Most of the women I know seem to want a vehicle that's powerful, that puts them up high, that makes them feel equal to the road. In a book Lisa gave me, called *Ladies, Start Your Engines: Women Writers on Cars and the Road*, writer Kate Culkin describes the lure of her El Camino: "half-car, half-truck, the mermaid of the automobile world . . . It screams both *pay attention to me* and *get out of my way*."

After saying good-bye to Augusta, I sat in her driveway for a few minutes and read up on the Porsche engine—a "2.5-liter, 201-horsepower (150kW), aluminum alloy, water cooled, horizontally opposed, 6-cylinder 4-valve mid-engine." The name Boxster is a combination of "boxer" (for the engine's horizontal design) and "roadster" (for the open, two-seat layout). Pretty quickly I skimmed past the hard specs ("rack and pinion steering, MacPherson struts, aluminum alloy lower control arms with stabilizer bar") to the options list: "seats with adjustable heating, on-board computer, sport package with 17-inch wheels, wind deflector, sound package, cruise control, CD player, alarm system. . . ." My Boxster had the wind deflector—a Plexiglas plate between the seats that had come loose and threatened to fly away until I stabilized it with electrician's tape—but it didn't have cruise control, which I dearly missed. Then I read about the "speed-dependent rear spoiler, which extends at 75 m.p.h. (120 k.p.h.) and retracts as the speed drops below 50 m.p.h. (80 k.p.h.)." Did my car have that? I got out and looked at the rear of the Boxster, and there I detected a separate slice of metal that might be it. But how could I ever know for sure? The existence of the rear spoiler seemed to me a Zen-like question: If I drive the Boxster 75 m.p.h. but can't look back and see the spoiler, is it really there?

On the way out of town, I noticed a police car behind me. My mind immediately went to a Halloween night in 1957 when my friend David and I blew up a service-station Coke machine with cherry bombs and Officer Shy Hartley picked us up a block away in his trusty squad car. He drove us around town as an object lesson for all. Remembering that opened up a floodgate of Hazlehurst car stories, all rushing over me in the length of time it took to drive through town and stop at the red light. One of my junior-high classmates was a nearly grown boy who "double-dated" with his parents by hanging a blanket between the front and backseat so he could make out with his girlfriend. Another friend made it a habit to direct traffic, as though the most heroic act in fifties life was to try to control the cars that were quickly outnumbering us. This boy, Richard, would step into intersections like a lion tamer, whistling and waving his directions at the oncoming traffic. Finally the authorities would arrive and escort him home to his parents. Richard died early. In later years, I've thought he might have been clairvoyant.

At the stoplight downtown, the cop pulled beside me on the right. When I realized he was looking at me, I lowered the passenger window.

"That the new roadster?" he said.

"Yep."

"I used to sell Porsches. It's a beauty!"

I waved, relieved, and drove off to find Hazlehurst's mayor, a man named Randy Kimball. In his private life he runs an auto-parts business, but I wanted to talk with him in his official capacity. I wanted to know how the interstate highway had affected his little town. When I lived there, a steady line of traffic zoomed up and down Highway 51, which cut right through Hazlehurst. It was the straightest route between Jackson and New Orleans. Now on quiet nights you can hear the muffled whoosh of cars coursing along I-55, about a mile west. Unlike Sneads, Hazlehurst is blessed with two exits, and at the north one a new kind of downtown has grown up, anchored by Wal-Mart. When I hooked up with Mayor Kimball, I told him the story about my last trip to Hazlehurst, about finding Sherman's Department Store closed and much of downtown boarded up.

"Yeah," he said. "On Saturdays, downtown, you can park anywhere you want to now." But then he went on to say that the interstate had revolutionized life in this town of 4,200 people. It's done that mainly by making the urban attractions of Jackson, thirty-five miles north, seem much closer. Before the interstate, "you pretty much figured it was killing a day" to go up and come back. Now it's a commute. People from Hazlehurst think nothing of driving to Jackson for dinner and a movie, and a lot of people live in Hazlehurst and drive to Jackson to work. It's supposedly the best of both worlds—they earn city salaries but live in a quieter, nonurban community. They also spend an hour or so more in their cars every day.

Hazlehurst's downtown has stayed afloat, the mayor said, by turning to a service niche instead of retail. "Lawyers' offices, health care, a furniture maker, even a church," he said, ticking off buildings I remembered as housing shoe stores, hardware stores, and other typical downtown outlets. "Trends have changed. People don't want to shop downtown anymore. They don't want to have to look for parking, or to park far away from the store they're going to. They'd rather shop somewhere else, even though they end up walking about the same distance, or farther. We've developed a whole new section of town since you lived here. Who'd have ever thought we'd have a Ramada Inn and another new hotel building out there? McDonald's pulls people off the interstate, and Wal-Mart is out there. Taco Bell and Burger King. I guess if I had to say whether the interstate was positive or negative, I'd have to say positive. Our sales tax is higher now than it's ever been. Bottom line, I think we get more from the interstate than we lose because of it."

Heading toward Jackson on May 15, I had the antsy feeling that this trip was unraveling. Everything had become difficult—my suitcase was too big, my dopp kit too small. I never knew anymore what compartment my underwear or socks were in, and I couldn't find dental floss without emptying everything out of the bag. Maybe I was trying to haul too much of home along with me—the rules, the responsibilities, the organization. Underlying this uneasiness was the fact that it was the middle of the month. Not only had I missed my stepdaughter's birthday yesterday, but today was bill day. I pay bills on the first and the fifteenth, and I really hadn't made arrangements for taking care of them while I was gone. I thought I would bring it up with Beth in Miami. But considering the conditions under which she left, it seemed a bad time to ask her to take on another of my jobs while I was out breezing around the country. I looked forward to getting home to regroup. I also dreaded it.

Arriving in Jackson, I got behind a black BMW convertible with the vanity license plate "Get One." *Oh, the arrogance,* I thought. Later that day, when I mentioned that plate to my friend (and host) Bill Allen—an assistant U.S. attorney—he told me he knows a lawyer who asks prospective jurors if they have bumper stickers on their cars. I assume vanity license plates offer the same sort of insight into the drivers' personalities, though perhaps more subtle than "When Guns Are Outlawed, Only Outlaws Will Have Guns." The information highway isn't a new thing.

David Sanders came over, and we sat outside on Bill's deck telling stories about the cars we had known and loved. I had hoped that Tom Miller could be there, too, but he was out of town. These three are some of my oldest friends, and our friendships are inevitably plaited with memories of cars. With David I first enjoyed that prized teen status of "permanent shotgun"—the one who always rides up front next to the driver. I've lived through so many of David's car seasons, from the era of his pink 1957 Chevy through his Black Bonneville Phase to his 1965 Jaguar XKE roadster, the very model now displayed at the Museum of Modern Art as a masterpiece of twentieth-century design. It was in David's E-type, as it was called, that we careened north on the Natchez Trace one spring night when the bugs were so thick on the windshield that David had to raise his head above the glass to see. A huge beetle crashed squarely into his forehead, and I thought he was going to roll the car. It's not a significant "car story," but it was one of the funniest moments I ever had with him. Bill, off and on my college roommate, owned a black 1962 Corvette, in which we logged many happy miles to the bootlegger (happier miles coming back) before Lafayette County, Mississippi, was voted wet. As for Tom, one incredibly dark night we drove—in whose car, I don't remember (probably David's)—from Oxford to Tupelo to visit one of my aunts. Tom's imagination being what it is, he had me convinced that we actually saw an alien space ship hovering in the highway ahead of us.

That morning on Bill's deck, David talked about his mother's champagne-colored 1957 Chrysler Imperial, a car that was dear to my memory as well. After a fall day and evening at the state fair in

Jackson, David's mother drove us home to Hazlehurst. Two girls were with us in the backseat, and one of them rested her head on my shoulder and went to sleep. She wasn't my girlfriend, and never would be (in fact, she would become David's). But forty years later I can still smell her hair, a sweet blend of shampoo and dust and cotton candy. And I can remember how *alive* I felt during that drive. I wanted it to last forever.

As David and Bill recalled their stories, Bill's wife, Betty, joined us for a time. She told about how, when she and Bill married in 1966, he still owned the Corvette. "But Bill's family said, 'Now that you're married, you need to have a family car.' So they traded in his Corvette for a 1966 Impala, which never worked. It wouldn't turn off—you could jiggle the key, but the engine would just keep on going. To make matters worse, the Corvette went to auction and was bought by a man who went to graduate school when Bill did. As we were parking in front of the graduate school, this guy in Bill's Corvette would whip into the space next to the Impala. Bill would sit there in our quivering family car, first looking at the Corvette and then at me. I think he wondered what kind of deal he had made."

I stayed with Bill and Betty for two nights. On Saturday morning he drew me a map for a shortcut from his house around Ross Barnett Reservoir to Highway 25, and then on to Maben, where Bill Ballentine had lived. I made a note of my odometer—4,044 miles, of which I personally had logged 3,842. Over twenty-one days.

It was a brilliant blue morning, still early, and cool. I had the top down and wore a sweater over my T-shirt. From where Bill and Betty live, the route Bill had drawn for me runs through beautiful country, rolling and hilly, with big old houses surrounded by white wooden fences. Those houses have been there probably seventy years. They were built out in the country, but the city is creeping, like the just-greening kudzu, inexorably toward them.

I found a good oldies station—*real* oldies (Ray Anthony playing "The Bunny Hop"; Rosemary Clooney singing "Stormy Weather"; Dean Martin crooning "Sway Me Now"). It was nice to listen to old-fashioned music on an old-fashioned road. It was the kind of road the Porsche was made for—winding, hilly, trees close on either side, the air rich with the smells of country. Equal parts honeysuckle and manure.

When I reached Highway 25, I discovered it was being turned into a four-lane. I gunned the gas and passed a truck that was creating a Chernobyl-like fallout of red clay dust. Amid the pines and hardwoods and rolling hills and red clay, I almost didn't notice a small auto graveyard on the left. Rusted pieces of metal languished among the weeds, plants curling around and through them. I wondered where Bill Ballentine's Mustang was.

If Bill had to perish in a car wreck in the sixties, the Mustang was the perfect car for him to die in. I thought back to what that decade was like. Everybody was experimenting—trying to "find themselves." At the beginning of the sixties we did what we always do—we decided we wanted the thing we didn't have. Through most of the fifties we had worshiped big, flashy cars. Then, in October 1957, the Soviets launched Sputnik and we Americans saw our confidence go into a tailspin. At the same time, the interstates were burgeoning, the suburbs were sprawling, and families needed more than one car. We suddenly wanted something small and sensible.

Detroit couldn't understand the backlash against the land yachts we had demanded since the war. GM issued this response: "A good used car is the answer to the American public's need for cheap transportation." When the public disagreed with that assessment, Detroit gave us the compacts. We didn't love them. They didn't express our souls. So John DeLorean dropped a powerful V-8 into a Pontiac Tempest and created the muscle cars. They were wildly popular during the mid- to late-sixties, and I've often wondered how much of that was due to our devastating lack of power in Southeast Asia.

In the sixties, there were too many cars, too many choices, too many frustrations. Little boys leaning on their rakes could no longer keep track. "Last year," wrote Hal Higdon in a 1966 issue of the *New York Times Magazine,* "a Yale University physicist calculated that since Chevy offered 46 models, 32 engines, 20 transmissions, 21 colors (plus 9 two-tone combinations) and more than 400 accessories and options, the number of different cars that a Chevrolet customer conceivably could order was greater than the number of atoms in the universe. This seemingly would put General Motors one notch higher than God in the chain of command."

The maroon Mustang that Bill died in was one of the Ford Motor Company's many attempts to connect with a drifting America. The car was light and peppy, more Jimmy Cagney softshoe than the muscle cars' heavy testosterone stomp. It's probably not beside the point that Bill was an Ole Miss cheerleader. I never could have done that. One, because I wasn't as self-confident as he was—to me it was slightly suspect for males to engage in such activities—and two, because I was cursed with a certain darkness of spirit that precluded a cheerleader's optimism. In any case, I liked being around Bill. He made me laugh at myself and everything else.

Bill was among those—Mendy was another—with whom I spent those last few halcyon days on the Gulf coast before hitchhiking home to get married. Back at school that fall, I naturally didn't see Bill as much. He lived for a time in an apartment south of town, and sometimes when my wife didn't grouse I went over and played guitar with him and a few other guys. Later Bill moved, with Erich and Mendy, to a house north of the Oxford city limits on Highway 7. Sometimes on

Friday or Saturday nights, my wife and I went there for parties, drinking too much and putt-putting home around the curvy two-lanes in our beige VW.

By midsummer 1967, I had finished one year of graduate school and was beginning to work on my master's thesis—the one about escapism and search in Hemingway's works. Bill had decided to go to graduate school, too, and had stayed the summer in Oxford to work for a professor and prepare for classes in the fall. The last time I saw him was the day he died. I had finished a class and was walking to my car when I heard him call out from his professor's office. "Hey," he said, "where you going?"

I stopped and propped myself against the doorjamb. I had to go home and work on my thesis, I said. He didn't want to hear that. "Y'all come to Memphis with us tonight. I've got a date. We're going to the Rendezvous." His date was someone I didn't know. *He* didn't know her well, he said. This was the first time they had gone out. "Come on. We'll eat some ribs, drink some beer."

Such an evening didn't fit into my life as much as it did his. I was married, earning no money, had my studies to attend to, and my wife was working. It was a school night. I begged off.

"You pussy," he said, with that sparkling smile.

I slowed for a man on a tractor just in front of the Bible Way Pentacostal Church—two trailers butted together. On the side of the road were crosses saying "Born to Save." It occurred to me that I wouldn't like to be driving through this country at night, especially in this car. I was very near Philadelphia, Mississippi, where in 1964 three civil-rights workers were found buried "in an earthen dam," as it was described in the still-haunting phrase of the time. "This section of highway sponsored by Calvary Baptist Church."

I passed through Louisville, pronounced "Lewisville," where Tom Miller was from. A few miles north I drove into Maben, a town I had visited only three times in my life—once when I spent a weekend with Bill at his house; then when I served as a pallbearer at his funeral; and finally, in 1989, when I took my son Matt through there on the way back from the beach. It's a small town, mainly one short wide thoroughfare where shoppers park their cars in a row in the center of the street. As I cruised around searching for familiar landmarks, people stopped what they were doing—mowing, walking, shopping, talking—and gawked at the Boxster. I pulled into a Shell station across from Jim's Auto Parts and went in to ask directions to Audelle Ballentine's house. The woman at the cash register didn't know her, but lent me a phone book. Suddenly the woman behind me in line said, "Audelle Ballentine? I think she died a couple of years ago. I work at the hospital, and I think I remember she died."

Someone in the store once lived across the road from the Ballentines, and soon I had general directions to the house. "I think Miz Ballentine's daughter has been staying there since she died," one woman said.

I found the small brick house easily, summoning it back from the depths of memory enough to *almost* see myself inside it thirty years before. No one was home. I had met Bill's sister, Betty, a couple of times, and I jotted her a note telling her I was sorry her mother had died and that I think of them all often. I left my address and phone number. I never heard from her.

This time I was struck by how short a journey it was from Bill's house to the cemetery—scarcely a mile. Audelle was buried next to Bill. It turned out that she had died seven years before, on December 28, 1990. I wished I had looked her up when Matt and I came through in 1989.

Standing by their graves, I thought back to that July night in 1967.

My wife and I were asleep, one or two in the morning. Suddenly the phone rang. I was twenty-three years old—an age when phone calls in the night didn't necessarily mean something ominous. That was the last night I ever felt that way.

I fumbled for the phone. "Hello?"

"Jim," said a voice, and even in my half-conscious haze I could tell that the voice was stressed almost to the breaking point. "It's Erich. Something terrible's happened. Bill's been killed."

He told me there had been an accident on Highway 6, coming back from Memphis. I asked if there was anything I could do, and he said no, we would get together in the morning. I told my wife what had happened and then lay there staring at the ceiling until dawn. The next day I learned that in the pounding rain the right wheels of Bill's Mustang had veered off the new pavement, which was an inch or two higher than the ground. He overcorrected, pulling the steering wheel hard to the left, and the car careened into the oncoming lane, head-on into a truck. Bill and his date both died instantly.

It was the era before photo IDs, and the girl was using a friend's driver's license. The police first notified the wrong girl's parents.

My mother, two months shy of her eighty-seventh birthday, told me she planned to renew her driver's license. We were at her house in Tupelo, a town that I had been nervous about driving the Boxster to. Tupelo is my automotive Bermuda Triangle. While driving to Tupelo over the years, I've suffered the following: three flat tires, two dropped transmissions, one speeding ticket, a collision with a deer, a burned-up engine, and a terrible sunburn. I suspect it has something to do with Tupelo's almost institutional religiosity and my almost institutional suspicion of pervasive piety. My cousin has suggested I try to fool the gods by pretending I'm really going somewhere else.

I tried that as I drove up the Natchez Trace from Maben, but then there it was, the sign for Tupelo. I told Mother I didn't dare stay long. I gave her a ride in the Boxster, though she wouldn't let me put the top down. I think she liked it. With age, my mother has become a much better passenger. Now I'm the one who gets nervous with her behind the wheel.

The truth is I've been her passenger only a couple of times in my life. It's still an alien experience, I guess because she didn't drive when I was a child. She was terrified of automobiles. Then one day at age fifty-eight she pulled into our driveway in Miami *driving her own car*. Phil and I were gone by then, and I remember reeling with disbelief when I heard the story. Always steely deep down, Mother had simply gotten sick of asking my father to drive her here, drive her there, and his acting ugly about it. I think now that Dad was going through a strange time, and he and Mother weren't as close then as Phil and I liked to think. She says he would rail at other drivers, tailgate, curse. So she had taken secret driving lessons and bought her own wheels. She had escaped him and reinvented herself. Never mind that from then on, when she wanted to go shopping in busy downtown Miami, she simply drove herself to the corner, parked, and took the bus.

Late the next morning, Sunday, I headed the Boxster west for the first time in days. Driving through Pontotoc, I suddenly remembered a trip home from Ole Miss to Florida at spring break. Every journey becomes a permanent part of you, no matter how deeply buried. I hadn't thought of this in years, but some image in Pontotoc triggered the memory. As a sophomore I accepted a ride with a fellow Floridian whom I remember only as Frank. He was burly and wild-eyed, and I suppose we had a class together. When the day of the trip arrived, I was to meet Frank after classes at his car. I arrived to discover that there would be two other passengers—another boy and a girl. I knew neither of them. Frank also announced that, on the way, he wanted to stop by Pontotoc and buy cowboy boots at the cheap outlet store where all of us had gotten our boots. Fine, we said—it was his car. We spent about an hour watching Frank try on every possible pair of boots before settling on the first ones he'd spotted. Then with his new boots on his feet, he floored the accelerator and we blasted off toward Florida at a speed the space shuttle would envy.

Before long, dusk closing in, Frank started drinking. Probably we all did, though it soon became uncomfortably clear that Frank and alcohol were a very bad combination. "I got a great big hawg," he said suddenly, leering over the backseat at the lone female among us. We were pretty sure Frank wasn't in the pork industry, so we tried to ignore his remark.

"Man, Frank," I said from the backseat, "what time you think we'll get to the state line?"

"Whoa," said the boy riding shotgun. "Did you see that 'Vette?" The girl didn't say a word.

"I got a *huge* hawg." Frank's eyes flashed into the rearview mirror and penetrated the girl's gaze.

There's a moment sometimes when strangers become family, and this was probably it for Frank's passengers. "Come on, Frank," I said.

"Yeah," said the boy in front.

"*Fuck* you guys," Frank said. "Can't you take a joke?" We were relieved, I suppose, by the word *joke,* and we all rode in silence for a while. Then Frank leered into the rearview mirror again.

"My big hawg's lonely. You think you can take my hawg?"

And that was only the first two hours of a twenty-hour trip. The girl found another ride back the next week.

In Oxford I pulled over and got out my camcorder so I could take pictures of the town square made so famous in the books of William Faulkner. It was also a place where I had spent much of my life, as had generations of my family before me. In fact, it was on this very square, in around 1913, that my maternal grandfather first took his family for a spin in an automobile. "The man gave him instructions and asked if he understood," my mother says, "and of course he said yes. But then once they started going, he couldn't remember how to stop. So he had to keep driving around the square until the car ran out of gas."

As I aimed my camcorder and started shooting, a policeman stopped his car next to mine and studied me through his passenger window. I waved and held up the camcorder, and he drove on. But I noticed that he waited at the next stop sign, right before the square. As I approached it, he motioned with his left hand for me to come past him. Not a good development, I thought. I figured he saw the hot Porsche and the Nevada license plate and now he thinks I'm here to sell drugs to the students. I put the camcorder away, made a full and obvious stop at the sign, and then pulled on past him.

He followed, as I suspected he would. On the other side of the square I took a right on North Lamar. He continued to follow me. I looked for a speed-limit sign, but didn't see one. At the next corner, Jefferson Street, I took a right. So did he. I drove twenty miles an hour. At the next light, in front of my mother's childhood home across from the cemetery, I turned left. The policeman followed. *Oh, shit,* I thought. I crept along, and he crept right behind me. Finally I let the speedometer nudge up just past twenty-five. He turned on his light— not his blue light, but his pulsating headlights.

I pulled over right next to William Faulkner's grave, where my friends and I had spent many a midnight drinking bourbon and toasting Mr. Bill. "What's the matter, officer?" I said as he eased up beside me.

"What kind of car is that?" he said.

"It's the new Porsche Boxster. I'm writing a book, and Porsche let me—"

"You mind if I take a look at it?"

"No, fine," and I turned into the little driveway to the cemetery.

When he stepped out of his car, I saw that he was a giant. I got out and asked if he wanted to see my driver's license. He didn't. He just wanted to look at the car. He studied it from every angle, then asked if he could sit in it.

Once I realized I wasn't under suspicion for drug dealing ("Drug dealers don't carry camcorders," he said), I told him what I was doing and asked why he pulled me over.

"I thought this was the new Dodge," he said.

Driving north on I-55 toward Memphis, I felt an excitement I hadn't experienced since the day Beth and I left for Miami. It was the imminence of adventure, and going home was only part of it. The closer I got to the Mississippi River, the more excited I became. Eleven years before, when I moved back South to start a magazine, the writer Willie Morris, who was instrumental in my moving, told me I should come to see him. "Cross the river at Greenville," he'd said. In those few words I heard music. It was the same music I heard one morning at home when a TV weather forecaster said, "It's gusty on the Plains." There rests in our souls a song of the open road, as Whitman put it, and occasionally someone or something hits the note that sets it free. Stephen Vincent Benet was right, not just about American names but about American words: *Great Plains, Loveland Pass, the lone prairie, the wide Missouri*. There's a flintiness in some sounds that ignites the urge to *go*.

Crossing the old bridge over the Mississippi meant I had finally left the congested East and was now entering the wide-open West. I cast a deferential glance right, where some 300 miles north, Lewis and Clark had begun their encounter with destiny. After traversing the depressing jumble of West Memphis, I bore left at the fork of two interstates, 55 and 40, and straightened west in the direction of Little Rock. Within minutes I was behind an eighteen-wheeler bearing a big hand-lettered sign across the entire rear of its rig: "SHOW ME YOUR HOOTERS!" The country had changed a bit since Lewis and Clark's day, but still, what an adventure! I laughed out loud and floored the Boxster toward the blazing sun.

SEVEN

Party in the Road

The best news at home was that my neighbor John had mowed my lawn for me. I arrived on a Sunday evening just as Beth and several friends were winding down an afternoon's croquet game in our side yard. The others seemed glad to see me, but Beth just proffered her cheek for me to kiss. I felt like a croquet ball that had been whacked into the rough.

I stayed home three days, one day too many. It's strange how the things you miss when you don't have them can seem overwhelming when you do. In rereading *Travels with Charley,* I saw that Steinbeck asked his wife to fly to Chicago to meet him in mid-journey. He loved being with her, but it threw him off his pace. Seeing Beth worked the opposite for me. I was thrilled to see her, but her fury had gathered steam. A hurricane born in Miami was now threatening to level the midsection of the country. I was cocky, she said. I had been cruel for no reason and wasn't contrite enough. After a few days of that, I was *eager* to get on the road again.

This time I took less of home along with me. I exchanged my big foldover bag for a small grip, one just big enough to hold a parka, Timberlands, shorts, jeans, a few shirts, underwear, and socks. I packed a different dopp kit, too. This one zipped around the edge so you could open it wide and actually see what was in it. I also picked up a passenger. Back when this trip was concocted, I had told John that I would be happy for him to come along for a while. During my hiatus at home, I mentioned it again. The day before I left, he announced that he had cleared his calendar for two days, Thursday and Friday, May 22 and 23. He would fly home Saturday. We had no idea where I would drop him off, which was part of the fun of it.

At about noon on the 22nd, John, Linda, Beth, and I gathered in our driveway. A labor lawyer about to set off in a foreign luxury sports car, John kept himself grounded by wearing a camouflage International Brotherhood of Electrical Workers baseball cap and his red, white, and blue Converse high-tops. Linda kissed him good-bye, but Beth and I didn't even hug. As we pulled away, I waved. Beth was talking to Linda and didn't notice.

Why is it that whenever you're leaving, you feel a pang of regret for the people who must stay behind? Jayne Anne Phillips touched on that in a story called "Fast Lanes"—the couple driving cross-country felt the euphoria of freedom, while "everyone else lived where they stood." I had that feeling as we left town: the gas-station attendant, the drive-through lady at McDonald's, the cop directing traffic, the postman making his routine rounds. All of them were stuck, while I had God knows *what* waiting for me over the next hill.

It never occurs to you that it might be another Manager's Complimentary Cocktail Party. That's the phenomenal power of the road. "There wasn't any place as pretty as the one that lay ahead," wrote

A. B. Guthrie, Jr. That's got to be an *American* feeling, and as the second half of the century picked up steam, I think that feeling has been expressed not just in car trips but in the broader journeys of our lives. In the house Beth and I live in, the first two families stayed there for forty-three years. But beginning in the late sixties, the relative turnover became phenomenal: six families in twenty-nine years. Something had happened in the culture, and moving on was just easier than staying put. When the mire of "living where you stand" becomes too much to bear, we try to fix it by changing jobs or getting a divorce or moving farther and farther away from what bothers us, from the downtowns to the suburbs to the *exurbs,* the last stop being the Unabomber's cabin.

Instead of cutting over to I-55, John and I drove up U.S. 67 through the Arkansas delta toward Missouri. At Walnut Ridge, Arkansas, we stopped for a bite, and then I let him drive. I worked on my notes and made a call to my agent, who was still trying to reverse the last bad bit of business news. After that I just rode and watched. The land in northeast Arkansas is very flat. We approached our first hill at 3:50 that afternoon just south of Poplar Bluff, Missouri, almost four hours after we left. Before construction of I-55, which lies many miles to the east, Highway 67 was the main north-south artery between St. Louis and many points to the south and southwest. The ghosts of those glory days still can be seen—run-down strip motels, their neon signs no longer bright, their once-festive pink-and-aqua paint now dull and peeling.

We decided to stay on 67 all the way to St. Louis. Winding though the twists and turns of Mark Twain National Forest, we couldn't help noticing the inordinate number of flowers and crosses on the sides of the road. The signs ticked off names like Lodi, Knob Lick, Cobalt City, Doe Run. In Desloge we stopped to look at a place that advertised antique automobiles. It was closed, but in the open lot outside were a dozen or so cars, including a 1968 Camaro convertible, a 1956 Ford, a 1961 Chevy, and an old El Camino for which they were asking $10,500. I pointed out a 1970-something Volkswagen convertible marked with a "sold" sign. It doesn't take much to set John off on automobile editorializing, and I had no idea we had just stumbled over one of his pet peeves: "*This,*" he said, pointing at the VW like the very reverse of a used-car salesman, "is a piece of *shit,* no matter how you dress it up. It's old technology, ugly, stupid, loud, and they ought to have been outlawed fifteen years ago. I thought when they started making them that by now we would never see one. It was an okay car in 1938, when Hitler was in full swing. Now it ought to be outlawed!" I laughed so hard I could hardly hold the camcorder.

We drove on, finally stopping at a Budgetel Motel some twenty miles south of St. Louis, on I-55 in Jefferson County. I wanted to go to the Museum of Westward Expansion at the St. Louis Arch the next morning, and we figured it would be easier to stay here than to push on into downtown. Interstate 55 shadows the Mississippi at this point, snaking left and then right again to follow the river into St. Louis. Because of the river, I suppose all these little towns in the vicinity of our motel—Festus, Crystal City, Herculaneum—had some reason for being before the interstate came along, though St. Louis commanded most of the big trade. Now these towns cater to the flow of interstate traffic, providing cheap, easy, and familiar lodgings to travelers far from home.

We ate supper at a nondescript restaurant in a nondescript strip mall, where John told me an amazing story about a friend of his, Bo Hawkins. Bo had grown up in Little Rock but now lived in Russellville, about ninety miles to the northwest. One of the loves of Bo's life was a 1969 Corvette that he bought in 1973, when he was a sophomore in college. Instead of selling the car when he graduated, got married, or began his family, he instead kept it. For years the Corvette was his everyday car, and he restored its upholstery, replaced its engine, made sure it received a lustrous new paint job. Over twenty years he put some 175,000 miles on the car, but it still looked great.

Then in 1993, Bo's responsibilities as a husband, father, and career man began to take so much of his time that he had none left for enjoying the Corvette. "I've decided to sell it," he told John on the phone one day. He hated having to make that decision, but he knew it was the right one. It wasn't fair to keep such a car and not be able to give it the time it deserved. He put an ad in one of the statewide papers published in Little Rock.

"The very first person who called him was an optometrist in Little Rock," John said. "His name was Clark Angel, and he had grown up in Russellville. Clark had owned a 1969 Corvette years before, but had sold it—an act he had regretted ever since. Now he had a little money and was looking for a car like the one he had let get away."

At first, Clark didn't give Bo his name. He just asked about the Corvette Bo had to sell. "What color is it?" Clark asked. "The one I had was Fathom Green."

"This one's Fathom Green," said Bo.

"What about the interior—mine was saddle tan leather."

"*This* one has a saddle tan leather interior."

"Well, how about the shifter?" Clark said, excitement rising in his voice. "I replaced the original one with a Hurst Competition shifter."

"That's what this one has. What's your name?"

"Clark Angel."

"Damn, Clark," said Bo, recognizing the name from the Corvette's papers, "*this is your car!*"

"Don't do a thing till I get there," Clark said. He wheeled into Bo's driveway an hour and a half later and bought the car on the spot.

I thought about that story in bed that night. It made me consider the concept of karma. Clark Angel had apparently lived a good life, not dilated his patients' eyes unduly, not overcharged for fancy frames. For an American male, this was a hint of heaven.

On a bright blue morning under the St. Louis Arch, we craned our necks and cupped our eyes as the silver glint soared and became one with the sun. It is an astonishing monument, this "gateway to the West." It is bigger, taller, more massive than it looks in pictures. I don't know exactly what its designer had in mind as its meaning, but to me it evokes not only a gateway but also the arc of a country unified through exploration—one giant foot planted on either side of a vast continent, with a vapor of mystery to be filled in between. It also bears a resemblance to a huge McDonald's sign, which isn't entirely inappropriate.

After a half hour in the museum, we searched out a phone so I could call the Missouri Department of Transportation. I wanted to drive the Boxster across that very first section of interstate highway, and I wasn't sure where it was. A young woman answered the phone at the Department of Transportation. She had no idea what I was talking about: "Nineteen fifty-six? *That's* when the interstate came in? I'm learning something!" Fortunately someone named Ed, in the department's "Building/Facilities" area, happened to be in the office and overheard her side of the conversation. She put him on the phone. He told me to cross the Blanchette Bridge and, as a guidepost, to "look for a big casino on the right." The westbound lanes of I-70 were the oldest, and soon after the casino I would see a big red, white, and blue sign marking the section.

We set out on what I figured would be an anticlimactic adventure (seen one interstate, seen them all), but I was determined to do this right. This section of highway was historic. In its mix were the very elements of the American character—energy, grit, determination, perseverance, pride, hope, self-delusion. Actually, driving among five lanes of interstate traffic while watching for a roadside sign and wielding a camcorder over the car windshield turned out *not* to be such a tepid adventure.

We approached the old steel bridge crossing the Missouri River, giving a rousing thumbs-up to Lewis and Clark and the starting point of their wild journey. As for ours, we missed the sign the first time. We must have lost it in the highway babel—"McDonald's, World's Largest Indoor Playplex!" "Vote Pro-Life!" "Fred's Yard of Concrete!" "E-Mail Me" (the vanity plate on a candy-apple red Sebring in front of us)—so we exited, headed back toward St. Louis, and turned around for another try. This time we spotted it, a relatively unobtrusive sign saying "Nation's First Interstate Started Here 1956." We parked, and I stood up in the seat of the Boxster to capture the landmark on videotape. The sign I photographed was green, not the national colors of Ed's description. Maybe there's more than one. Or maybe "interstate green" and "flag red, white, and blue" have become interchangeable in Ed's mind.

John drove west, pushing the Boxster to near 100. I was nervous about it because if we were stopped and the policeman had to speak to the Porsche people, I didn't want them to know someone else had been driving. There was a lot of traffic that day. A woman in a car with New York plates leaned out the passenger window and blew John a kiss, then took our picture. In three whole weeks of driving, no one had blown *me* a kiss. I decided it had to be John's sexy IBEW cap.

As he drove, John told me some of his favorite memories of cars and the road. He came of age in the muscle-car era, running the quarter mile by the river at midnight and racing at high speeds on curvy national forest roads in pitch dark, headlights slashing through the blackness like shooting stars. "It was insane, but it was great fun," he said. He always loved cars. "My dad loved yellow Fords. We always had one. In the fall when the new cars came out, we would go to the dealerships on Saturday morning and look at the cars in the show-room. We would spend hours doing that, admiring the new features, checking out the new options. But we wouldn't stop there. We wan-dered out into the back lots, peering through and over fences, trying to see if they had anything else hidden away back there."

John's father was a broker of construction machinery, and every summer he drove around the country looking at equipment he might want to buy. John, eleven years old in 1962, sometimes rode with him on those cross-country jaunts. "I loved to go on those summer trips with my dad. Some would be two weeks, others a few days. One time we went to Chicago, another time to Wichita. I remember others in Colorado, in Lubbock, in way far east Tennessee. He liked to go buy road equipment at auctions out of state, because they were in so much better shape than in Arkansas. They weren't beat up by rocks. I re-member back then, as the highways were being opened a little at a time, Dad once pulled up to a stretch of pavement with a 'Road Closed' sign on it. 'I bet this thing is finished,' he said, and he pulled that big yellow Ford up onto the new pavement and away we went, zooming along this brand-new highway that no one had ever driven on. It was great."

It's also a memory that fewer and fewer Americans will ever have—riding in the only car at any time on any section of interstate highway. John and I talked about how, shortly after that halcyon jour-ney he made with his dad, many of their countrymen who once had loved both cars and the road had begun to question their own devo-tion to this particular American dream. I told him that both Frank

Turner and Tom Adams recall those as tough times for building roads and selling cars.

Turner's tenure at the Federal Highway Administration overlapped with a wider realization of the social cost of the dream. People were being put out of their homes. Entire neighborhoods were being razed to make way for highways. And the cities were already seeing the pattern of the future—the inexorable movement to the suburbs. "Americans have been conditioned to respect newness, whatever it costs them," wrote John Updike. The highway, it turned out, wasn't just the unfurling ribbon of Woody Guthrie's soaring song. It was also a scar.

That realization had been building for years, starting in some places in the very early sixties and gathering steam as more and more communities grasped what it really meant to have an interstate highway system. I came across a newspaper clip from the *Arkansas Gazette* of October 22, 1961. Aerial photographs show various angles of Little Rock roads in progress—bulldozed swaths cut into the earth's crust all the way to the horizon. They look like sky views of a tornado's path.

But the ongoing promise was that the hellish traffic would one day decrease. In 1963, a Little Rock newspaper article reported that "the 1962 traffic volume map of the state Highway Department is out, and at the year's rate of increase, traffic threatens within a year or two to go right through the top of the traffic trend graph." The article indicated that "based on a 1939 average of 100, Arkansas traffic now has increased to 344 percent and it has shown no letup since 1944. From 1940 to 1941 it jumped 32 percent, then during the World War II years of 1942 to 1944, it dropped to a low of 69 percent of the 1939 average. Since then, the rise has been continuous."

Finally, by the early seventies, the truth was out, and it was shocking. This was the headline in a Little Rock newspaper.

VOLUME OF TRAFFIC IS MUCH HIGHER
SINCE CONSTRUCTION OF INTERSTATES

Comparing the 1970 Traffic Volumes Map with the 1963 map, the report listed increases in various locations around the state: "The largest increase in the Little Rock area is shown going southwest to Benton, east to Memphis and northeast to Jacksonville. A point on U.S. Highway 70 just north of the Pulaski County line showed a daily traffic volume of 11,000 vehicles in 1963. The same spot, incorporated into Interstate 30, showed 19,200 vehicles daily in 1970."

The same story was playing out all over the country.

Frank Turner took over the top federal highway job in 1969, the culminating year of a long period during which "the environmentalists were sticking their noses into something they didn't know anything about. They started with the premise that we didn't need a road program at all—people were supposed to use mass transit in the urban areas. We asked them, 'What about in Kansas?' "

Still, the environmentalists demanded and got from Congress—in Turner's words—"authority to be one of the supervisors and overseers of the highway program." He refers to 1969's National Environmental Policy Act, which required an environmental-impact statement before any federal funds could be spent. It was an epitaph for the heady era of the engineers and their good-old American pragmatism, and marked the rise of interest groups and double-talking politicians, the latter with *their* good-old American pragmatism—they wanted to please every voter. Despite the numerical traffic standards Turner and his men had for deciding such issues as where interstate exits would go, the process became more and more politicized. The result was more red tape over a longer period at greater cost. Says Turner: "My blood was pretty much boiling all the time during those years."

Meanwhile, in Detroit, Tom Adams and his team at Campbell-Ewald were dancing as fast as they could. Chevy was still outselling everything else, but the American car market in general had its own problems with environmentalists and consumer advocates. It was 1965 when Ralph Nader published *Unsafe at Any Speed*, which basically did in the Corvair. But Adams doesn't recall Nader as being his biggest obstacle in those days. "In the sixties," he says, "the automakers' corporate management decided they could make more money without putting as much quality into the product. Instead of putting four screws into the frame, they put two. It started to show up. The public saw direct evidence that the vehicles weren't trustworthy and as attractive as in years gone by. Because somebody with a budget was making a lesser car."

The imports began flooding in. "It was troubling," Adams, the former Navy pilot, recalled. "People who had fought the Japanese and the Germans were suddenly buying their cars. It was like being on a sinking ship without understanding why it should sink."

As John and I headed west, I thought back to where I was during all this turmoil. For much of it I was in Kansas City, having driven my ugly, stupid, but extremely progressive Volkswagen bug up from Mississippi in the summer of 1968 to begin my plum job as a "writer-editor" with Hallmark. There at the dawning of the Age of Aquarius, the fact that I drove a humble VW probably made my new colleagues think I was idealistic, and truly I was: As soon as I could possibly afford it, I planned on buying a big old great-looking American car.

It's worth noting that the only vivid memory I have of that VW is of the incredibly poor heater in the impossibly cold Kansas City winter of 1968 to 1969, when my wife was pregnant with our first child. I drove fast to try to heat the car, but it seldom got warm before I dropped her off at her office.

In the spring of 1969, with our baby due in June, we traded the Bug for a sleek new midnight-blue Chevelle Malibu Super Sport two-door with a naugahyde interior so blindingly white that no *wonder* the picture of me with the car on the day we got it shows me wearing shades. To me, this was my first car. I was twenty-five years old. I chose it, I was paying for it, and throughout that spring and summer I spent every possible moment washing and polishing it. There was an elegance and a sportiness to that Chevelle that made me feel not merely prosperous for the moment but well on my way to a successful life.

Unlike the Volkswagen, the Chevy plays a tremendous role in my memory. It coincided with the starting of my family, and so it edges into the backgrounds of numerous snapshots and eight-millimeter home movies. There it is, bright and shiny on a matching fall day, as my son David stumbles through golden leaves. It gleams behind beaming former college pals raising brews to toast their new adult lives. It noses into family gatherings in which I am no longer a child.

What I didn't know about that brilliant blue dream on the day of that first snapshot was this: In that very car I would travel the entire length of my day-to-day life with my sons. Seven years later, far north in another state, I would steer that old Chevelle away to a new life as my wife and children drove the other direction toward theirs.

I wanted to know if kids in mid-America still cruise on Friday nights, so John and I pulled off I-70 at Columbia, home of the University of Missouri. Unfortunately, we'd arrived after spring classes were finished and before summer term had begun. The high school was out, too. College towns without the students are lonely places. *Crash* was playing at the movie theater—I'd read about how bizarre it was, involving a group of friends who get sexual thrills from car wrecks.

Lurking around campus on Columbia's Avenue of Columns, we ran across a university policeman on a bicycle. "Officer Matt

Marshall," his name was. "Call me Matt." He told us there wasn't much teen cruising in Columbia, especially at night. Amazingly, the high-school kids were allowed to leave the school grounds for an hour at lunch. "Now they cruise at *noon*," he said.

We studied the map and decided to try Boonville, on the Missouri River some twenty miles west of Columbia. The atlas said it had 7,095 residents. Downtown Boonville is about a mile off the interstate to the north, approached through rolling hills dotted with red barns. The hills eventually give way to a tree-lined residential area of large old houses. After that comes a newer commercial area (Wal-Mart on the right), and then you descend a steep hill to the business district, at the end of which is an old steel bridge over the river.

It was about 4:30 P.M., close enough to day's end for us to be attracted to the Stein House Cafe on the left, catty-cornered across from the Butternut Bread bakery. The aroma of fresh bread gave this town a homey quality. I pulled the Boxster into a spot in front of the Stein House, and as we got out a voice said, "Nice car. You wanna trade?" I looked up and saw a man with a beard leaning out a second-story window. We joked about trading cars, and then I told him why we were there. "I'm writing a book about cars," I said. "Do kids here still cruise on Friday nights?"

"Go on in," he said. "I'll be right down to join you."

We took stools at the bar and ordered beers. The Stein House looked like one of those classic saloons from the old West, with rich wood and a backbar mirror and front booths and slow fans rotating just beneath an ornate ceiling. Neon beer signs gave the room a cozy glow. The man from the window walked in a few minutes later with another man in tow. "Steve Thomas," the bearded man said. He was editor of the local newspaper. The other man, the "town administrator," was also named Steve—last name pronounced "Gayle" but spelled Goehl. "The old German spelling," Thomas said, nudging Goehl.

"So," I said to Thomas, "you live above the store?"

"Yeah. It cuts down on a lot of unnecessary drinking and driving."

I ordered a round of beers and asked them about life in Boonville. Steve Thomas, originally from St. Louis, had been there since 1989. "If you hate history," he said, "don't hang out here." The town, founded in 1839, was named for Daniel Boone.

"But didn't he spell his name with an *e*?" I said.

"There's a lot of argument over that. Some say he did, some say he didn't. Others say he spelled it both ways."

Boonville, we learned, has 400 buildings on the National Register of Historic Places. The Santa Fe Trail started just across the river. Down the street was the "oldest operating theater west of the Alleghenies." The barn behind the old jail on the corner was the site of the last hanging in Missouri. Jesse James's brother was locked up in that jail for a time, awaiting trial, "but he beat the rap." Lewis and Clark came through, of course, and so did Harry Truman every time he traveled from one end of the state to the other. "Before I-70 was built, that bridge at the end of the street was the link across the Missouri River between St. Louis and Kansas City. This was old Highway 40. There was a restaurant here that Truman never passed up."

It is a tight little town whose German ancestry you can hear in the clipped words of the locals. When Wal-Mart came in, the downtown merchants "got together and started a Main Street program," Thomas said. "They levied a tax on themselves, rebuilt downtown sidewalks, redid some of the building façades."

"Main Street is thriving," said Goehl.

And it certainly looked that way from our perspective. It was the end of the day on a Friday, and cars were parked all up and down the street. Traffic was picking up. People were out on the sidewalks, visiting with one another. You could hear laughter from time to time.

"Today was the last day of school for the year," Thomas said. "There'll be a lot of cruising tonight. His boys in blue will be out in force." He nodded toward Goehl.

"Cruising begins at dusk," Goehl said.

I felt a chill go down my spine. It was eerie the way they talked about it. I felt that maybe we had stumbled into a Stephen King novel, a little old homey town in the heart of America that turns into a wild pagan orgy when darkness falls. Maybe the police close off access to the interstate so no one can get in or out. Maybe the townspeople dance naked in the middle of thriving Main Street, and at midnight they sacrifice a tourist (or two) to the gods of agriculture and commerce. Maybe they string them up first in the barn behind the old jail. Maybe then they boil them in schnapps.

"At dusk, huh?" I said.

The two Steves nodded. (Maybe they're *all named Steve*.)

"Well, we'll be back."

We checked into the Comfort Inn near the interstate, where John made a reservation to fly home from Kansas City the next afternoon. I worked on my notes and rested for a while. Finally, as the light grew dusky in the room, we decided it was time.

Main Street was already crowded, and this didn't feel like the desperate cruising that springs from ennui. This was a parade. The street pulsated with the pent-up energy that marks the changing of the seasons. I could imagine how these people felt. The kids, those who were out for the summer and not for real life, needed to flaunt their freedom. Their parents had their own causes for celebrating—a hiatus from surly conversations about grades; an extra hand on the farm or at the store.

Our parking space in front of the Stein House was still available, so we resumed our perch at the bar and watched the goings-on. Soon Steve Thomas came in, accompanied by a group of friends. He introduced us all around (not another Steve in the bunch), including to the two owners of the Stein House, Jeff and Tim, who said they'd been open only two weeks following the death of the previous owner. The Stein House was fifty-one years old, and they were the fourth to run it.

For a time I stood out in front videotaping the procession. A waitress brought me a glass of wine while I was shooting. Peering through the eye of the camera, I felt that what I was watching *was* a ritual, and that it *was* ancient. In cars, station wagons, minivans, and pickup trucks they came, over and over, north and south, south and north. There was a commonly accepted route for the cruising, and no one deviated from it. In their endless circle they seemed to be mimicking some rhythm of life itself.

John and I took Steve's advice and ordered steaks for supper. Before, during, and after our meal, various people stopped by the booth to talk. I'd noticed that the cars cruising by bore a certain mundane similarity: There were very few of the "character cars" that Olin had talked about. "When I was in college in the late seventies," said Steve, "I had a 1972 Grand Prix. I put nice wheels on it and fixed up the engine. But it was the only car that looked like that. Today the cars don't seem to make the same statement we tried to make with *our* sets of wheels."

Steve said he had noticed three things about the local kids and their cars. One, they have access to either more money or more credit, because they drive a lot newer cars than past generations of teenagers did. Two, they all work to pay for their cars. "It's a helluva family issue in towns like this. Kids want wheels, and they want nice ones. I know teenagers today who have car payments." Finally, they don't race the way their parents did—or do. "Across the river, Highway 40 parallels the Missouri through bottomland so flat you can see for a mile and a half. I know guys my age who still go over there and hammer it out. But the kids don't. They're into stereos and sound. We were speed freaks. They're *sound* freaks."

In short order, Jeff summoned a teenage worker from the kitchen in a spirit of show and tell. "My name's Jesse Cotting," the young man said. "I'm a lonely dishwasher in this restaurant [cutting a wry smile at his boss]. We could use another one."

Jesse, just turned eighteen, said his car was a "Pontiac Sunbird, metallic blue, '89. It's got 119,000 miles on it, but it's real nice—perfect except for a little crack. I put a thousand miles on it in two days, taking it to Columbia, taking it to Fayette to get something fixed. I'm putting my own stereo in it. I like loud music." He was customizing his car with sound. He would stand out in town not because of how fast or how sexy his car was, but because it had a sound system that could split an atom.

Jesse said cars are the big thing for kids in Boonville. "Cars and beer and drugs. Mainly marijuana and acid." Those kids cruising by out front would probably end the night by going to somebody's farm and having a party, he said, or stopping on a country road or bridge with the music blaring from the cars. Maybe they would pull up beside a creek and strip off their clothes and swim. "If I didn't have to work, I'd cruise all the time," Jesse said.

We paid our bill and walked out by the Boxster. The chain of cars kept coming, the music louder now, the headlights brighter, the occupants noisier. They waved and shouted. Horns tooted in the timeless pattern: *beep bee-bee beep beep—beeeeep beeeeep*. John and I looked at each other and smiled. We got into the car, and I dropped the top, then pulled the Porsche into the steady stream. Our spot, our place in the pageant, was behind a carload of giggling girls in a maroon Neon. A white pickup with three boys followed us. The girls waved, and the pickup honked. They seemed to understand that our presence was a tribute, not an intrusion. For a half hour or so we made the loop, down to the river, then right, right, left, and back, turning in formation at the other end of Main, then looping back for another run. After a time, the drive began to feel surreal, as though we had steered into some national dream.

Later, lying in bed at the Comfort Inn, I imagined those kids dancing on a bridge in the dark river bottomlands, their car lights ablaze like a bonfire, their precious stereos tuned in unison and sending their special signal into the heartland night. The form had changed since Kerouac, but the heated message was still the same.

John nudged the Boxster to 102, a record for the trip. He gunned it on a suddenly sparse stretch of I-70 between Boonville and Kansas City, and the only consequence was that his IBEW cap blew through our slipstream into history.

We reached Kansas City about 11:00 A.M. and drove through downtown, which was less lively than downtown Boonville. Then we went to the Country Club Plaza a few blocks south. The Plaza was one of the first shopping centers in the United States. But calling it a "shopping center" doesn't do it justice, not with the current connotations of that term. It's a beautiful place, like an old Spanish city, with decorative tiles, wide sidewalks, and flowing fountains. From what I could tell, the Plaza had, for all purposes other than business, become the city's downtown.

We went to Barnes and Noble, where I bought a *Hemmings Motor*

News. It lists car shows all over the country, and I thought it might prove useful in finding people to talk with on the rest of the trip. Later, walking around looking for a restaurant, we passed the parked Boxster. Three men were hovering over it, peering in. "At least fifty thousand dollars . . ." one of them said. Eventually we ate at Winstead's, Calvin Trillin's favorite burger place, and then crossed the Missouri again to make the twenty-mile trek to Kansas City International.

When we got there, John's flight wasn't scheduled to leave for another hour, so I parked and went in with him. It felt a little strange to be putting John on the plane. I had enjoyed having him along. Beth and I had had fun together on the road to Miami, but there was an added advantage to having another male on the trip. I felt a little more comfortable among strangers. And of course there was no danger that John and I would get into a lovers' quarrel and stop speaking. When his plane was called, we shook hands and I headed back to the car. I felt a twinge of envy, knowing that he would sleep under his own roof that night, and that his roof was just next door to mine.

I didn't plan to stay long in Kansas City. It was a town I'd lived in for five years at the start of my adult life, and I still had good friends there. But I wanted to move on, to push westward. My only agenda in Kansas City was to go out to the suburb of Overland Park, on the Kansas side of the state line, and see where my wife, son, and I had lived in the late sixties and early seventies. I doubled back to downtown and tried to remember how to hook up with I-35. At one point it was my commuting highway, and I knew it intimately. I knew the colors and patterns of the strata on the bluffs through which Frank Turner's men had carved this road. I knew the curves, the speeds at which they were navigable. I knew the houses in the hollows and the signposts on the hills. And yet, whenever I think of I-35, the memory that most often comes to mind is a disembodied scene from my rearview mirror. Coming to work one winter morning, I glanced at the rearview at the very split second that a car behind me careened through the air and over an embankment. I never slowed down.

I hardly recognized the highway now. What once had been a quilt of farmland—I remember, vividly, a field of sunflowers—was now displaced by giant furniture marts, screaming outlet malls, brazen discount centers. My benchmarks were lost in the crowd. My specific memories of street names and numbers had faded in the fog of time, and I drove past an interchange that looked vaguely familiar, only to turn around a mile later when I knew beyond doubt I had gone too far. I got off at what I hoped was the street I once had traveled daily. Like Lewis and Clark's guide Sacagawea sensing terrain she had known long ago, I suddenly felt a twinge of recognition, a pentimento of the living world: *I took my son to a Kiwanis pancake breakfast in that grocery-store parking lot.* Just past there, a half block to the right, I spotted the brick façade and mansard roofs of an apartment complex I remembered: Louisburg Square, our first postcollege apartment, the one-bedroom unit where my first son was conceived, the parking space where the VW huddled during that snowy winter, the corner where I posed in shades with my new blue car.

It had looked so new back then. Now, though still nice, it showed its years. I parked and took pictures, then tried to find the other places. We lived at Louisburg Square for a year, then moved to a townhouse for two months before I had to leave for basic training at Fort Bragg, North Carolina. When I came home in January 1970, we rented a house for a few months before moving to a two-bedroom apartment very near here. I couldn't find the townhouse, but I did stumble upon the two-bedroom apartment. I almost didn't recognize it, so changed were its surroundings. When we'd lived there, in 1971 to 1972, the complex was fronted by a vast field, a meadow almost, in which my son and I flew kites and where I used to jog in the evenings after work.

Now that field was gone, given over to a spur of the interstate. At some point bulldozers came and ate into the meadow, creating a valley later scraped smooth by road graders and paved over by trucks oozing progress.

I looked for two hours for my first house, the one we'd bought (for much less than the price of this car) after the two-bedroom apartment. I should have written down the address before I left home—not that I would know even now where to lay my hands on such information. For someone so attuned to the meanings of houses, I was surprised that I hadn't a clue, not even the vestige of a slippery memory, as to the name of the street my first house was on. It too was in this general area, but the area had grown so, sprawled so, that almost nothing looked familiar.

While I drove, I thought about our life in that house. There, during the early seventies, we realized we needed a second car. We lived in the suburbs, ten or fifteen miles from our offices. It was getting just too difficult now, with day-care schedules, for the three of us to touch all our daily bases in one automobile. The Chevelle was four years old. I had long since learned that white upholstery wasn't the best choice for accommodating babies and toddlers. I spent long Saturday mornings wiping the seats with various products that promised miracles, but never again were they as white as I wanted them to be. After the seats, I carefully went around the car touching up nicks with my little bottle of midnight-blue paint. With every passing year the spots I dabbed stood out more and more, as the blue of the body faded and dulled.

One night, after teaching a writing class at a local school, I came out to find the rear of my beloved Chevelle pushed violently into the backseat. A hit-and-run driver had hit me and run. The car was drivable (and ultimately fixable), and I crept home with the rear dragging and scraping, like a squashed bee trailing his insides behind him.

So when it came time to buy a new car, I had lost some of the starry-eyed wonder of four years before. The climate for buying had changed, too—and this time it was noticeable not just to the Tom Adamses of the world, but even to me. In 1973, Arab nations had cut off crude-oil sales to the United States in retaliation for our support of Israel in the 1973 Yom Kippur War. Suddenly there was an "energy crisis," and it actually showed up at my neighborhood gas pump. For the first time since World War II, Americans had to restrict their travel. Not by law, but by practicality. Many service stations closed on Sunday, which meant gassing up on Saturday or staying close to home until Monday. The gas-guzzling muscle cars, the last hurrah of America's quarter-century postwar bluster, now looked simply irrelevant. Since the late sixties, car buyers had turned increasingly to foreign brands. Now they flooded into the foreign dealerships—especially the Japanese ones—looking for something that would give them thirty miles to the gallon. I wished I still had the old VW.

At Campbell-Ewald, Chevrolet's ad agency, they tried to put the best possible face on the situation. "You've changed. We've changed" was the headline on one of their ads from the early seventies. "Change. That's what putting you first is all about. These are uneasy times. . . ." The ad featured both the Chevrolet Caprice and the Vega.

Even today, studying a too-light photocopy of a Vega advertisment from 1972, I find the car surprisingly good-looking. The lines are straight and bold. Mine had the sport wheels and a tight manual floor shift that made me feel like I was driving at Le Mans. Besides, it was $18 cheaper than an American Motors Gremlin, $58 cheaper than a Dodge Colt, $79 cheaper than a Ford Pinto. Oh, what company I was suddenly in.

The day I brought the Vega home, I parked it in the driveway and went inside to get my wife. When I came out five minutes later, my four-year-old son, David, and several of his friends were climbing on the trunk of the Vega. I screamed at them and chased them off, but it was too late. The little copper rivets from their blue jeans had gouged a wandering trail in the finish. It was etched there from then on, a map to nowhere, growing rustier with every passing day.

I had been blessed with good weather most of the trip, but that afternoon the sky grew a blackish purple and soon let loose in torrents. I crept along I-29 toward St. Joseph, trying to keep going even though other cars had pulled over to weather the storm.

Almost as quickly as they had blown up, the dark clouds cleared, and the sun shone through. The rich rolling farmland looked lovely in the fragile light. A haze of baby green dusted the furrowed fields, first sign of the crop to come. I rounded a curve and saw a bright-red barn on a deep-green hill, with a slice of blue in the sky behind and yellow flowers splashed in front. It was as though Henri Matisse had painted the American heartland.

St. Joseph would be the first part of this journey that represented a break with my own personal path. From Kansas City, my family and I had moved to Minneapolis—despite my wife's protestations—in the winter of 1973 to 1974, so I could take a magazine job there. The day the movers unloaded our possessions, the snow blew sideways through the open door of the new old house. Soon I discovered we had moved to a land so frigid that office workers plugged their parked cars into radiator heaters so the blocks wouldn't freeze by quitting time. I watched autos race on frozen lakes. In a world of dispassionate Scandinavian practicality, I soon became aware of the high social status of Volvos, and of my inability to afford one.

After my dispiriting afternoon in Kansas City, I was glad to split off and head into uncharted territory. I rolled into St. Joseph—"Home of the Pony Express"—late in the day and tried to get my bearings. Nothing I saw evoked the old frontier. The closest thing to Pony Express was Federal Express. Four-lane streets beckoned with the uncomfortably comforting signs of home away from home. I nosed the Boxster into a space at the local Sonic drive-in, where a disturbingly young waitress soon brought me the lemonade I'd ordered.

"How do I get to downtown?" I said. "The old downtown."

She gave me directions, and then said, "I'm not sure how *old* it is."

But it *was* old, old and beautiful, a charming turn-of-the-century residential area with alleys in back and cars parked in the alleys—just the way the new urbanists want the world to be. The downtown commercial area started quaintly enough, but then rapidly turned into run-down buildings with bars on the windows. A couple of guys sipping from paper bags gave me the eye as I made a U-turn and went back the other way. The downtown area was all but deserted.

Driving back toward the interstate, I passed a Western-looking building with a picture of a man on a horse. The Pony Express Motel, it was, and I liked the looks of it. But I wasn't sure about the neighborhood. I have the Porsche to worry about, I told myself. I'd better drive a bit farther. I was ashamed already, because I knew what I was going to do.

I decided on the Days Inn next to the interstate, but when I got to the parking lot I saw that the roof was being repaired. Some beams were even exposed, and since more rain was predicted, I opted for the Ramada Inn next door. A sign said, "Happy Hour Till 7." The only room available there was a second-floor smoking room, for $54 plus tax. Monday was Memorial Day, and the fact that the Ramada was almost booked made me nervous. I hadn't paid that much money for a room since Miami.

Shortly after the desk clerk processed my credit card, I learned (a) that this Ramada had no elevator, and (b) that the bar was an "interactive sports bar" with not a soul in it but a lonely bartender. I walked out to the vast motel parking lot and surveyed my possibilities. Downtown hadn't looked promising. Nothing there had beckoned with the old-fashioned warmth of the Stein House. I was ashamed again. I knew in my heart I was about to walk across the parking lot to Applebee's.

A perky barmaid named Lucinda served me a Jack Daniel's on the rocks. While I sipped it, I recalled something my cousin Augusta had told me. She has a friend who changes his name when he's traveling. Instead of George or Pete or whatever his real name is, he becomes Billy Bilkins. It's his *nom de road*. It frees him of his past, of his failures or successes, of his or others' expectations. Maybe, I thought, now that I was across the river away from my past, I should adopt a *nom de road*, too. What would the name be? I would have to think about that.

Lucinda lent me a pen so I could catch up on my notes. Reading them back today, I cringe to relive that evening. Not that Applebee's is a bad place—in fact, I highly recommend their local chicken fajitas. But here I was, driving cross-country in arguably the hottest automobile in the world at the moment, and I had slunk over to a chain restaurant to drink whiskey alone and watch cutely dressed waitpersons perform their insipid birthday-treat ritual: Clapping like cheerleaders surrounding the blushing Birthday Girl (or Boy), they unveil a dollop of chocolate with a single candle in it, then chirp the Happy Birthday Song. Never mind me, what's happened to *America?*

That night I didn't sleep well. The unceasing traffic on the interstate sounded like the ocean tide, though not nearly as comforting in its timelessness. The next morning I drove over to the Pony Express Motel and parked under the overhang. It was a rustic place, with leather Western furniture and old prints of Pony Express riders on the walls. The paneling looked as though it had come from one of the barns those ponies had been boarded in.

The manager, an Indian (as in Bombay), came out from a back office.

"I just want to say, I'm sorry, sir," I said.

"Sorry?"

"No, *I'm* sorry."

"Pardon?"

"I should have stayed here. I didn't *see* this place," I lied, "and so I went to the Ramada. This is the kind of place I look for."

"You do?" He seemed shocked. "You like old places?"

"Yes, I do."

"Most people today want new."

"I know. I'm sorry. How much is a room here?"

"Twenty-seven dollars."

"Ohhhh."

"Say, what kind of car is that?"

I turned and looked to see his view of it, through the picture window. "Porsche," I said. "The new Porsche."

"Very nice."

"Yes, it is. Well, thank you. I'm sorry. I'll stay here next time."

He waved as I left, probably wondering what kind of fool does what I had just done. I recognized it as strange even when I was in the middle of it, but I had woken up in Ramada's stale room that morning with an overwhelming feeling of self-reproach. In spite of my plan to travel the way modern America travels, I felt it was time somebody apologized to *some*body.

EIGHT

Strange Freight

Sunday, May 25. Paula Cole's whispered challenge dogged me like a shadow, and I flipped the dial to news. In North Dakota, Air Force lieutenant Kelly Flinn, dismissed from the service for fraternizing with a married enlisted man, said that all she wanted to do now was "get in my Jeep and drive."

Before leaving St. Joseph, I searched out a parkway I had read about, a pretty tree-lined route built in 1918 and still preserved as it was then. It was nice to take a Sunday drive on a road without fast-food signs, but the trip ended too quickly. I also went to the Pony Express Museum, where I met a family from Omaha. They commented on the Porsche, and I told them I won it playing blackjack in Reno and now was giving it a christening drive across the country. I don't know whether they believed me or not. They didn't ask questions. The woman, a schoolteacher in her forties, volunteered that she still lusted for a red Firebird. Her husband said he drove a Ford truck but wished he had a GMC. Their second-grade son said he didn't care about cars at all. We entered the little museum together and generally moved through the exhibits in a group, me trying to tread the line between distant friendliness and desperate hanging-on.

One last thing I hoped to do in St. Joe was catch a bit of the Indianapolis 500, which was scheduled to start that morning. A desk clerk at the Ramada had suggested I try a place called Legends, a "sports bar out on the Belt Highway." I got there a couple of minutes past noon. The room was dim and gloomy, with heroic pictures of American sports stars staring down from the walls. Two men at the bar nursed beers, not even talking to each other, while a bored bartender read a newspaper. A horse race, probably the Preakness, flickered across the TV screen. It was too sad a place for me to stay.

As I entered I-29, I checked my mileage—5,424 for the car, which meant 5,222 for me. Soon I was in the rolling hills of northwest Missouri, bound for Nebraska. The day was overcast, but the colors of the rich farmland stood out even through the dark wash of gray. On one stretch I pushed the Porsche to 104, and that was going uphill. It felt good to speed in a place where space permitted. I could feel the sky getting bigger by the mile.

Shortly past the Iowa line ("Iowa, You Make Me Smile!" read the welcome sign), I left I-29 and went west on Highway 2. The rain had started up again. In my rearview, the eastern sky was a murky blue, but straight ahead the horizon looked light. The road was desolate. I drove for what seemed five minutes at a time without seeing another car. On either side of the highway, the farmland was flooded. Soon I crossed the Missouri River again—into Nebraska. I thought of Lewis and Clark, who passed this very spot in midsummer, 1804. On July 21 of that year, a few miles north of here, they reached the mouth of the Platte River. "This was a milestone," Ambrose wrote. "To go past the mouth of the Platte was the Missouri riverman's equivalent of crossing the equator. It also meant entering a new ecosystem—and Sioux territory."

I had no idea what kind of territory I was entering. Twenty-five years earlier I had driven across Nebraska one way in a rented Winnebago with my wife, our son, and my wife's mother, brother, and sister, but I didn't remember a thing about the state except an astounding expansiveness through which the highway seemed to run forever. I stopped the Boxster and studied my map. The bottom right part of it, where I was, showed the usual tangle of red, blue, and black lines— civilization. To the west, the Nebraska map faded to white.

One of the things I hoped to do in Nebraska was talk with a highway patrolman about his take on Americans and the road. In 1972, one year after I drove across the state, deaths due to highway accidents reached their highest number ever in the United States, before or since—56,278 people. By the time Frank Turner retired from the Federal Highway Administration in 1972, the open road had become an open wound. Detroit was bleeding, too. Five years earlier, in 1967, Japanese import sales in the U.S. had been only 70,304. By 1972, they were 697,788. Nobody seemed to be having much fun on the road. In 1971, a prescient young director named Steven Spielberg had captured our mood in his first movie, a TV thriller called *Duel*, in which a traveling businessman is chased by a demonic Mack truck. You never see the face of the mysterious driver. That's because he's us.

Nineteen seventy-two was an important year also because of something that happened in Portland, Oregon. Until the early seventies, Portland was on a track with Atlanta, facing the same problems and solving them in the same ways—building more highways and razing its past for tomorrow's parking lots. Both cities had dying downtowns, commercial blocks left behind at the end of each workday as suburbanites fled by car to their outlying hideaways. In 1970, *New York Times* architecture critic Ada Louise Huxtable visited downtown Portland. She later described it as a collection of "towers, bunkers, and bombsites."

But in 1972—sparked by a proposal to add another ramp to the existing acres of pavement along the Willamette River, and also to build yet another parking garage downtown—the kinds of environmentalists who'd been making life difficult for Frank Turner nationwide emerged as the establishment in Portland. The result was something called the 1972 Downtown Plan. A writer for the Portland *Oregonian* called it "Portland's declaration of independence. Breaking with more than thirty years of American urban planning in which the automobile had highest priority, the 1972 Downtown Plan knit together transportation, land use, historic preservation, and design under the clarion call of livability." The plan called for light rail, not more highways. And the next year, 1973, the Oregon legislature passed a law requiring each of the state's cities to draw a line around itself, beyond which the law would not allow development. This is the Urban Growth Boundary (UGB) for which Portland, especially, would become famous among new urbanists. Urban sprawl, they decreed, would stop right there.

Near the town of Dunbar, Nebraska, purple and yellow wildflowers drank rain while men in bright shirts hit golf balls on a course devoid of trees. Prairie putting. The links were green, but strange in their baldness, a golf course at the end of the world. Soon I passed a little cemetery whose wrought-iron fence was adorned at each post by a tiny American flag. Memorial Day tomorrow, I remembered. In Nebraska, for the first time on my journey, I noticed rust on the cars. Not a lot—just tiny specks here and there, like cancer.

The rusty spots took me back again to my own past. On an icy night in January 1976, my wife asked to meet me for an after-work drink at the Sofitel Hotel in Edina, Minnesota. That was unusual. We had two sons to get home to, and we didn't have money to be going out on Monday nights. Over that drink she told me she wanted a divorce. She didn't love me anymore, she said. She swore there was no one else. She planned to take the boys and go home to her mother's house in Miami. She wanted to do it in June, after David finished first grade.

For the next six months we lived together with that secret. Once I had accepted that the divorce would actually happen, I began making preparations for the change. She would take the Vega, we decided. It was newer, and she had farther to drive. But in the two years we'd been in Minnesota, the daily barrage of salt had begun to eat away at the bottom of the car's lightweight body. Not just the floor, but the lower part of the doors and rear panel. I took the Vega to a body shop, and the man repaired it the best he could. The new gray paint covered the lesions, but the scars were clearly visible, like reconstructive surgery performed on a leper.

By then my beloved Chevelle was old and tired, too. Looking at it in my narrow driveway, I could hardly remember the beautiful new car with the blinding white upholstery. Now its paint was nicked, its interior soiled and gray, its engine coughing smoke and drinking oil. During those Minnesota winters, I'd had to call AAA many times to come jump-start the Chevelle in the morning—sometimes as often as twice a week. At some point in the course of that six-month holding period, I started thinking about buying myself a new car. I was beginning a new life, and something inside said I needed a different vehicle to take me into it. My soon-to-be ex thought that was a fine idea. She was so agreeable because she knew a secret that I didn't know. Soon her new wheels would include a BMW five-series, courtesy of her next husband.

One evening she and I drove to the Fiat dealership not far from our house. I yearned for a convertible, naturally, but it was my ill fortune to have my divorce and subsequent midlife crisis at a time when America and its automakers were losing their sense of play. From a record high of 509,415 convertibles produced in 1965, by 1976 the number had sunk to 14,000. That alone said something about the sorry state of our romance with the automobile. But since my romance with my wife was over, I needed a car I could love. Tom Adams and his advertising team were reduced to using the slogan "Chevette, Chevrolet's new kind of American car," focusing on such practicalities as wheelbase (better than the VW Rabbit) and headroom (more than the Toyota Corolla). I ran across a telling quote from the mid-seventies from Ed Cole, the man who had created the magnificent, best-selling 1955 Chevy. By then he was the chairman of General Motors. "The fun is gone," Cole said. "I wouldn't go into the automobile business again."

But Fiat produced a convertible called the 124 Sport Spider, and that's what drew me to the showroom that night. There, not on the floor but in the slick brochures, was a car that made me sense the possibility of someday feeling whole again. It was white with a black convertible top and black interior. The dealer would have to order it, which would take a few months. When the Spider came in, he would credit me a few dollars in trade on my old Chevelle.

From then on I harbored a slightly different view of the impending split-up. I hated it still, but there was a silver lining. I was being forced to reinvent myself. I'd never owned a car as a single person. I was thirty-two years old, had a good job as editor of *TWA Ambassador Magazine,* and was about to become the owner of a sports car. I still would see my boys (though Matt, born in 1975, would be too young to travel for a few more years), and they would love the Spider. Once my wife and I told my older son, David, about the divorce, I showed him the car brochure and we planned a trip together later that fall. He would fly to Minnesota, and the two of us would drive to Mississippi for Thanksgiving. Nineteen seventy-six was the nation's bicentennial year, and we would follow our mightiest river through the country's racing heart—just us, old pals, on the road in my convertible. The idea made both of us feel better.

Sometime in the month or so after they left, I met a woman at my new apartment complex. She invited me over for pot roast, and I went. Then I asked her to go with me to see Garrison Keillor's "Prairie Home Companion" at a nearby lakeside bandshell. By then the Minnesota summer had come, and there was no way to hide the Chevelle's pitiful condition. In the winter, the same salt film that had caused the cancer also could cover its effects. Now the car was simply what it was—exposed, weary, seen better days.

Part of my sense of self was represented by the condition of that Chevelle. But I also felt that hope was on back order. I took the Fiat brochure to show my date that night—my first real date in a dozen years. And even when I had to stop the Chevelle and add oil from the case I kept in the trunk, the very *picture* of that white Fiat Spider was promise enough to fend off terminal despair.

I rolled into Lincoln a little past three in the afternoon and stopped at a Texaco station. The man behind the cash register—Charlie—told me how to get downtown, to the state highway patrol headquarters, and to a motel he said was a classic in Lincoln. It was called the Villager, out on 52nd and O streets. Though it had been bought by Best Western, it was an old place with real character. It wasn't on the interstate.

The highway patrol building happened to be on my way to the motel, so I stopped and wandered around, knocking on doors and peering through windows, trying to find somebody home. No luck. Lincoln being the state's capital city, I had assumed the state patrol headquarters would be manned around the clock. The patrolmen I met a couple of days later in North Platte would have a good laugh over that one.

I drove through downtown before going to the motel. Lincoln is a pretty city, with broad sidewalks, big trees, and handsome old brick buildings. I liked the way it looked. It was easy to get around in, too— a grid system of blocks and lines, well marked, simple in the best sense of that word. By that I mean not overthought. In my head I contrasted Lincoln with Boston, a much larger city, certainly, but with a road system that's all but undrivable. I know how to read road signs, and I've driven in cities all over the world. But one time in Boston I literally had to abandon my car and hail a cab to make it to an appointment. Nothing in the way the roads were laid out made sense. That, of course, is in a town with more high-powered colleges per capita than any other place in the country. I suspect too much analytical, and not enough practical, brainpower at work there—too many eggheads in one basket.

Lincoln's trees stopped at about 16th and O, and then the predictable part of town began—the car dealerships, the gas stations, the motels. But it was still unlike the new commercial strips along the interstates. It seemed real. The Villager was on the left, a fifties-looking building with an elaborate sign and a manager's office in front under a drive-through carport. I pictured my dad going into just such a motel office while the rest of us waited in the car. Would there be room in the inn? Here, the office light looked appealingly bright on that gray day. Is there any time of life more depressing than a rainy Sunday afternoon? Its very bleakness portends the inevitability of duty.

There were rooms available, and mine was in a secluded wing at the back, off a courtyard. I drove around and parked as close as possible to my door. The Villager was a big motel, but very few people seemed to be staying there. The room was nice, more spacious and better appointed than any I had stayed in on this trip, and the walls were a rich yellow—a nice contrast to the interchangeable white walls of most chain motels. After settling in, I tried to figure how to make this day count for more than it had so far. The answer I came up with was to phone one of the people whose names I'd seen in *Hemmings Motor News*. Lincoln was home to a car club, and this man was listed as the contact.

It was an awkward conversation, and I probably woke him from a nap. For a second I thought about just hanging up, but instead I plunged ahead, identifying myself and telling him what I was up to.

"How long you staying?" he said.

"I don't know. It may depend on you."

He said he would check with some of his people and get back to me. He never called.

But that night, after a lonely dinner at the sparsely populated Villager bar, I dreamed that he had called back. In the surreal way of dreams, at first he was a lanky black man with a nub for a right hand. Then he became a cowboy-hat-wearing badass with a leer, who said to me: "You're really going to see something now. Just blend in and don't say a word."

"Can I bring my tape recorder and notebook?"

"Yeah—okay."

The next morning, I couldn't remember what actually went on at the meeting of his car club. But I did remember that when I tried to leave, one of the club members grabbed my camcorder and note pad. That man was naked. I wrestled with him, but others jumped in, and I ran away. I remembered trying to make my way up the hill to the state police headquarters I'd visited the day before. I hid there in the bushes, and finally the naked guy threw my camcorder and note pad in a ditch and left. When I retrieved them, all my footage and notes about the meeting had been deleted.

On Monday, Memorial Day, I planned to try the state police again. As I was dressing, "Headline News" featured a story about how over-crowded the national parks had become. Too many people were driving too many cars. A spokesperson for the Park Service said, "The marriage between the American public and their automobile is going to have to undergo a separation." She talked about setting up mass transit in the parks. The story then segued to a related feature about Portland and its efforts to fight the automobile.

When I called Beth to wish her a happy Memorial Day, she told me about all the fun she and our friends had planned for the day. She didn't say, "Wish you were here." Feeling sorry for myself, I went across the street to a restaurant, where I ordered a ham and cheese omelet with hash browns that came served in what can best be de-scribed as a pile. I picked up a newspaper, and an item in the *Lincoln Journal Star* caught my attention: " 'Yield' creator dies" was the head-line, and the Tulsa-datelined piece went on to report that "Clinton E. Riggs, a police officer credited with creating the 'Yield' traffic sign, has died at age 86. The first sign, reading 'Yield Right-of-Way,' was installed at a Tulsa intersection in 1950. . . ." I hoped Mr. Riggs hadn't spent much time in traffic in recent years.

Apart from a roving female security guard, nobody was at state pa-trol headquarters again. I felt bogged down in Lincoln, that I wasn't talking to enough people, wasn't doing my job. Then I walked back to the police parking lot and the very sight of the Boxster thrilled me. I decided at that moment to just get in and push on—where to, I had no idea. It was a small epiphany, a realization that even towns I don't live in start to oppress me if I feel I have unattended responsibilities there. Being on the road passes for progress.

One thing bothered me, though. As I drove to the highway patrol building, the coolant light on the Porsche dash blinked on. I pulled over immediately, read the manual, and checked the clear coolant indicator in the rear compartment. I could see blue liquid. After a while, the light went off. But from then on, I had acquired a traveling companion—a nagging worry that something was going to happen to the car.

The Nebraska plains pack a cumulative power. After a while, the low loping hills gather force and break into a gallop. Driving west on I-80, I thought of Willa Cather's *My Antonia,* one of my favorite books. In the introduction, she writes about growing up in a little town like the ones I was passing (long before the interstate made their entrances all alike), dusty towns plopped in the midst of miles of ripe wheat in summer and bleak bare ground "gray as sheet-iron" in the cold months. I was glad to be there for the warmer time. The sky was huge, and I knew that if the sun were out today the heat would already be unbearable. Nebraska in summer must be like living in perpetual noon.

The security guard at patrol headquarters had told me five fatalities had already been logged for the holiday weekend. She said it was the worst Memorial Day weekend on record for Nebraska, and it wasn't even over yet.

Driving 90 in a steady drizzle, I passed a sign for a town called Pleasant Dale. I hate the name "Pleasant" attached to any place name—Pleasant Plains, Pleasant Valley, Pleasant Hill, Pleasant whatever. Pleasant is such a tepid word. I preferred Beaver Crossing, McCool Junction, Aurora, Wood River. About every ten miles, I saw a dead deer on the side of the highway. A pretty little white clapboard church had a saying painted on it: "God Is Always With Us." Soon after, there was a motel with a real tepee out front. Then a sign advertised "North Platte—Home of Buffalo Bill Cody." I pulled over and looked at my map. North Platte was two-thirds of the way across the state—a healthy distance from Lincoln—and I liked the idea of spending the night where Buffalo Bill once roamed. It was still a hundred or so miles away, but I decided it would be a good place to stop.

Unless you've been there, it's almost impossible to convey how straight and flat and wide the country is in lower central Nebraska. Even with the day's limited visibility, I could see freight trains coming for miles. At most, only one or two trees at a time broke the horizon. Rising from it, the cottony sky spread out like a fan before me. Suddenly, or so it seemed, a fog rolled in and settled low on the land. The plains became ghost terrain, with only a hint of green on either side of the white-edged highway. I slowed down and kept it steady at the speed limit—75.

The cars that passed me bore Iowa, Indiana, and Nebraska plates. None of the passengers in them craned his or her neck and looked my way. I thought of Garrison Keillor, what he would say about that. "Midwesterners are practical people. Not easily impressed." Even in Lincoln, the Boxster attracted few admiring glances. These were brogan people, work-boot people, *truck* people. Out on the highway, the one hard stare I got, from a man in a GMC pickup, was marked with clear disdain.

At Kearney, I decided to leave I-80 for a while and drive on U.S. 30, the old road that parallels the interstate. The fog had lifted some, and I wanted to see more of the land. I put the top down, slipped on my cap and parka, and flipped the Boxster's Tiptronic transmission to manual. It was fun passing cars on the wide flat land, moving out and thumbing the accelerator, hanging in the left lane a bit longer than necessary. Once, passing a truck on a lazy curve, I kept the pressure on, pushing the Porsche to 115—the fastest I'd gone so far. I was beginning to enjoy the speed.

The farther west you go in Nebraska, the hillier the land becomes. The trains, Union Pacific, kept rumbling by—I counted six of them in less than an hour—and each little town I passed through (Lexington, Cozad, Gothenburg) had its own tin-roofed grain elevator by the tracks. Past Gothenburg, to my north, the treeless rolling hills reminded me of female bodies lying on the plains. As I neared North Platte, the sky grew dark again—with an eerie glow along the horizon. It gave me shivers. I was glad to be pulling into the town where I would lay up for the night.

Most travelers don't come into North Platte on Route 30 anymore. It's no longer the best section of town. The Platte River splits there, the north fork coursing across the plains toward Wyoming, the south fork turning toward Colorado. I passed over the wide marshy North Platte River and followed the signs through town to Buffalo Bill's home, the estate known as Scout's Rest. Faded little motels (the Rambler, the Western, the Chalet) recall an era when this was a main route across the nation's midsection. When I stopped at a light, a truck in front of me was adorned with two bumper stickers: "You either is, or you ain't," and "Sober and crazy." The car in the next lane bore a sticker that read, "Out of estrogen and packing a gun." I wondered if those were hints to what had made the West so wild.

I hadn't really planned to go into Buffalo Bill's house, but when I saw it, I couldn't resist. You might expect the famous Pony Express rider and cavalry scout to choose a self-consciously rustic house whose eaves dangled with fringe. Instead, he lived in a green-trimmed white mansion—Second Empire style—which sits on acres of land adorned with elaborate gardens. Built for him in 1886, it displays all the fine furniture and appointments of a nineteenth-century gentleman. The man was obviously tired of camping out.

The furnishings intrigued me, but I especially enjoyed seeing the artifacts from his Traveling Wild West Show. One framed poster, showing men in Russian hats riding horses, and with an insert of Cody at the upper left, proclaimed:

> BUFFALO BILL'S WILD WEST
> CONGRESS OF ROUGH RIDERS OF THE WORLD.
> THE BRAVE COSSACKS OF THE CAUCASUS
> IN WILD STRANGE FEATS AND FEARLESS EQUITATION.

By the time I reached the top floor, I felt a strange sense of déjà vu. Then I saw the original white buckskin suits, the garish belts, the elaborate boots—all encased in Plexiglas. It was just like being at Graceland.

After Buffalo Bill's, I explored North Platte, population some 22,000. Crossing over the tracks toward the interstate, I found the town less faded, more vital, cleaner, more friendly-looking. Split one-way streets bisected the downtown area, and the closer I got to I-80, the more familiar the landmarks became (Wendy's, Pizza Hut, A & W, Dairy Queen, Applebee's, Holiday Inn). It's the paradox of American travel today: In the real parts of town you feel like an alien. Near the interstates you feel at home.

At the I-80 exit, the South Platte River is a shallow slash in the earth with channels of water cutting around sandbars like pieces of rent cloth. It reminded me of the rivers in cowboy movies, streams my childhood heroes forded on horseback. I turned around at the river and went back toward the older section of downtown, whose main thoroughfare is paved with brick. There I spotted a sign that called out to me. Maybe it was the neon Miller Beer logo in the window that did it, or perhaps it was the pair of leggy can-can girls painted on the window itself (accompanied by the legend "Home of the Frontier Revue"). In any case, it was after 5:00 P.M., and Doris's Tavern looked like a good enough place. I parked out front and went in.

What I saw inside almost brought tears to my eyes. Doris's is a classic saloon, rich with smoky light the color of bourbon, a high-ceilinged rectangular room with a burnished bar on the right and red leather booths along the long left wall. Beyond that, past two vertical strips of pink neon, there's another room where men and women shoot pool together. But none of that caught my eye at first. All I saw, the image that stunned me speechless, was the wall of photographs of American servicemen (and women, though I didn't absorb that immediately). Starting at tabletop level, the arrangement rises eight feet high and stretches forty-three feet long. Some of the black-and-white pictures had yellowed with smoke and age. On Memorial Day, I had stumbled into an American time capsule.

Taking a seat at the bar, I was immediately waited on by a pleasant-looking woman who I guessed was Doris. When she brought my Jack Daniel's, I told her I was touched by the pictures. I asked how this wall of fallen heroes came to be.

"Oh, they're not all dead," she said. "In fact, my husband Wayne's up there, and he's still kicking. *Wayne, come here!*"

They were Doris and Wayne Dotson, they said, and while she waited on customers, he told me their story. Originally from Oregon, he was on his way home in the late forties when he stopped off here to earn a little money. He took a job with an electric company, met Doris, and never left. They married in 1951 and raised their family in North Platte. While Wayne worked at the electric company, Doris ran a tavern. Ten years ago, she bought this place.

As for the soldier photographs, the previous owner had hung some forty of them on the wall. That gave Doris a bigger idea. North Platte has a sweet history with servicemen, a past linked to all those trains I saw during the drive over from Lincoln. "We have the largest railroad classification yard in the world," Wayne said. "During World War II, most of the troop trains came through here on their way west. There was a National Guard unit from here that was about to ship out, and so the local people decided to meet them with sandwiches when their train came through. They fixed a big spread. When the troop train arrived, the North Platte unit had been shipped on a line farther south. But the soldiers who came through appreciated the hospitality so much, the people of North Platte decided to meet *every* troop train. That was the start of the North Platte Canteen, which served every troop train that came through here for the entire war."

Doris's idea was to celebrate this past by hanging a framed picture of every North Platte soldier who had been to battle, in any war. Today there are 650 pictures on her wall, covering the years from World War I ("One picture, Sam Street") and World War II, Korea, Vietnam, Grenada, and the Gulf War. When one of the soldiers dies, Doris sticks a little gold star at the bottom of his or her photograph.

Wayne and I discussed cars, including his 1964 Mercury Comet, and he started making phone calls to people he thought I should talk to. One of them was a man named Lowell Fenster who taught automotive mechanics at Mid-Plains Community College. We planned to meet at Doris's the following morning for breakfast. Wayne also told me where the highway patrol office was and said that several of the officers were Doris's customers in their off time. I was beginning to like North Platte a lot.

When Doris had a minute, I asked her where a good place to stay was. "You know, you should *never* ask a woman what's the best motel in her own town," she said. I laughed, and she directed me to the Husker Inn, just four blocks away.

It was very small, fifteen rooms total. I checked in, washed up, and flicked on the news. After several rain delays over the past two days, the Indy 500 had finally been run that afternoon. While I was watching, I heard rain and pulled back the curtain to look. Five feet in front of my room, two teenage boys were standing over the Boxster, shading their eyes and trying to peer inside. The rain didn't seem to bother them.

When I opened the door, they looked startled. "Hey," I said.

"This yours?" the taller one said.

"Yeah."

"I *love* your car."

"Me too," said the other kid. He was dark-haired, handsome, a little shy. Not so the taller boy. I asked what kinds of cars they would have if they could have anything in the world, and the tall boy answered without hesitation. This was a subject he had spent many hours mulling.

"A BMW or a Lexus," he said.

"Why?"

"Speed and luxury."

"But *why?*"

"That's what girls like."

We talked a few minutes more. I learned from them that (a) kids still do love cars, especially boys; (b) boys like speed and luxury because (c) that gets girls; (d) girls like cars, but mainly because boys like them; (e) dorks cruise while cool kids go to parties on Friday nights, except (f) if you have a cool stereo, you can cruise and turn it up for a while, but (g) you don't want to do it too long because then it becomes uncool; (h) kids still race, sometimes 90 miles per hour on North Platte's one-way streets (it's called "dragging the ones"), even if lots of police are around, because (i) "kids risk it."

When the rain got harder, the tall boy said, "So, should we go inside and continue this conversation?"

Something about his forwardness made me wary. "No," I said, "I've got some phone calls to make."

When I got back to Doris's, she and a bunch of friends were dealing cards at a big table in the corner. "It's cuckleburr," she said when I asked what game they were playing. "A combination of bridge and pitch." The tavern was getting lively now, and Wayne brought several people over to meet me—some whose pictures were on the wall. We went out front and looked at the Porsche. For supper, I ordered a barbecue pork sandwich and a couple of beers, and was back at my room by nine. It was still light out.

I watched "The McConnell Story" on television, a tearjerker I love with Alan Ladd and June Allyson. Beth and I talked a couple of times, the last at 12:15 A.M. I couldn't go back to sleep. I kept hearing cars rumble by, and I imagined they had something to do with the two boys I had talked with earlier. Several times I got up and peeped out the window to check on the Boxster. The taller boy had said he lived in one of the apartments next door, and at 2:30 I heard a loud car pull in over there. Then the trains started. At 4:20 a big truck rattled down the street and stopped in front of a house half a block away. It was a rigger home from a run. He banged things and slammed doors. Naturally, I dozed off just in time for my 7:00 A.M. wake-up call.

Doris's place didn't look quite so appealing early in the morning. It reminded me of a car trip my friend David and I had taken in 1964, from Miami to the New York World's Fair and back. We planned to save money by camping along the way, except in the big dangerous cities, where we would stay in hotels. The first night, someplace in Georgia, we stopped off at a diner to get a cup of coffee before sleeping in a nearby roadside park. We happened to mention the park to the man behind the counter, and he said *he* wouldn't sleep there. "Not since that hitchhiker was murdered." That comment flip-flopped our plans. We stayed in motels all the way to New York and back, and the only place we "camped out" was in Greenwich Village, at the famous Gaslight Cafe, which was owned by the father of a friend of mine. The problem was, before we could pitch our sleeping bags on the floor of the Gaslight, we had to wait until the music was over and the customers had left. I remember waking up in the dirty daylight, realizing my hand was lying in someone's spit. Like most such places, the Gaslight looked magical at night. The early morning was a different story. I don't mean to say that Doris's was like that, but in general I don't like to eat breakfast while whiskey bottles are in view. Eggs and toast should have their own space.

Lowell Fenster came in on time, a tall man in sweatshirt, jeans, and black wingtips. He told me he'd been a teacher for twenty-five years, and before that had "pulled wrenches" for a living. It was fascinating to listen to him talk because his interest in cars was so different from mine. He was drawn to the mechanics of them, to the cerebral and visceral thrills that come from the precise clicks of a ratchet. His specialties were the four basics: "brakes, engines, electronics, suspension systems." Unlike most of the nostalgic laymen I had talked with, Fenster didn't yearn for the good old days when people still could work on their own cars. He felt that automobiles were better now than ever before. "Back in the sixties, we had lots of horsepower," he said, "but we also had lots of pollution." I told him I thought it odd that someone from the Great Plains would even mention pollution. Then he told me a story. Many years ago he got his pilot's license. Occasionally he would need to fly in and out of Denver, and it was during those times that he could actually see what was happening to the wide open spaces. "A dirty cloud stretched from Denver up the Platte River valley, all the way to about Ogallala. That pretty much parallels the interstate.

"We have to worry about pollution," he said. "North Platte has a lot more cars now than it did when I first came here. Everybody has two or three. Yeah, we have to worry, too."

After breakfast I drove out to the state patrol office near I-80. I figured this was a long shot, that miles of red tape would be involved in getting to interview a trooper. When I told the duty officer what I wanted, he made a phone call and then took me down the hall to see Lieutenant Fred Ruiz, who looked to be in his mid-forties. Ruiz agreed immediately—if I wanted to ride with one of his troopers, that would be fine. Come back in an hour, he said.

I checked out of the Husker Inn, made a phone call to my agent, and was waiting back at the station when Ruiz came out with Officer Mark Larson, who was friendly but guarded. Larson and I spent the next three hours together in car 105, beginning at a place he called "the fishing hole." To get there he drove east on I-80 about five miles, then exited and positioned himself some fifty yards from the entrance to the interstate. Had you been driving by, you wouldn't have seen him. But using radar, he could clock how fast you had passed between two premeasured poles. He could catch you speeding from half a mile away.

It was strange riding with a state trooper. I'd been stopped on only a few occasions in my thirty-seven-year career as a driver—one of the first times being on that trip from Ole Miss to Florida with weird Frank, the man who talked incessantly about his "hawg." His speedometer was broken, and a policeman stopped me at midnight for speeding. When I mentioned the faulty speedometer, the officer gave me a piece of advice I've never forgotten: "Son," he said, "if you're passing everybody on the road, you're going too fast."

I wanted to talk with patrolmen because they, more than anyone else, have the chance to discover our secrets. We all have a sense of how invisible people feel in their own cars. Look to the next lane at a stoplight, and someone will be picking his nose—"digging for gold," as my stepdaughter puts it. Or he'll be singing at Carnegie Hall along with a voice on the radio. But what else might someone be doing? One summer during college, I drove a mail truck for the Dade County school department. It was a big truck, like FedEx trucks today. Driving up U.S. 1 on a sweltering August afternoon, I glanced into the car next to me and saw that the woman driving had her skirt hiked to her waist, and she was wearing no panties. I almost wrecked my truck trying to keep up with her, but soon she disappeared into the rushing constellation of cars around me. I wanted to talk with a trooper because they have license to invade our private space. They apply gravity to our headlong orbits. For at least the time it takes to write a ticket, we return to earth.

"I'm going to stop that blue car," Larson said, and number 105 roared to life. He entered I-80 going east, then U-turned across the median and began his pursuit. "I'll clock his shadow at that overpass," he said. I looked up just in time to see a car disappear under a bridge far, far ahead. The second it did, a shadow flicked across its top and Larson began his timer. The patrol car picked up speed, and soon the blue car, an Oldsmobile from Illinois, pulled to the shoulder. I asked Larson if he wanted me to get in the backseat, and he said because the driver was a woman, he would leave her in her car—"to be politically correct." I waited while he wrote out a ticket for a twenty-two-year-old girl on her way to Cheyenne, Wyoming, with two of her friends. The digital screen below his radio showed 81.7 in orange numerals.

When he got back in, I asked him to explain what had just happened. He sketched it out for me, drawing the overpasses and so on. It sounded like one of those math problems I always hated in high school. "Right when she got to that overpass, I started her distance on VASCAR (a device whose acronym means "visual average speed computer and recorder") by hitting the time button when I saw the shadow of her car. I already had her clocked on radar. I turned around on the median, and then when I got to the same overpass I hit the distance switch. Using another overpass at the North Platte interchange, I shut her time off. I already had her time in the computer, but I had to come up to the same point and shut off the distance. Her radar was 82, and she slowed down for construction, but her average speed was still 81.7 over 2.57 miles."

Larson and I roamed for many miles over the next few hours. He showed me the road where a wagon train of Mormons reenacting their people's westward trek had passed just the week before. Very near there he stopped to investigate an old car parked on the side of the road, and the young man tinkering under the hood told him the car was his "vo-tech project." He was just adjusting something in the engine. I wondered if he was a student of Lowell Fenster's.

For some reason, Larson called in the license plate, and he discovered that a pickup order had been issued for this guy's revoked license. Conveniently, he happened not to be carrying it that particular day. Larson had him phone his brother-in-law to drive him home, and then gave the young man a kindly lecture.

"You hit someone, and you'll work for him the rest of your life."

"I know."

"Today, I know what you're doing. Next time, we'll have to see a judge."

"Yessir."

We left the young man to wait for his ride, and drove around some more. Larson's radio crackled with a report that headquarters had received three 911 calls from a woman out on one of the small side highways, and Larson decided to drive out to the area where he thought she might be. He never did find her, not while I was with him. The land was beautiful, rolling, and very desolate. I wouldn't want to be out here in winter, I thought. Years ago, the idea of being stranded in such a place wouldn't have occurred to me, but after living in Minnesota it became one of the first things I thought of whenever I encountered such terrain. Every winter during those years, we heard two or three horror stories about people whose cars had stalled during a blizzard and who had frozen to death twenty-five yards from a farmhouse they couldn't see. In Minnesota the weather was beautiful but dangerous, and no matter how prepared you thought you were— tune-up, full tank of gas, blankets, provisions, candles, flashlights, flares—the natural hazards of the road could add up to disaster. One frigid night, I was parking my white Fiat in front of a restaurant when the radio announcer said, "The windchill index is eighty-five degrees below zero." *Why did I come to this place?* I thought. *Why am I driving a ragtop car?* In Minnesota, for the very first time—and not just because of the weather, I suppose—I began to consider my own vulnerability on the road. Security is a fragile concept.

After a couple of hours, Officer Larson had warmed to my presence, and he began to talk more. I asked if he had seen a lot of changes in the traffic patterns over his nearly nineteen years as a trooper. "It's a lot easier than what it used to be for speed enforcement," he said, "because when I started we still had that dreaded fifty-five-mile-per-hour speed limit. Violators complained something terrible. The truckers hated it. They'd get in pissing matches with you over it. After we got rid of that, everything got easier." He said he thought today's cars were *too* comfortable, with ergonomic seats, cruise control, thermostats, and such. The comfort level is especially dangerous on Nebraska's straight flat interstates. Lots of wrecks are caused by drivers falling asleep. Gadgets create problems, too. "I once saw a car swerving all over the road, and I assumed the driver was drunk. But when I stopped him, the man was trying to read an incoming message on his in-car fax machine."

He told me about the time four drunks were rolling along the interstate with three flat tires. "As soon as I stopped them, two of the tires burst into flames. I put them out with my fire extinguisher. It could've been a lot worse." Then there was the inebriated driver who, when told that he was being taken to jail, said, "Could I change clothes first? It'll be a lot less embarrassing for both of us." Turned out he had on women's underwear beneath his clothes.

But the story I couldn't get out of my mind, the story that compelled me to study the vehicles around me for the rest of the trip, had nothing whatsoever to do with cars. It was instead about a truck driver arrested in central Nebraska a few years back. Larson said troopers still talk about this case, and no wonder. Inside our little boxes of glass and steel, we all are such strange freight.

The trucker picked up a prostitute at one of those all-night truck stops, and after having sex with her, he killed her. But he didn't just dump her body on some desolate stretch of highway. It was winter, and Nebraska winters can be brutal. A man can get lonely. The trucker strapped the woman's body to the bottom of his eighteen-wheeler, where she soon froze stiff as a board. "But when the trucker wanted a little companionship," Larson said with a shy grin, "he would bring her back into the cab and thaw her out."

I left North Platte in mid-afternoon on May 27, heading for Casper, Wyoming. There was a story I wanted to investigate there. At Ogallala I got off the interstate and picked up Highway 26, a two-lane that curves and winds along the North Platte River over the increasingly rolling plains. Far to my right, and down below, was a big blue body of water that I thought must be the river, but it wasn't. It was Lake McConaughy, obviously a lake created by a well-placed dam.

Highway 26 is part of the old Oregon Trail. The flaxen hills are treeless for the most part, and the gray cloudy sky was as big as I had ever seen it—an Ansel Adams sky. The road ahead seemed, for the first time in my life, absolutely perfect. Pieces of it peeked over the upcoming hills, a disjointed but continuous ribbon. The perfect road, the perfect car. I edged the transmission to manual and gradually bore down on the accelerator. Eighty-five, 90, 95, 100. Lyle Lovett was blaring from the tape player—"I'm lookin' for a cowboy . . ." One-oh-five, 110, 113. Then an open stretch unfolded in front of me, and I pushed it harder. One-eighteen, 120, 122, 125. A curve was looming fast, and I dropped back below a hundred. My heart was pounding. I had never driven that fast in my entire life. This car made speed easy.

The moment evaporated quickly, as bad roads and heavier traffic intervened. I got behind a tractor of some kind, and there was no place for him to move over. Soon I was in a slow line of cars and trucks. Everyone was slowing down to gawk at the Mormon wagon train that was camped on the side of the road. This was the same group Officer Larson had seen in North Platte the week before. They hadn't traveled very far.

I was glad I had seized the chance to speed when I saw it. It was the best time I'd had in an automobile since I owned my white Fiat Spider. But for all the good times I'd had driving the Fiat, I didn't get to keep it for long. In 1978, less than two years after I'd bought it, I got a call one day asking if I wanted to move to Chicago and become articles editor of *Playboy* magazine. It was the job of my dreams, the chance to edit writers like Norman Mailer, Truman Capote, Irwin Shaw, Kurt Vonnegut. I told my Southern Baptist relatives that it was the most important job at the magazine, since everybody *says* they buy it for the articles.

Wanting a taste of the urban life, I decided to sell the Spider and live in the city. The woman I was dating in Minnesota sold her car and went with me. We took buses to work in the morning, cabs home at night. For a couple of years I convinced myself that I liked public

transportation. It made me feel righteous for the first time in my selfish life. The feeling didn't last. On summer days, tall men with body
odor would inevitably sidle up next to me and reach for the overhead
rail. The first time I stood to offer a woman my seat, she cursed me
for being sexist. The next time I tried it (with an older woman), a man
dashed into the seat before the old lady could rattle her brittle bones.
This was during the late seventies, early eighties—a confusing time.

In 1980, the woman and I married and I began dreaming of owning a car again. I wanted to get out of town on weekends. We went to
look at Fiat Spiders, which had doubled in price between 1976 and
1981, a result of the cost of imports and the government's new environmental requirements. We bought one anyway. By then my sons
were twelve and six. David had become tall. It was clear that a small
two-seater with a tiny back bench wasn't the most practical car for
even a part-time dad. But since when had practicality been part of my
car-buying equation?

My change of heart about the Fiat came in the late summer of 1983.
By then my wife and I had renounced our full-time urban experiment
in favor of a big old expensive house on the North Shore. It was the
suburbs, essentially, even though our street was paved with brick and
the house was seventy years old. We were escaping the city—the
noise, the crime, the crush and now on weekends we could drive with
the top down on winding shady lanes. One night at the end of August,
we did just that. The next morning I woke up and my face wouldn't
work.

I went to the doctor. "Have you ridden a bicycle lately?" he said.
"No."
"Have you ridden in a convertible?"
"Yes."
"When?"
"Last night."

"Well, that's it. The wind on your face gave you Bell's Palsy."

It seemed like a simplistic answer (it was), but between that and the family seating problem, the Spider was doomed. Within days, my wife and I traded it for that Audi 4000, the closest I'd ever come to owning a luxury car. Even though it had plush seats and a great stereo, I had a hard time squaring my self-image with my preconceived biases against four-door automobiles. It didn't help that just four months after buying it, I would turn forty.

Was it true? Was I no different from other people my age?

Just outside Northport, Nebraska, I saw a sign for "Carhenge." I had heard about it but had no idea it was anywhere in the vicinity. Some crazy artist had re-created England's Stonehenge using automobiles, which he'd painted all flat gray. The sign said it was north of the little town of Alliance. I studied my map. It was a total of eighty miles out of my way.

But how could I skip it? I spurned Casper and turned north on Highway 385. Mountain Time had taken over just west of North Platte, so the hour was only a little after four. Even so, with the sky gray and cloudy, there was a hint of day's end in the air. It wasn't cold, but the sky itself looked more like late fall than like late spring. A blue mountain range rose in the distance.

The drive to Alliance took less than an hour. I followed the signs through town (McDonald's, Holiday Inn at one end, blending to a brick-street downtown at the other) to Carhenge, which was a couple of miles north on a little highway. I didn't see it at first, which struck me as odd. The sky is so big, the land so flat, the view so long that it seemed impossible to miss anything that stood above the horizon. But the gray formation of cars was lost against the brooding gray of the sky. When I finally saw it, it wasn't what I had expected.

Carhenge sounded like a funny idea, and I thought I would find it merely amusing. But this strange formation has a portentous power to it. The cars—probably a couple dozen of them—are scattered around and stacked atop one another like boulders. The endless plains provide a vast backdrop for this display, like a high wide wall in an art gallery. I left the Boxster in a little gravel parking area and approached the monument on foot. It was larger than I expected—taller, more massive, the same size as the actual Stonehenge. There was no music, no packaged commentary, no fanfare of any kind. Just the whistling wind and the big gray sky and the eternal silence of the monument itself.

I spent an hour there, looking and thinking. The cars in front of me represented an era in American life—the postwar dream, giving way to the disillusionment of the seventies. A big-finned Plymouth from the fifties perched atop a boatlike Caddy from the sixties. Elsewhere there was a scaled-down Vega, and then a sculptured Valiant—both sad attempts to hold the dream together. I found myself imagining future generations rounding a hill and coming upon this enigmatic formation. I heard them puzzling over it the way we puzzle over Stonehenge. *What did these ancient relics mean? Where did they come from? What were they for? Why was this such hallowed ground?*

Then I caught a glimpse of the Boxster in the parking lot. No, I thought, even future generations of Americans won't have forgotten the answers to those questions.

NINE

Green River Blues

The automobile isn't a team player. There was a time, a less frenetic time in this country, when it appeared to be—when its advertised purpose was to bring families together by providing shared adventure or spanning a gap of miles between loved ones. But at its cold steel heart, the car has always been an instrument of potential anarchy. Home is about digging in, at least in the ideal. It requires teamwork, generosity, selflessness. You can bend a car to the rules of home—the ubiquitous minivan of soccer moms, for example. But at the end of the day, wheels are for moving.

Such were my thoughts after Beth and I fought on the phone from Alliance and I did something totally uncharacteristic of me: I hung up on her. I don't think I've done that—to anyone—more than a couple of times in my life. I phoned her back and apologized for hanging up, but the conversation didn't improve much. She was furious. The next morning when I called again, she'd been up all night writing me a five-page letter. I could only imagine—a blistering litany of every sin I had ever committed (only five pages?). She wanted to fax it to me, but I refused to receive it. I had to concentrate, I said.

It wasn't easy. I sat in the lobby of the Holiday Inn Express and worked on my notes. The night before, I had been too tired to write. This morning I felt distracted. I worried that I was letting myself slip, that I was succumbing to the temptation to gloss over too many details of the trip because all I wanted to do was to get on the road. I made myself spend an hour working on my notes, and then I checked out of the hotel.

When I loaded the Porsche and turned the ignition, the coolant light came on again. I stopped at a Kmart to buy some, but they carried only gallon sizes. The Kmart salesman said, "I noticed your car out in the parking lot. From what I've read, you can drive that thing across the desert without adding coolant." I remembered that the manual said it was okay to add a little water if need be, and that's what I did. Mileage: 6022 for the car; 5820 for me. I dropped the top and headed for Denver.

There were many times on my journey when I forgot my purpose in being on the road. This was one of those times. What, exactly, was the point of getting up every morning and driving to another town? Sometimes the reason seemed conditional—it depended on what I found when I got there. But then why, after finding much the same thing over and over again, should I go on to the next town, and the next, and the next? "I travel not to go anywhere, but to go," wrote Robert Louis Stevenson. "I travel for travel's sake. The great affair is to move." Somewhere on the barren Nebraska plains, I thought about the statistics the people at the highway administration had sent me the previous winter. In 1955, there were 62.7 million cars registered in this country. By 1985, there were 171.6 million. According to the 1990 Nationwide Personal Transportation Survey (NPTS), in 1969, a man my age (between thirty-five and fifty-four, in fact) drove 12,841 miles a year. In 1990, that number had increased 47 percent—to 18,871 miles annually. In his book *Self-Consciousness,* published in 1989, John Updike said that every seventeen years the average American male drives the distance to the moon—238,855 miles. By the 1990 NPTS, the rate was every *thirteen* years. For women, the increase has been even more dramatic. In 1969, females in that age range drove 6,003 miles. By 1990, with the changes in their lives, they were driving 10,539 miles a year—a 76 percent increase.

What can you make of such numbers? I'm no sociologist, but I lived those years and watched others live them. It was a feverish time. Ever more cars, and ever more miles *per* car. One thing I know for certain is that an automobile provides personal freedom, and personal freedom changes everything. In my research for this book, I found a study on American mobility by an Arizona State University geography professor named Patricia Gober. "From the end of the last century until 1940," she said, "between 75 and 80 percent of the native-born population of the United States resided in the state of their birth. After a small uptick in 1940 due to low mobility in the Depression era, this figure has steadily dropped. In 1990, 67 percent of native-born Americans lived in the state of their birth."

Recently I heard a woman on television making the case to bring back "fault" divorce. California started the trend toward "no-fault" in 1969. Thirty years later, some 50 percent of first marriages and 60 percent of second marriages end in divorce. "It's time to put personal responsibility above personal freedom," the woman on TV said. But personal freedom—including the freedom to move on—is at the core of what makes us American. We will destroy everything for our right to become Billy Bilkins.

Highway 88, which I turned onto just south of the town of Bridgeport, was the most desolate road I had been on in the entire trip. Then, scanning the radio stations, I heard a talk jock from Scottsbluff lambasting Bill Clinton for his "immorality" in selling computer chips to the Chinese. I laughed. *The world is still spinning,* I thought. On Highway 71, just before I was to reconnect with I-80, I spotted a huge automobile graveyard off to the right—Rick's Wrecking, north of Kimball, Nebraska. Something, maybe my mood, made me stop. I pulled the Porsche inside the gate and parked next to an old blue pickup. The office was a metal building, dim and cool inside. At a front counter, a man in jeans, glasses, and a Rick's Wrecking cap was talking on the telephone.

"Right. Sure, we've got that. Four hundred fifty dollars. Okay, by Friday. Thanks."

When he hung up, I introduced myself and told him what I was up to. His name was Lacey Broussard—he was Rick's partner, he said. He seemed wary at first, but he gave me permission to look around. "We've got ten acres."

I picked up my camcorder and wandered through the neat rows of twisted metal. At first, what I saw was a harvest of death. One black Thunderbird had obviously been rolled, crushing it and everyone inside. I cringed at the thought of what the occupants' last moments must have been like. Then I came upon an old Mustang with its front bumper pushed nearly to the driver's seat. My old doomed friend Bill Ballentine came inexorably to mind. But after a few minutes of walking and looking, I noticed that the steel bodies began to take on a life of their own, separate from the hapless drivers who had consigned them there. They were just shells, like the locust shells I used to find in my yard as a boy.

Back in the office, Lacey seemed a little more open now. He was from Louisiana originally, so we had a Southern upbringing in common. I asked how his business worked. "This is where I sell everything," he said, pointing to the computer. "Everybody in the country who has this system can pull up what I've got. If they're looking for a fender for an eighty-five Chevy pickup, they can locate it on the computer and give me a call."

As if on cue, the phone rang. "Rick's Wrecking," Lacey said, and within a minute he had closed a deal for "a 7.3 diesel engine. Twenty-three hundred dollars. All I had to do was answer this phone." I was impressed. "People are always going to be driving automobiles," Lacey said. "And they're always going to need parts."

Before leaving, I asked what was the one automobile part he didn't have but wished he had. He didn't even have to think. "A Ford Taurus transmission, eighty-six to ninety-two. There was a flaw in the Taurus trannies. I could sell as many of them as I could get, for five hundred bucks a pop."

I-80 took me west to Wyoming. Place names become more evocative to me the farther west I go. Maybe it's because as a child I played cowboys and Indians, not pilgrim or planter. *New Hampshire* doesn't do it for me, and neither does *Virginia*. But *Nebraska, Montana, Colorado, Dakota*—they stir some inner restlessness. They speak of open spaces.

I remembered having a similar feeling when I left Chicago for Arkansas. The year was 1986, and my dream job had turned into a nightmare. For a year before I quit, it was all I could do to force myself to go to work. I began worrying about standing too near those big windows in my office, the ones overlooking Michigan Avenue from ten floors up. I stayed in that office at least two years too long. Part of my decision to stay put was pure will, a desire to break the American cycle of looking over the next hill for happiness. And part of it was indecision. I didn't know which hill to look over.

Then in early 1986, through a series of contacts and coincidences, I made a momentous decision. I would leave *Playboy* and move to

Little Rock to help start a magazine about the South. I knew almost nothing about Arkansas, except that even Mississippians made fun of it. But my exhilaration was such that at times I could hardly breathe. I felt that I had found a new frontier. We would need a second car, and the image that flashed into my head was of an off-road vehicle.

As it turned out, my boss at *Playboy* had decided to trade his company car, a blue 1984 four-wheel-drive Jeep Wagoneer with 22,000 miles on it. One snowy February day, I went to the leasing agency and wrote a check for $7,500. In return I got a two-year-old Jeep with an amazingly bad sound system and a big dent in the front left fender, put there by my boss's teenage son. But I didn't mind either flaw, and never had them replaced or repaired. To me, the flaws were a kind of bonus—constant reminders that the journey wasn't all smooth roads and pretty vistas.

I had given up the best job I'd ever hoped to have. I had stepped off the beaten path into no-man's-land. And I remember vividly the nasty day my wife and I finally left Chicago, the Wagoneer packed to the roof, eighteen-wheelers whooshing all around us. My wife was coming with me so we could look for a house, but even that didn't matter much to me. All I knew was that I was *going*. Whatever happened before, or later, didn't matter. The moment was the thing. Sleet, snow, and ice pummeled the windshield, and the wipers beat like hummingbird wings. I was as happy as I had ever been in my life.

Zooming toward Wyoming in the Boxster, I contemplated the fact that both my divorces came during a period after we'd recently moved to another state. Would they have happened otherwise? Who can say? In the first case, my wife met someone else. In the second, my wife hated Arkansas and wanted to return to Chicago. As part of my early research for this book, I talked with Dr. Sidney Blatt, a Yale psychologist who specializes in depression. "The automobile has its advantages," he had told me, "but we pay a big price for it. In mobile societies, there are no supports at home or at work. Life becomes an endless process of saying hello and good-bye." It sounded like a country song, but I knew it was true. When my second wife said she was returning to her old job in Chicago, I just couldn't go back. So one day in 1988, she loaded up the Audi and pointed it toward the big city. After she left, I drove my Jeep to the top of an Arkansas mountain and looked out over the valley below. Another beginning, I thought. I had tried to negotiate the last one in a sports car, but that now seemed naive. In the dozen years since, I had learned that the road was longer, less predictable, and quite often more dangerous than I had imagined. *This* beginning wasn't about chasing lost youth. It was about survival. That would require tougher wheels.

In Cheyenne, a roadside sign said, "All dealer vehicles and saddle mounts must exit." Cheyenne looks industrial, but in a Western way—buildings are lower, more spread out. The sky is still huge. Something about that perspective gives you a sense of personal power, of being tall. Maybe that's what it feels like to be a cowboy.

I picked up I-25 south toward Denver. It was 2:45 P.M. when I pulled into a Flying J Travel Plaza for a late lunch. I also had to phone my friend Ron King in Denver, who had told me to stay with him when I got to Colorado. Of course, I had given him no warning as to when I might show up. I didn't have any warning myself. This time the day before, I'd thought I would be in Casper by now.

The Flying J is the oasis of choice for the modern American nomad. It is a combination Wal-Mart, Safeway, Waffle House, Conoco station, and Motel 6. You can take showers, wash your car, and buy anything from books on tape to refrigerator magnets, from toys to jewelry, from chewing gum to socks. When I entered the restaurant, the man who greeted me said, "Would you like a telephone?"

"Sure," I said. He picked up a menu and retrieved a sturdy little cell phone from a rack behind the counter and escorted me to a booth overlooking the vast parking lot. The menu listed just about any greasy fried comfort food a lonely, reality-suspended traveler could want. I ordered a cheeseburger and a Diet Coke and phoned Ron at his office. A phone card is part of the traveler's basic equipment these days.

He was glad to hear from me but already had plans for the evening. He gave me detailed instructions to his house and spelled out what he called "the Bedouin Rule": If a stranger shows up at your door, you must invite him for three nights; if he doesn't leave after three nights, you're entitled to kill him and steal all his belongings. I promised I wouldn't be turning the Boxster over to him that easily.

On the drive into Denver, a couple of guys in an old gray Mustang pulled beside me and began revving the engine. I thought to myself, *Do Frenchmen do that?* I couldn't imagine it, but maybe they do. It seems so tediously *American* to want to race all the time. I smiled over at them, and they smiled back. I punched the Boxster, then let off the gas. The Mustang lurched forward, then slowed. Smirks all around. We were side by side on I-25, going about 70, when we took off. I had forgotten to drop the Boxster into manual, and the Mustang peeled out ahead. Finally it was clear that I could overtake him if I kept speeding, but I backed off just before hitting 100. This was, after all, a crowded interstate highway. I apologized aloud to my boyhood racing mentor, Teddy Neuweiler.

When I got to the Loveland turnoff, the terrain changed. Off to my right, I could see the Rockies rising in the haze. But just south of the turn to Loveland, some forty-five miles from Denver, the land fronting the interstate began to feel crowded. Not strip malls yet, but the seeds of them. I passed one of those ubiquitous mini warehouse complexes, one of hundreds I had seen across the country—"U Store It. U Lock It. U Keep Key." I may be wrong, but I don't remember seeing such personal storage facilities when I was growing up. Now they're everywhere, whole villages built around abandoned possessions. Where are their owners? When will they come back? What secrets have they locked behind all those sliding metal doors?

Before long, construction on I-25 brought traffic to a dead stop. While we idled, road graders picked and carried, dropped and scurried, earnest as ants.

Ron's was the first private home I had entered in a week. He showed me to a spacious guest room, and then he and his girlfriend, Leslie, left for a concert. I drank a beer and sorted out my dirty clothes. Everything in my bag was beginning to smell musty. It was past time to do laundry.

I called Tina Poe, a friend of Beth's and mine, to make a date for lunch the next day, and then I phoned Beth. We argued again, and I accused her of "haranguing" me. She accused me of not being supportive. That's one of those female trump cards that always puts me on the defensive. She wanted to fax me the letter she had written the night before, and I pled ignorance of Ron's fax number. Finally she insisted on reading it to me. It wasn't a harangue at all. Instead, it was essentially a love letter—sensitive, eloquent, totally candid. And totally effective. It made me feel awful. Later I walked to a yuppie bar Ron had told me about—Hemingway's Key West Grille—where I ate dinner and wrote my day's notes. One entry said, "In the battle between home and the road, home is scoring major hits."

The next morning I felt more hopeful, though when I phoned Beth, she didn't answer. I washed clothes at a Laundromat, then drove to the new Denver library to do some research. The library is striking—the architect designed it to look like a whole village in a single building. Inside, I went to the reference section to find clips on a man named Spicer Breeden. He was a rich young scion of an old Colorado family, who bought expensive new cars every three or four months. One night in March of 1996, a dark BMW speeding at 110 miles an hour struck a Toyota 4Runner on I-25 in Denver, causing the Toyota to roll. The Toyota driver, a columnist for the *Rocky Mountain News* named Greg Lopez, was killed. The BMW sped off into the night. The driver, Spicer Breeden, thirty-six, later shot himself just as police were closing in. They had tracked him through his unique "cosmos black" car—only 100 BMWs were manufactured in that particular make, model, year, and color. Of those 100, only three were shipped to Colorado. Of those three, one was later sent to Texas, one was still on a dealer lot, and the third was sold to Spicer Breeden.

A short version of the story had appeared in my local newspaper, and I had been fascinated by it. It spoke tragically, classically, of a life lived in the gap between inadequacy and hubris. And it offered a fittingly ironic conclusion to Spicer Breeden's need to be known by the car he drove. I didn't have time to look up and interview the remaining characters, but I wanted to see what more I could learn in the time I did have. For an hour I pored over a clip file, absorbing the sad saga of Breeden's high-living family, his oft-married father and *his* exotic automobiles, and the episode in which Spicer canceled a marriage the night before his wedding because his fiancée got angry and threw rocks at his car. Once again I wondered why, apart from the specter of libel, any writer ever need resort to fiction.

Then the story took one more incredible turn. In a small clip, a *Denver Post* writer outlined a bizarre connection between Spicer Breeden and Greg Lopez, the man killed in the hit-and-run. Thirteen months before the accident, Lopez had written a profile of the man who sold Breeden the black BMW. The car salesman, despite earning some $50,000 a year, preferred to live in his retrofitted Ford camper. "I drive past my old house sometimes and wonder how I used to live like that," the salesman had told Lopez. "If a neighborhood goes bad on me, I change neighborhoods. My biggest worries are finding a level parking space close to a bathroom."

I wandered off to lunch feeling that somewhere in that twisted tale was a moral trying to break free.

I met my friend Tina in the lobby of a hotel near her office, and together we hopped a downtown tram and were transported to an Italian restaurant a few blocks away. Denver was the biggest city I had been in since Miami. Being out of the Boxster, riding mass transit, felt a little unsettling. It wasn't unpleasant—the trams seemed to come by frequently enough, and they were free. But I noticed a subtle difference in how I felt as I waited for the cute little circuslike wagon to stop and pick me up. I felt like part of a herd. Not an enlightened feeling, but not one that's easy to escape, either.

Tina perceived a different herd. Over lunch, she described the traffic in Denver as not just terrible but dispiriting. She described the agitated faces of people caught in horrendous traffic jams, row after row of them, drivers alone in their little curved caves of painted metal, as Updike called them, trying to escape in the very instruments that now made escape impossible. "We are driving twice as much as we did in the 1970s, yet the result seems to be less mobility and more frustration," writes new urbanist Peter Calthorpe. I thought of what my brother had said about the elk. They used to run free, and now they don't. No wonder they're angry. Tina wondered if I would suffer an identity crisis when I had to drop off the Boxster. I didn't want to think about that. "There's a chance I'll buy it," I said.

That afternoon, stopping by the rejuvenated old section of lower downtown ("LoDo") to see Ron's office, I had to park the Boxster four blocks away. When I rounded the corner on the way back, four tough-looking guys were crowded around the car. "Like it?" I said, trying for a tone of cool-but-friendly nonchalance. One of the men, a big guy with a dark black ponytail, wearing shorts, T-shirt, and boots like my Timberlands, said, "Yeah. I was thinking of buying one." I was frankly skeptical—the way he was dressed, he could have been a construction worker. But there was an explanation for that: He was in the fashion industry. Derrick Finn was his name, and he was distribution manager for a sportswear manufacturer, whose building I had parked in front of. His car at the moment was a $48,000 Dodge Stealth. This man was serious about buying a Boxster.

I rolled back the top and showed him all the features. Then I asked for his card. He invited me into his spacious office, where he retrieved a business card from his desk drawer. "I'm thirty-six," he said. "Married, two children, a homeowner—all the responsibilities that come with life. Kids play ball, one's in ballet. My wife's car is an Isuzu Rodeo. We did the van thing, had an Astro, but didn't like it. Didn't want to be stuck in that mold. As you can see from my appearance, I dress young, I am young, I try to act young. From that we went to a big conversion van, captain's chairs, the works. I loved that. I would drive it every weekend, to go play ball and stuff like that. But she drove it every day. Just hated it. You could imagine, four miles to the gallon. So she got the Isuzu Rodeo.

"But I don't think women appreciate cars the way we do. When I was in high school, I had a chance to buy a sixty-seven Mustang fastback, built to the gills. Fifteen hundred dollars. I begged my father to buy me that car, but he said, 'No, I'm not going to let you kill yourself in that thing.' And I probably would have. It was a lot more car than I could handle. Later, when I graduated, my dad bought me a 1967 Plymouth Belvedere 500, with a big 440 in it. It was cherry red with a white vinyl interior. It was the end of the muscle-car era. I graduated in 1979. By my senior year, gas prices had gone from roughly twenty-five cents to sixty cents a gallon. It was the oil embargo and all that. People were dumping these cars. My dad paid five hundred dollars for it. I drove it for four years of college, then sold it to my cousin for two thousand dollars.

"Those wants are inbred in us, I think. I always wanted a sports car. And I wanted it when I was young enough to really push it. There are times when you get out on that open road, and you put your favorite CD in, and you just *go like hell*."

Of course, he doesn't get to do that very often. He lives close enough to work that he drives his beloved Stealth only "eight to ten minutes in the morning, eight to ten minutes at night."

"Do you ever wonder if it's worth it? The traffic, the expense, the hassle?"

"Yeah, I do. In Denver, we're very lucky. We have a great bus system. But you'd never *ever* catch me riding the bus."

"Why? Would you be embarrassed?"

"No, it's not that. I come in here every morning at seven-thirty. I cut out and go to the gym every day at four-thirty. The bus runs right down here a block away. I *park* three blocks away. The gym is *four* blocks away. I could walk to the gym, walk back, and catch the bus, and it would dump me off right by the park and ride. But I think it's just knowing that if I wanted to, I could leave at any time. Not having to be on a set schedule. You know? It's asinine the things we do. It's just the freedom."

"One final question," I said. "Do you ever think about just getting in your car and driving and never coming back?"

He laughed. "I think *every* American male does."

That night I took Ron and Leslie to a restaurant called Coos Bay. Great yup food at great yup prices. "I'm like my dad," Ron said at dinner. "I buy the least expensive used car and drive it till it falls apart."

"That may say something about your relationship with your dad," I said, and ordered a second bottle of pinot noir.

When we got home, I phoned Beth. My stepdaughter Blair answered and said she was sleeping. Later I found out that Beth told her to tell me that. I read *Undaunted Courage* until I fell asleep, right in the middle of an Indian uprising.

The next morning, Friday, May 30, I got out of bed early and went running for the first time since Pensacola. I should have been getting way more exercise than I was. The irony was that I'd become more sedentary on the road than I was at home. That's part of the lure, of course: The road absolves you of responsibilities. I jogged through Ron's nice old residential area, a place that reminded me of where I live in Little Rock. Handsome cottages, front porches, big trees. But even so, Denver was getting to me. This was the first time I had spent two nights in one place since my hiatus at home. Ron had been the perfect host, but I was beginning to feel closed in by the crowds, the traffic, the expense. I was too old and too marginally employed to be a yuppie. Plus, this thing with Beth. Sitting around Denver, I had too much time to think about it. We had never been in a fight like this when one of us was away.

I thanked Ron as he left for work, and then I loaded the Boxster. More trouble. Even after the car had warmed up, the dashboard oil gauge showed the oil level as low. I'd been instructed to use only synthetic oil, if I needed any at all, so I stopped at an auto-parts store and bought a couple of quarts. By then, the dash gauge showed the oil level as fine. I popped the trunk and measured the level on the dipstick three times. Each time, it seemed okay. *At least I have oil with me,* I thought. The coolant gauge looked okay, too. I wanted everything to be perfect. Today I would cross the Rocky Mountains.

The first time I ever laid eyes on the Rockies was in 1971, guiding that lumbering Winnebago across Kansas. After hours and miles of numbing flatness, I began to notice a change in the far horizon. I wasn't even sure my eyes weren't playing tricks on me. But the horizon kept growing, slowly but surely, as though I were present in a different eon and was actually watching the mountains crack through the earth's crust like chicks breaking free of their shells.

Now, heading west on I-70 again, I watched the mountains literally emerge from the haze—first as blue, then green, then gray-brown with creamy snow on top. A red Acura driven by a blond woman passed me going at least 80. Her license-plate holder said, "Save a steer, eat a cowboy." I passed a Jeep sporting the bumper sticker "Mean People Suck." Then came an old VW van with a sign in the rear window: "Don't cheat, don't lie, don't steal. Congress hates the competition." Suddenly a man in a green Lotus pulled up next to me and gave me the thumbs-up. It was the first time in days. Nebraska had seemed singularly unimpressed with the Boxster. The stares had picked up again in Denver. Now this Lotus driver was speaking the road language I had learned on the way to Florida. I felt like I had come home again.

Whenever a shiny new car passed me, I glanced at its finish to see if I could make out the reflection of the Boxster's spoiler, but I never could. We all were going too fast. Seeing that spoiler had become a miniquest for me. In Denver, I had driven by a mirrored building specifically for that purpose, but downtown traffic had prevented me from going fast enough for the spoiler to engage.

Ron had suggested I take the Loveland Pass instead of going through the Eisenhower Tunnel. I had been unsure. At almost two miles long, the tunnel was the most ambitious one built during the interstate highway program. I felt I owed Frank Turner the compliment of driving through his men's handiwork. Then I realized that no matter whether I took the pass or the tunnel, my route would eventually lead me through Glenwood Canyon, one of the most challenging projects in the interstate highway system. It was challenging not simply because it was a seventeen-mile gash through the Rocky Mountains, following the Colorado River. The challenge had come in adapting the pragmatism of the road builders to the demands of the environmentalists. In the late sixties, the Glenwood Canyon project had been the topic of dozens of meetings and hearings and environmental studies. I decided I could skip the Eisenhower Tunnel. Glenwood Canyon was where American ideals collided.

The Porsche seemed to be working hard in the mountains. I was feeling lethargic myself. About ten miles east of the Loveland cutoff, a couple in a sedan passed me and the woman gave me a look that her husband would have hated to see. At least *I* would have been stunned to see Beth eye somebody else that way. Of course, it was the car, not me. Secrets and lies and automobiles. It made me wonder about that couple's journey together. Would they opt for the sunny pass, or would they be more comfortable in the tunnel?

They kept going as I exited to Highway 6, Loveland Pass. I pulled over, kicked back the top, and put on my parka. I wanted to be able to see this road. It was about twenty miles of curves and switchbacks, climbing higher and higher. I flicked the transmission to manual, which turned out to be very helpful. It felt less dicey being able to shift while keeping my hands on the steering wheel. There was no guard rail. At any time I could have gunned the Porsche and sailed into thin air as Susan Sarandon and Geena Davis did in *Thelma and Louise*. At the summit, I stopped and photographed the plaque marking the Continental Divide—11,990 feet above sea level. All around me were snow-covered mountains. On the way down I held my camcorder above my head in an attempt to photograph the drive. It was hard steering and shifting with one hand, and I captured mostly snow and sky and a soundtrack of wind rumbling like an avalanche.

Back on I-70, I noticed the Porsche felt freer on this side of the Continental Divide. It was all downhill now, from there to the sea. Not everyone was enjoying the drive so much. I passed an eighteen-wheeler whose brakes were smoking. Huge billows roiled out from beneath his trailer.

Vail soon came up on the left, a mountainside village of condos and smart cafes. In the green valley between the interstate and the bluffs, a giant screened cage, like a man-made box canyon, invited vacationers to practice their golf drives without losing their balls in an eagle's nest. I wasn't sure if what I was seeing was actually the Vail of renown or simply the less exclusive sprawl situated near the highway. Probably the latter. I hoped we hadn't reached the point of setting ritzy vacation sites along the interstates.

The signs to Glenwood Canyon began showing up miles ahead—a good omen, I thought. This was supposed to be one of the places where, after an extended battle, the amended system worked. Frank Turner had told me how his people "bent over backwards" to accommodate the human and environmental challenges. Once the road men's consciousness was raised—once they realized that simply moving more traffic faster wasn't an acceptable end-all—they found ways to deal with the problems. "Sometimes we moved the highway," he said, rather than run it through someone's property. "In the little towns, especially, we encountered fierce arguments and hard feelings. The worst was in New Mexico, which refused to let us build roads through or alongside communities. Basically, they said, 'Take your damn tractors and go somewhere else.' We eventually built the highways a reasonable distance from the communities." As for Glenwood Canyon, "it was one of the most spectacular projects. We made a scenic thing out of it. We put more money in it than could be justified on pure economics."

The canyon cuts right through cowboy country. When I was a child, my family never drove West, so the first time I saw big rocks like the ones I'd seen in the Westerns was in 1968, when my wife and I drove into southern Missouri on my way to take a job at Hallmark. Then in 1971, I saw the Rockies, and later the Badlands of South Dakota. In 1989, Beth and I sat atop a blood-red mesa in Sedona, Arizona, watching the sun set. It's almost an American duty to go witness such sights, where you can still see something of what stirred the early settlers' blood. Even today, the landscapes still match the magnificence of the dream that Lewis and Clark were chasing two hundred years ago.

I held the camcorder above the glass and caught the roaring wind. The sparkling Colorado River sets the highway's course, which is as it should be. For seventeen miles the interstate follows the river, twisting and turning, rising and falling, splitting and coming together in a way that doesn't intrude on the natural splendor of the river, mountains, and sky. Tunnels cut through yards of rock. High bluffs display layers of history. Glenwood Canyon is a beautiful drive, but it's more than that. It's also eloquent testament to the American need to *go*, no matter what stands in the way.

Just east of the town of Glenwood Springs, the traffic began backing up. Either a wreck or road work lay ahead, I guessed. But for fifteen minutes, all cars heading west were stopped dead in their tracks. We were gridlocked in God's Country.

Past the canyon, the land flattens and spreads, forming wide pastures where horses roam. The mountains recede into the distance. Scrub brush grows along the highway, drying and turning into tumbleweeds. I caught a glimpse of an old Thunderbird from the fifties in a rancher's garage. Throughout this journey I had spotted such vehicles—a '55 Chevy half covered near a barn in Missouri; a car from the forties pulled beside a garage in Denver.

Near Grand Junction my nose caught the scent of something sweet, and I decided it must be wildflowers. It reminded me of a night two decades earlier when I had gone to Victorville, California, to interview my childhood hero, Roy Rogers. Until then I hadn't known that the desert, the high desert, was so fragrant. But that night, as I nervously waited for daybreak, I sat outside my motel room studying the stars and inhaling the sweet air, which mixed with my memories of Roy and Trigger. The next day, the King of the Cowboys showed me both his old and new museums. The old one, a former bowling alley, was now completely empty. Everything had been moved to the new place. Still, Roy escorted me around the entire floor, saying, "And this is where old Nellie Bell was, and here's where old Bullet was, and . . ." It was bizarre, a tour of a vacant room. Then when he drove me in his truck over to the new one, which was shaped like a cavalry fort, he gave me a second tour. Most everything was still under wraps, and at one point in the tour he stopped and said, "And you remember old Trigger, don't you?" He was pointing to a big white tarp covering something on the floor. He lifted the flap, and there was his legendary golden palomino, the miracle horse who could count with his hooves. My mother once had taken me to Memphis to see him. Now Trigger was mounted and bucking but lying on his side, a roadside attraction waiting to be set upright for the paying public.

The sweet Colorado air made me wonder if the desert was near. At Grand Junction I pulled into a gas station and studied my atlas. Utah wasn't far, and sure enough, the country I was about to enter was nearly all white on the map. I filled up with gas, even though I wasn't down half a tank. The desert is no place to take chances. While I was topping off my tank, two separate carloads of people stopped and came over to ask about the Boxster. First, two young guys in a pickup. "That's the first one I've seen," said one.

"I hear they're hard to get," said the other.

"Yeah, they are. I just lucked out." By now my Nevada plates were less conspicuous. Then an old VW van stopped and a group of older people piled out. "Great car," the men said. The women just walked around it and smiled.

I approached Utah on a stretch of highway that was "Maintained by the Church of Jesus Christ of Latter Day Saints." At 5:50 P.M. I crossed the state line doing 90, then pulled into the first rest stop to survey the countryside. The sky was blue in the distance, but the white fluffy clouds showed pockets of rain. The terrain was all sandy brown and scrubby green, with hazy purple mountains ranging far to the north and west. After a few minutes of taking in the new scenery, I got back in the Boxster and headed out in search of lodging.

Green River was sixty-two miles away, and that seemed to be my best bet. The land was incredibly desolate, and the sudden difference between Utah and Colorado was astounding. Just a few miles east, water had been running out of the mountains, filling rivers and streams. Now I was in high desert—all cracked creekbeds and sand, nothing green but the road signs. The interstate was as flat and straight as I had seen anywhere. There were very few exits, and most of them were to private ranches, not towns. The exit to Moab, a town I had heard of, appeared simply to trail off into the desert.

Twenty miles out of Green River, two girls in a maroon pickup passed and smiled, then kept watching me in their rearview mirror. I felt a strange excitement now about their presence. I settled into cruise position and watched them from behind my sunglasses. Home felt a long way away. Sometimes I couldn't even picture it clearly. In the meantime, the road stretched on ahead.

The maroon truck kept going when I turned off, following a sign that advertised Green River, population 866, as "The Watermelon Capital of the World." That would come as a shock to the city fathers of Hope, Arkansas, I thought, since Hope bills itself the same way. Then a Comfort Inn sign beckoned in the early evening light. The sign was very comforting on the surface, but down deep I considered it a bit disturbing, too. Is there no place left to get away from civilization? I thought of the time Beth and I had driven from Sedona to the Grand Canyon. After miles of rural highway, we passed into a twilight zone of utter desolation. Few cows, fewer people, seventy-five miles that made driving across South Dakota (a stretch the CIA could use to force people to talk) seem like rush hour on U.S. 1. At the end of that highway, in front of a faded gas station, we came upon a spanking-white *USA Today* box full of that day's papers.

Following a winding approach road to Green River, I saw the motel standing out to the right. It must be hard to build to scale in the West. This Comfort Inn, just two stories high, seemed plopped down and alien, not growing out of the land itself. It made me think of the big house in the movie *Giant*, the mansion that stands alone and incongruous on a vast prairie. The new urbanists preach about how today's homogeneous, scaleless, chain-store architecture undermines the cozy sense of community we all seek in our souls. That's how I felt about the Green River Comfort Inn, but I checked in anyway.

"We have a rate for seniors," the woman at the desk said.

"No, you younger-the-dumber, you don't understand. *Step outside and look at my car!*"

That's what I wanted to say. Instead, I said, "Fine, I'll take it." She didn't even ask for my AARP card.

After I washed up, I drove the half block to the restaurant the desk clerk had suggested—the Tamarisk, on the banks of the Green River itself. I didn't want to eat yet, but I did feel a powerful hankering for a dust cutter, as the cowboys would say. A gin and tonic, icy cold and smelling of juniper berries, was the image that came to mind. Surprisingly, the Tamarisk parking lot was almost full at 7:00 P.M. There was a line of people, mostly families, waiting to be seated. I asked the young hostess if I could get a drink.

"Yes," she said.

"I don't want to eat yet," I explained. "Do you have a—"

I didn't even get the word out before a grim-faced woman with a black-dyed beehive hairdo came up and interceded. "We don't have a *lounge*," she said, and she spoke the last word as though she were saying *whorehouse*. She did tell me about a place called Ray's Tavern, down the road in town. I got back in the Boxster and went to find it.

The main drag of Green River ambles past a park with some sort of missile in the center. What, I wondered, could *that* be about? Across the street from the park, a double-wide trailer houses the city hall. Vin's Cafe, advertising great steaks, was closed on Friday night. For some reason, I thought of that Mormon wagon train I had seen back in Nebraska—what a leap of faith their ancestors had made to settle in this depressing country. But that was unfair of me. I knew nothing about this place, this town, this state, the good people who live here. I did love being in the West. The difference between driving in the crowded East and through the open West is remarkable, exhilarating. How could a society that dreamed of the latter create the former? And yet, here in the tiny town of Green River, Utah, I found myself wrestling with what I considered my native ambivalence. When do open spaces become too open? Why is it so hard to find a perfect middle ground? I think often of Thoreau's line: "The mass of men lead lives of quiet desperation." Would I think of it even more, I asked myself, if I lived in Green River? Probably no more than usual, I answered. The desperation is within me.

Ray's wasn't hard to find. It was the place where the cars were. A cool bar-cafe catering to the many boaters who come to enjoy the Green River, Ray's has been around forty years, the menu said. One of the specialties of the house is its astonishing selection of beers. I decided to try one, choosing a dark and heavy pint of something called Cutthroat. It was more beer than I wanted, but it was good. It served the purpose.

After that, I went back to the motel and phoned Beth. I wanted to pace my evening, not swallow it in one gulp at Ray's place. The sky wasn't even dark yet. Beth wasn't home, so I tried calling our friends Joe and Ellison. Beth was there, but when she came to the phone, she didn't sound happy to be talking with me. Call me later, she said. It had been two nights since we'd spoken, since she had read me that remarkable love letter of rebuke. *Jesus,* I thought, *when is this going to end?* Groveling was starting to look like my most direct route home.

Before heading out for dinner, I stopped at the motel desk and found a new person, named Connie, in charge. I asked her to tell me about that strange missile in the park. "It's an Athena missile," she said. "Twenty years ago, we had the Green River Launch Complex here, just east of town. At one point, two thousand people were employed there. These missiles were fired, for testing, from here to the White Sands Missile Base in New Mexico. When the military went on to new and fancier missiles, they shut down this complex. It was 1972, I think. They presented the town with that missile when they left."

Connie also said there was talk about opening another launch base in Green River, but that the environmentalists "went ballistic." No, she didn't use those words, but I amused myself by pretending that she had.

I drove back to the Tamarisk and was shown to a table next to the window, overlooking the river. The water was pretty, a dusky blue, with a very fast current. I had brought my copy of *Undaunted Courage,* which I was plowing through with about as much speed as Lewis and Clark were discovering the wild West. I had reached the part in the book in which Lewis celebrates his thirty-first birthday in present-day western Montana with unusual introspection and gloomy self-criticism. Ambrose said that Lewis felt he had reached the halfway point in his life's journey, but in his physical journey of exploration, he had traveled nowhere near halfway. Adding to his glumness, he still had to lead his party across the massive Bitterroot Range of the Rocky Mountains. "Physically tired and emotionally exhausted after the tension of the past few days," Ambrose wrote, "he was in what is still today one of the most remote places on the continent. . . ."

I closed my book and, hoping for more cheerful reading, picked up the menu. At the table next to me was a family with three very pretty children—dark eyes, dark hair, engaging smiles. I prayed that they wouldn't engage me.

The beer listed said "nonalcoholic" beside it. A troublesome sign. A waitress came over to take my order. "Can I get a drink?" I said.

"We don't have a liquor license," she said. At that moment it dawned on me that I was in a state where if you ask about getting a drink, some people think you mean iced tea. Which is, finally, what I ordered. I could have gotten up and gone back to Ray's for a burger and a beer, but I didn't really need either. *Imposed moderation*, I thought. *Fine, I'll sleep better*. I ordered grilled chicken and a salad. As I went back to my reading, a red-haired woman, probably in her mid-forties, took a seat at the table next to the big family. She was facing me. We didn't make eye contact.

As the sun set and the river mirrored the pink-purple sky, a flock of birds began swooping over and diving into the water. "What kind of birds are those?" I said as the waitress brought my salad.

"Just little birds," she said.

"Oh," I said. "Thanks."

Soon the little girl at the next table began fooling with the window blinds. At one point she almost lowered it on my head, but her mother made her stop. The red-haired woman and I caught each other's glance and smiled. I rolled my eyes.

From then on we couldn't stop looking at each other. It was often awkward, getting caught with food in your mouth and then smiling about it. She was obviously local, because several people stopped to talk with her. I noticed she had a nice laugh, which she used often. For the second time that day, I thought of Susan Sarandon.

Finally I was ready to leave. I had handed the waitress my Amex card some time back, but it was the beehive lady who finally walked into the dining room and announced, "Whose card is this?"

"It's probably his," the red-haired woman said, pointing at me. We laughed again. She was obviously aware of how absurd this place was. God, what must it be like to live there?

I signed my check and gathered my things. Then I stood and looked her way. She smiled back. *It's now or never,* I thought. I could go over to her, introduce myself ("Hi, I'm Billy Bilkins"), sit down and have a cup of coffee, then offer her a ride into the wild Utah desert in my silver bullet. We could turn up the music and dance under the stars.

Instead, I looked her in the eye and mouthed the word "Good-bye." I needed to go back and call Beth.

"'Bye," the red-haired woman said, and her eyes crinkled sweetly. Her fabulous smile was knowing and understanding and yet wistful, all at once.

TEN

Physics of the Heart

A t the Comfort Inn, I started the last day of May with two Styrofoam bowls of corn flakes, plus coffee, fake sugar, and nondairy creamer in a Styrofoam cup. After that, I gassed up the Porsche, washed the bugs off the windshield, and hurtled into Utah's taupe desert.

After dinner the night before, Beth and I had talked on the phone for an hour. We argued; she hung up; I called her back. We ended by telling each other "I love you." It was a fragile peace, but a welcome one nevertheless. Now my plan was to veer north on U.S. 6 to Provo, and from there through Salt Lake City to the Bonneville Salt Flats. I wanted to see the place where crazy men drove cars at airplane speeds.

I didn't know whether it was the vastness of the physical landscape or a quirk of the mental terrain, but I had noticed that a lot of daredevils came out of the West. Evel Kneivel hailed from Butte, Montana (where there's no set speed limit), and a Texas stunt driver called

Captain Midnight drove the car for Robert Mitchum in *Thunder Road*. The same man did the stunt work for the old TV show "Highway Patrol." I talked with him once. His real name is Patrick O'Brian, and after his Hollywood career was over, he reinvented himself as "Captain Dynamite." Appearing at baseball games and car shows, he would climb into wooden boxes loaded with explosives and blow himself up.

But it was my brother, Phil, who told me one of the strangest stories about cars and the wild West. Phil had read of this incident on the Internet, on something called the Darwin Awards—so named because the recognition of the judges is given to the person whose demise most obviously strengthens the gene pool. Phil regaled me with the tale, perhaps apocryphal, he admitted, of his favorite awardee. "In about 1996," he said, "the Arizona Highway Patrol came upon a pile of smoldering metal embedded in the side of a cliff above the road at the apex of a curve. The wreckage resembled the site of an airplane crash, but it was a car. The type of car was unidentifiable at the scene, but the lab finally figured out what it was and what had happened.

"It seems that the driver had somehow gotten hold of a JATO unit (Jet Assisted Take Off—a solid-fuel rocket used to give heavy military transport planes an extra 'push' for taking off from short airfields). The man had then driven his 1967 Chevy Impala out into the desert and found a long straight stretch of road. He attached the JATO unit to his car, jumped in, got up some speed, and fired off the rocket. The facts, as best as could be determined, are that the operator of the Impala hit JATO ignition at a distance of approximately three miles from the crash site. Investigators established this from the prominent scorched and melted asphalt at the take-off spot.

"The JATO, if operating properly, would have reached maximum thrust within five seconds, causing the Chevy to reach speeds well in excess of 350 miles per hour and continuing at full power for an additional twenty to twenty-five seconds. The driver would have experienced g-forces usually associated with dogfighting F-14 jocks under full afterburners.

"The automobile remained on the straight highway for about two and a half miles (fifteen to twenty seconds) before the driver applied and completely melted the brakes, blowing the tires and leaving thick rubber marks on the road surface, then becoming airborne for an additional 1.4 miles and impacting the cliff face at a height of 125 feet. The wreck left a blackened crater three feet deep in the rock."

The ultimate muscle car, I suppose.

Leaving Green River, I noted my mileage as 6,726 for the Boxster; 6,524 for me. The drive from Denver the day before had been my longest one-day trek so far—close to four hundred miles. I could have stopped someplace between Denver and Utah, but I was growing restless with my restlessness. I'd been away from home more than a month.

The two lanes of Highway 6 rolled out across a timeless terrain. I wouldn't have been surprised to see pterodactyls nesting on distant mesas. The traffic was heavier than I expected, and a maroon car from Texas was taking enormous chances. On straightaways, one could see for long distances, but this road curved often, around and over hills. More than once the Texan passed blindly, tucking himself back into the right lane just in time.

An oncoming driver flashed his lights, and everyone slowed down. I had forgotten how much I love getting that signal. We all knew what it meant—a state trooper was lurking somewhere ahead. But what I liked about it was the sense of community it expressed. Here we were, solitary travelers sailing through time in our individual capsules, but a mere blink of headlights united us for a few moments against a common foe. It was a language we all spoke, a language of the road.

Around a turn, I saw the trooper stopped behind a car with its hood open. Both the driver and the trooper were bent over the engine cavity, peering in. That driver was lucky, I thought. He could have been stranded at night, or in the winter, at a time when no one would find him. Through all my years of driving, I had wondered about people I saw on the side of the road. What happens to them? How do they get help? How do they know what to do? For more than thirty years, I had been lucky enough not to have to count myself in their number. Then in 1993, that changed. On a gray rainy December day on I-40, bound from Little Rock to Tupelo, I learned firsthand what happens to people on the side of the road.

Beth and I had been married four years by then, having met at the magazine I moved south to start. When I recall the moments of our relationship, the old blue Jeep hovers inevitably in the background the way my 1969 Chevelle once did in another life. There was the freakishly snowy day I gave Beth a ride home from work, my four-wheel-drive Jeep—like my father's blue Daphne from half a century before—able to traverse the slick streets when most vehicles could not. There was the rainy day we went to lunch and I locked my keys inside. There were winter days in the mountains, summer days at the beach, trips with my boys and with her girls. On the fall day we married, I drove us home in the blue Wagoneer.

By 1993, the Jeep was nine years old and had more than 100,000 miles on it. It had had some problems. On a trip to Mississippi, the temperature gauge hit the red zone and we had to wait for hours in Pine Bluff while a mechanic installed a new water pump. The exterior was nicked and faded, and a piece of rubber designed to prevent rain from penetrating the rear door had disintegrated to the point where moisture had invaded the inner sanctum. Sometimes the car smelled of mildew. The cloth covering the ceiling sagged from the humidity.

A friend of my mother's had just died in Tupelo, and Mother was distraught. Even though I was pushing the deadline on my first book, I decided it was important for me to pay her a visit. That's how I happened to be on I-40 east that December day in 1993. Everything had been fine the first eighty miles of the trip. The rain had been steady but tolerable. At the little town of Brinkley, I made my usual stop at the McDonald's drive-through for a cheeseburger and Diet Coke. Then I blasted back onto the interstate, turned up the rock and roll on the radio, and tried to eat my sandwich without spilling mayo all down my shirt.

The sky grew darker, and the rain picked up. Still, I felt pretty good about things. I was making good progress on my book and was proud of myself for going to see my mother in her time of need. The rain made more noise, so I turned up the music. When I finished my sandwich, I sipped my drink and beat time on the dash with my free hand. I was on a *road trip*.

I don't know what caused me to look at the dash, but suddenly the car felt different. When I glanced at the readings, the temperature gauge was way past the emergency zone. I immediately pulled to the shoulder. As soon as I stopped, the Jeep was enveloped in a great cloud of smoke from under the hood. I hadn't seen any smoke while I was driving, presumably because of the hard rain. Now it was all I could see. I turned off the car and for a long moment just sat there, trying to figure out what to do. It was 4:30 P.M., less than an hour before dark. I could make out one ramshackle house in the distance across a fence and pond, but nothing that looked promising. I had no telephone. Until that moment, I had thought cell phones were pretentious.

I turned on my emergency blinkers and decided I had to get out and lift the hood—if for no other reason than to cool off the engine. Also, I hoped some passerby would alert the police. The rain pounded. I pulled my jacket over my head to try to keep dry. As I stood staring dumbly at the smoking engine, a car slid to a stop on the shoulder about twenty yards away. I turned and looked. It was a beater of an Oldsmobile, Oklahoma plates, part primered, part not, probably older than my Jeep. There were two people in the front seat. I ran toward the Olds, not really knowing what I was going to say when I got there. From five feet away I saw that the driver—a man with dirty-blond hair, wearing an earring and a T-shirt—was brushing empty beer cans off the backseat so I could get in. His passenger was a small dark man in a beat-up military field jacket.

"What's the trouble?" the earring man said.

"Engine overheated. Do you know if there's a service station near here?"

"The next one's twenty miles east. I'm going that way. Get in."

Oh, shit, I thought. *It's nearly dark, and I don't want to be alone with these guys.* "The car's cooled down some," I heard myself say. "Maybe I can drive it to a phone and call Triple A."

The earring man shook his head like he couldn't believe what he was hearing. "Well," he said with a near smirk, "there's a bar about a mile away, at the Hughes exit. If you want to try it, I'll follow you there."

"Great," I said, and I ran back to the ailing Jeep, slammed the hood, and turned the ignition. In fact, the temperature gauge *did* show a significant cooling, but the line still hovered too near the hot side. I gripped the wheel and pulled my trusty old Jeep onto the interstate for what would be its last hurrah.

It tried, it really did. The problem was that the Hughes exit was two and a half miles away, not one mile. I held my breath as the gauge showed a slow but steady heating. "Please," I said out loud. "Please

please please." Finally, the Hughes exit appeared through the foggy windshield. The Jeep was still living when I turned onto the off ramp, but halfway into that curve the steering wheel stiffened in rigor mortis. I coasted my old car through the turn and onto the shoulder. The bar, a lonely white-block building barely visible against the darkening delta sky, stood fifty yards away.

The Olds pulled alongside my Jeep. The earring man leaned across his passenger and said, "Well?"

"Dead," I said.

"Looks like these are your choices," he said. "You can stay at the bar there, or you can go with me to Marion, twenty miles away, where there are motels."

Marion! Beth and I have friends in Marion! I decided to chance it. "Let me lock up," I said. While I surveyed the Jeep to see what I needed to take, the earring man got out of his car and opened his trunk. I locked the Jeep and threw my overnight bag in. As I was about to climb into the Olds's backseat, the earring man said to the other guy, "Get in the back. Let him sit up front." Without a word, the dark man in the fatigue jacket got out and slipped into the backseat. As I eased into the seat in front of him, I heard the light clatter of beer cans when he shifted his feet.

The man with the earring stuck out his hand. "Bob Woods," he said. I told him my name, and we shook. That's when I noticed the tattoos. I couldn't make out what they were, just that there were a lot of them. The man in the backseat didn't say a word.

"I know these guys at this bar," Bob said. "I'm going to stop and tell them to watch your car." My mind was already racing. How does someone with Oklahoma plates know people at a bar in the Arkansas delta? Why did he tell the other guy to sit in back? While Bob was inside, I asked the man in the field jacket where he and Bob were heading. He said he was a hitchhiker. Bob had picked him up in Oklahoma.

If that were true, it made me feel better, knowing they weren't a well-honed serial-murder team. *If* that were true.

Bob came out and said, "They'll keep an eye on it." Then he did something very strange. Instead of getting on the entrance ramp to I-40, he crossed over the interstate and began driving into the dark delta farmland.

"Where you going?" I said.

"I'm taking the back way." When he cut his eyes at me, he was smiling. For a split second his earring glinted in the fading light.

I'm a goner, I thought. *They will never* ever *find my body.*

The Texan in the maroon car blew by a log truck on the right shoulder of the highway, kicking up a cloud of Utah dust. I had never seen anything like it. The man was crazy. After we got beyond the state trooper, the Texan couldn't seem to contain himself. He began swerving into the oncoming lane to see if he could pass. He zoomed by cars while traffic bore down on him dead ahead. There was no need to pass. We all were going fast. At one point I got the Boxster up to 110, then let it drop when I topped a hill and saw a line of cars behind a slow RV. The Texan bobbed impatiently in the traffic, flooring, braking, flooring, braking, then shooting around two or three cars and depending on the kindness of strangers to let him back in the lane before he collided with an oncoming truck.

I thought again of Milan Kundera's theory—that we speed to forget, that there's something inside us we need to outrun. More and more, we see people like this Texan on the road. But he wasn't merely a speeder. He seemed angry. I remembered a report the AAA Foundation for Traffic Safety had sent me. "Aggressive driving" incidents increased at a rate of 7 percent a year between 1990 and 1996. Twelve thousand six hundred ten people were injured, 218 killed. Guns, knives, tire tools, even a crossbow were involved. People got in fights over parking spaces, refusing to allow passing, over being cut off in traffic, using the horn too much, tailgating, failing to use a turn signal. Most of the people responsible for those statistics were between the ages of eighteen and twenty-six, but hundreds were between twenty-six and fifty, and in eighty-six cases the drivers were between fifty and seventy-five. Most were men, many with histories of violence, but many with no such history. "Violent traffic disputes are rarely the result of a single incident," the report said, "but rather are the cumulative result of a series of stressors in the motorist's life." I wondered what malady of the late-twentieth-century soul manifested itself in such a trend.

I was happy to let the Texan be in front of me. It's better to have the crazies where you can keep an eye on them. That reminded me again of my strange experience with Bob Woods. As early-winter darkness fell, I shifted slightly in my seat so I could watch the man in the field jacket if he lifted a gun to my head or a knife to my neck. After going about a mile north, Bob turned east onto a narrow road that cut through black furrowed fields. "This is the way I always go to Marion," he said.

"I thought you were from Oklahoma," I said.

"I work there. On the railroad. But I live outside Forrest City." That was a town some twenty miles west on I-40.

"What do you do for the railroad?" I wanted to keep the focus on him. I didn't want him to ask what I did for a living and me have to say, "I'm a writer." Bob didn't seem like the type to suffer aesthetes gladly.

"Construction. But I hurt my back. That's why I'm home."

"When you think you'll go back to work?"

"Don't know. Meantime, my damn ex-wife is busting my balls for back child support. She even had me thrown in jail in Marion."

"That where she lives?"

"Yeah. I'm going there now to get my daughter for the weekend." His mood seemed to darken.

"How old's your daughter?"

"Sixteen."

"I've got two stepdaughters," I said. "One twelve, one nine." He didn't respond, and for a while we all rode in silence.

When we got to the Marion city limits, Bob turned to the man in the backseat. "Where you want to get off?"

"Can you take me back to I-40?"

"Yeah." And then to me he said, "I'll drop him off and then take you to your friends' house."

I was glad to see the man in the field jacket get out. We left him at a truck stop in the rain. The last I saw of him, he was looking forlornly through the window at the truckers eating supper. Then Bob remembered he had to go pick up a form at the post office, which was nearby. I waited in the car while he went in.

When we got to my friends' house, he parked the Olds in the driveway and I went to the door and knocked. No answer. Had the garage been open, I would have stayed there, but it was locked tight. I feared that my friends were out of town.

"Tell you what," Bob said. "Come with me to get my daughter. Then we'll bring you back by here."

I got in and we headed toward an older part of town. "My ex-wife's a goddamn bitch," Bob said.

"I know how that is," I said, ever the social lubricant. But the closer we got to the ex-wife's house, the more Bob brooded. "Fuck," he said, for no apparent reason. I didn't want to look at him directly, but I cut my eyes to the left slightly to see if I could gauge his mood. "Fuckin' rain," he said, and I stared straight ahead.

The ex-wife's house was a small sixties-style ranch in a neighborhood of similar homes. Bob pulled the Oldsmobile into the driveway behind a relatively new minivan. He didn't get out. Instead, he tooted the horn. "I'm not supposed to go to the door," he said. Inside the house, someone pulled back a curtain and peeped through the blinds, but nobody came out. We waited, then waited some more. "Goddammit," said Bob under his breath.

After maybe five minutes, the door opened and a cute young girl with a ponytail emerged carrying a backpack. Bob and I both got out, and I slipped into the backseat. When we all were in the car, Bob said, "Sheila, this is Jim. He's had car trouble." The daughter and I exchanged glum hellos.

On the way back to my friends' house, Bob asked his daughter, "What were you doing in there?"

"Mom and I were watching a movie." I could see his jaw tighten.

"Oh, Dad!" Sheila said, then, "Mom wanted to know if we could go by the school and pick up the boxes of fruit the band sold."

"What?"

"The fruit—oranges, apples, pineapples. We sold them as a band project. The boxes came in today."

"Well, honey, we need to get on back to Forrest City. Can't your mother go pick them up?"

"She's going to be really busy. Please, Dad."

"How many boxes are there?"

Sheila cocked her head. "Ummmm, four, I think."

Bob sighed. "*Awwww*right," he said. He didn't ask if I minded. In a few minutes we pulled up to the band room at the local high school. All around us, parents in nice new cars and vans and utility vehicles were loading crates of fresh fruit. "You better back it in, Dad," said Sheila.

I went inside with them. There was a line of parents waiting for a confused student to figure out the bills of lading. Bob wasn't in the mood to wait. "Hey, shit!" he said, and everybody turned to look at him. At us. "We got some fruit to pick up, and we're in a hurry!" It did no good. We had to wait our turn. Bob stepped outside under the overhang and smoked a cigarette. I hung around inside, trying to become invisible.

When it was Sheila's turn to pick up her fruit, we discovered that she had made a slight miscalculation. There were sixteen boxes, not four. A couple of hefty band boys toted the crates out to the Oldsmobile, and Bob began trying to figure out how to get it all in. He popped the trunk, and I retrieved my overnight bag. As the rain poured down on us, I helped him load the crates in, trying not to make a mistake that would set him off. We got six in the big trunk, eight in the backseat, and two in the front seat between Bob and Sheila. After we had almost finished loading the backseat, I got in and Bob put two boxes on my lap, and my bag on top of that.

Back at the ex-wife's, Sheila went in and got her mother's keys so we could load the crates into her minivan. I took the lead in stacking, and Bob pretty much stood and watched. Then we headed back to my friends' house.

This time they were home. In fact, their six-year-old daughter had been there when we stopped by earlier, but she didn't know the car and wouldn't open the door. Once I made sure I could stay the night there, I came back around to Bob's side of the Oldsmobile. "Listen," I said. "I really appreciate this. Let me give you some money." All I had with me was thirty dollars.

"Naw, naw, naw," said Bob. "I just hate seeing people stranded on the road. Stop and help somebody else sometime."

"I will," I said. Then I handed the twenty-dollar bill to Sheila.

"Here, you and your dad go get dinner." She smiled, and he didn't object. Me, I was just glad to be alive.

Southern Utah was wide and dry and beige, the only relief an occasional dark stratum of rock showing through on the cliffs. Once, I saw a white tepee high on a bluff. The landscape got prettier the farther north I drove. From desert monochrome, the terrain took on colors and texture, with green trees and a topping of snow on distant peaks.

At Provo, I connected with I-15, the highway that stretches from the Canadian border to Los Angeles. It runs down the center of Utah, a swath of development that seemed more scarlike than any interstate I had driven on. On either side of the highway, low houses and commercial areas and government buildings sprawl toward the horizon. I had heard that Utah was beautiful, but I was obviously in the wrong part. Provo made me think of Gary Gilmore, the killer whose story Norman Mailer told in *The Executioner's Song*. Mailer was the first big writer I worked with when I moved from *TWA Ambassador* to *Playboy,* and I obviously had a lot to learn. We were excerpting *The Executioner's Song,* and Mailer insisted on setting the type with extra space between paragraphs. That was his way of capturing the wide flat land that had produced a Gary Gilmore. Believing that part of my job was holding the line against prima donnas, I told Mailer no. He threatened to pull the excerpt, and my boss stepped in with a bit of diplomacy that I would emulate many times in the ensuing years. "Well," he said, "let's just set it and see how it looks." The Gilmore book appeared in the magazine, in three installments, with extra space between every paragraph.

Now I saw what Mailer had seen. If you come from the East, it's hard to imagine the openness of this part of the country. I have no idea what effect growing up in such a place has on people. But if density promotes community (as the new urbanists claim), then what does vast space promote? Is the American dream of Going West a blatant attempt to escape the shackles of human interaction?

Driving along this artery in the heart of Utah made me think of something the architect Peter Calthorpe had written about the suburbs we've created since World War II:

> Today the public world is shrunken and fractured. Parks, schools, libraries, post offices, town halls, and civic centers are dispersed, underutilized, and underfunded. Yet these civic elements determine the quality of our shared world and express the value we assign to community. The traditional Commons, which once centered our communities with convivial gathering and meeting places, is increasingly displaced by an exaggerated private domain: shopping malls, private clubs, and gated communities. Our basic public space, the street, is given over to the car and its accommodation, while our private world becomes more and more isolated behind garage doors and walled compounds. Our public space lacks identity and is largely anonymous, while our private space strains toward a narcissistic autonomy. Our communities are zoned black and white, private or public, my space or nobody's.

Just south of Salt Lake, I saw a sign for Park City, where Robert Redford established his Sundance resort and holds his annual Sundance Film Festival. On the spur of the moment I decided to make a detour. Beth is a talented screenwriter and in 1995 was a semifinalist in a prestigious screenwriting competition, the Nicholl Fellowship, sponsored by the Academy of Motion Picture Arts and Sciences. She's always wanted to go to Sundance for the film festival. *I'll buy her a Sundance cap,* I thought. *She'll love it.*

The sign advertised a turnoff some miles ahead, so I kept my sights set for it. But when I got there and exited, a big notice had been hung over the road sign: CLOSED—USE I-15. I doubled back and reconnected with the interstate, and when I reached the Park City exit I was met with another CLOSED sign. Afraid of going too far north, I got off in Salt Lake City and drove around, looking for someone to ask. A woman at a convenience store told me I could get there by going six blocks (three lights) north, then turning right. I did, and drove a mile or two toward the mountains. Then the road dead-ended at an interstate overpass. I asked a second person, a man in a car-rental place. He told me to head south a few blocks. There I found another CLOSED sign. Finally I stopped at a Texaco station, where I filled up and asked the cashier about getting to Park City. "I think the road is closed," she said. A customer standing in line said, "Yeah, they're working on the road. You can't get there." Surely that wasn't absolutely true. Still, all of this searching had eaten up an hour. I decided it would be easier for Beth to get to Sundance writing screenplays than it would be for me following Utah road signs.

The truth is I was fed up with Utah. My atlas told me that the Bonneville Salt Flats were eighty miles west, out in the desert. What guarantee did I have that they wouldn't be CLOSED, too? On the spot, I decided to escape Utah and head for Montana. I was tired, hot, and hungry. I hadn't eaten since my Styrofoam corn flakes six or so hours before. But I didn't want to spend another minute longer than necessary in Utah, not even for fast food. The only fast thing I wanted was my elusive spoiler crossing the Idaho line.

I shot north at 85 and 90, hoping I would get a ticket so I could write about one final Utah insult. But nobody paid the slightest attention to me. In steady traffic I aimed the Porsche toward a thunderhead that seemed to be settling on the highway miles ahead of me. It was gray and churning, with layers of blue above a white line at the horizon. I could see rain falling from a section of it, like fringe.

At around four I crossed over into Idaho. My memory, and my notebook entries, indicate that I had crossed from beige into greenness. Part of that impression perhaps had to do with the storm, the deep-blue roiling clouds that spewed rain and shot lightning onto the far hills. But in Idaho I could feel the presence of water nearby. The land seemed more compact—still mountainous, but tighter, closer in. One hill by the interstate looked like a giant gray elephant who had stayed in one place too long. He had patches of green moss growing on his back.

I exited at Pocatello and stopped at a tourist-information center to pick up a map. Pocatello bills itself as the "Gate City," the man there told me, because it was one of the first settlements on the old Oregon Trail this side of the Rockies. The man directed me to the original section of town, on the southwest side across the railroad tracks. "That's where the town began," he said. I drove over the Union Pacific tracks to take a look. Like the strata of rock on nearby cliffs, the layout of Pocatello offers a capsulized lesson in the predictable passage of time: First there was the river, the Portneuf, and the river brought the settlers. The settlers brought the railroad, and the railroad brought business. Business brought the suburbs, and the suburbs brought the interstate. The interstate brought more suburbs. Today Pocatello has some 46,000 residents, plus 11,000 students attending Idaho State University, and most of the city has moved north, away from the old town, following the flow of the new river of commerce, I-15.

Sticking to my usual pattern, I looked for a cafe or bar where I might find people to talk with. The first one that caught my eye was a place called the Round-Up Room, but I decided it had an aura of seediness about it. At a restaurant next door, the maître d' recommended the Oddfellows Bar one street over. Though I drove around the block several times, I never found it. I finally settled for Dudley's Sports Bar, a cavernous room in what once was Pocatello's federal building. The ceilings must have been twenty feet high, and the people sitting at tables looked small and lost. TV sets blared from every direction. The clicks of cues on balls and the tinny *whrrp-whrrp-whrrp* of video games added to the atmosphere of disconcerting confusion. Everybody seemed desperate to be entertained.

I took a seat at the bar and ordered a beer and a small pesto pizza. Next to me, two women played a video trivia game with what looked like little laptop computers. They were mesmerized, racing each other—and players online in other states, apparently—to answer such questions as "Which actress besides Grace Kelly married royalty?" (The answer, I knew, was Rita Hayworth.) I thought back to the good bars I had gone to on this journey, the Stein House in Missouri, and Doris's Tavern in Nebraska. Those were places where the townspeople came together to *be together*—to talk, to play cards, to interact. They were real places. But these "sports bars" were different. They seemed to cater to lonely isolated people who wanted to remain isolated in the company of others. In that case, the decor at Dudley's was entirely successful.

The young bartender couldn't think of anyone with "car stories," so I just sipped my beer and ate my pizza. I didn't want to talk with anybody anyway. By the time I finished eating, it was 8:00 P.M. I needed to find a motel. Neither the bartender nor the man at the tourist center recommended that I stay downtown (in fact, they recommended that I not), but instead directed me to the third Pocatello exit on I-15, the Pocatello Creek area, where the city has moved and where most of the locals go at night.

I settled again on a Comfort Inn, this one overlooking both the interstate and the blue-black mountains, both of which were shadowed by a gathering thundercloud. There was a rainbow in the distance. I stared out my motel window for a long time, watching the cars rush along the highway. It wasn't dark yet, but most of the cars had their lights on. Back in Little Rock, some of my longtime neighbors were moving, and that night they were throwing a big going-away party, with a live band, in their back yard. Beth would be there. My friends were *dancing* while I stood at a motel window watching cars pass on an Idaho freeway.

I gathered my notebook and *Undaunted Courage* and walked across the street to a restaurant called Sandpiper's. A beautiful blond hostess directed me to the lounge, where I took a table and set up shop. Soon my waitress came over, a tanned redhead named Alexis. When she took my order, she put her hand on my arm. From then on, I found concentrating on my notes difficult. I was pathetic, of course, but clearly I had entered some new phase of the road experience. The night before there was Susan Sarandon in Green River, and now here was Alexis in Pocatello. A warm smile, a simple touch—away from home they weighed more than they would have otherwise. Call it physics of the heart.

Alexis's legs were long and tan, and she wore an ankle bracelet. I ordered two or three drinks, I don't remember, and every time she came over she touched my arm or shoulder. Then another waitress appeared—younger, blond, and very pretty. She was tan, too. They both looked incredibly healthy, as if they had spent most of their lives outdoors. I surveyed the room. Every woman there was beautiful. There were even two tables of lesbians (I know because they were being very vocal about it), and every one of *them* was good-looking. I decided I needed to take a drive.

A bad idea, no doubt, but I dropped the top on the Boxster and drove back to town, this time on the surface road. Suddenly I found myself cruising among several carloads of teenagers. Two guys in a fast car pulled next to me, and the driver shouted, "What kind of car is *that?*"

"Porsche!" I yelled.

"Holy shit!" he yelled back. That is *bad!*"

We parted with a mutual thumbs-up, and then a couple of carloads of teenage girls pulled in behind me. They started honking and waving, and when they passed, the girl riding shotgun in the second car lifted her T-shirt and showed me her breasts. It lasted only a second, and then the car sped off trailing laughter in the soft spring air.

Strangely enough, none of this made me feel as good as I might have thought it would. I felt feverish, frustrated, and a bit buffoonish, a pitiful fraud far from home. I drove for a while longer, hoping the air would clear my head. Then I got back on I-15 and turned toward the Comfort Inn. It was 10:00 P.M. or thereabouts, but I didn't really want to go to bed yet. I hadn't decompressed from the day. Then I remembered the bartender at Dudley's telling me the locals hang out at the Best Western, which was just behind my motel. It was a depressing thought, a Best Western lounge on Saturday night, but if that's where the American dream would lead me, so be it.

The place was packed, and very quickly I learned why. Saturday is karaoke night in Pocatello. I suppose they do karaoke somewhere in my own hometown, but it's not an activity I'm drawn to, as either a participant or an observer. My wife would tell you I can spot the dark cloud behind every silver lining, but karaoke has always struck me as especially sad and needy, a showcase of dreams fallen short. I took a stool at the bar and ordered a Jack Daniel's and water. The karaoke contest was just getting under way.

A young bearded man doubled as the disk jockey and the master of ceremonies. Apparently there were to be several rounds of competition. For the first round, the entries included the following:

- Sean, a tall dark-haired man with blow-dried hair and a mustache, wearing jeans and boots and a blue-and-white diagonal-stripe-and-solid shirt like ones I've seen in photos of Garth Brooks. Sean was smooth, very practiced. He held the microphone the way stars do, casually, open-palmed, the mike floating between his thumb and fingers as his other hand painted a broad stroke on the far horizon. He sang a Garth Brooks song (which one, I'm afraid I don't remember—I was scribbling notes on cocktail napkins but also trying not to look like a reporter; I missed some things), the lyrics projected on several monitors around the room. They reminded me of those old follow-the-bouncing-ball singalongs you used to see at the beginnings of movies;

- Darrien, a shorter, stouter man wearing a striped shirt, Duck Head slacks, and dorky Cole Haan moccasin/loafers. He didn't look like a superstar, but he did have a good voice;

- Ellen, a pretty brunette wearing shorts. She had brought her own cheering section, consisting of a frizzy-haired redheaded woman in jeans, boots, and vest, and a man in a white T-shirt with an unfortunate long "tail" protruding from the back of his short-cropped hair;

- Roderick, a skinny black man who did a rap number. Two of his friends, one who looked like Darius from Hootie and the Blowfish, backed him up. On another rap song, Ellen and her coterie provided backup;

- A nondescript girl who sang a couple of songs;

- An overweight man with dark hair who didn't know the words to his selections, even with their being projected on the screen in front of him;

- A man with a physical handicap and a very good voice;

- Rob, a medical technician sitting next to me at the bar. Rob was very serious about the competition, constantly reevaluating his chances as the others went through their paces. He wasn't great, though when he came back to the bar I told him otherwise. I was alone in America and had lost my soul.

The lineup of strangers risking public humiliation had seemed like plenty of entertainment to me, and I figured that while the judges deliberated, people would do what they usually do in bars—laugh, talk, drink, visit with one another. But no, a belly dancer provided a kind of sorbet between karaoke rounds. She shimmied and shook while the room watched in rapt silence. Finally the judges announced the finalists: Sean, Ellen, Darrien, and Steve, I believe his name was, the man with the handicap. They received warm applause. Perhaps it was the drinks, but I began to reconsider this phenomenon I had happened upon. So what if singing karaoke is about dreams fallen short? It is also about taking home, like Hemingway's old man on the sea, at least the skeleton of those dreams. It is one more way to escape the grip of real life, of settling down and having a family and a job and a house and endless responsibilities. In that sense, that Best Western bar on a Pocatello Saturday night wasn't all that different from the Porsche I'd parked in the lot outside.

Sean and Ellen tied for first, with Steve third and Darrien fourth. Ellen sang "Baby, It'll Be All Right." When Sean's turn came, he sang "Lady" just like Kenny Rogers. The spotlight bathed his face, and his eyes closed tight when he hit the high notes. I wondered where he was inside.

ELEVEN

Westward Ho

June 1, 1997. I woke late feeling guilty, hung over, and a bizarre compulsion to wash the car. After dining with the church crowd at Perkins, I searched out a coin-operated wash and spent nearly an hour cleaning up the Boxster. It was filthy, covered with Utah dust and road film. I took great pains to make the mag wheels shine. When they did, I felt much better.

Just after noon, I left for Montana. North of Pocatello, the interstate was bordered on either side by acres of farmland—potato fields, I guessed. The country reminded me of Arkansas, except for the size of the mountains in the background. A couple of girls in a Jeep Wrangler passed and smiled. By then I knew what to expect. The Boxster elicited different responses, depending on gender. Women generally smiled admiringly, perhaps longingly. There was a softness to their countenance when they beheld the car. Men revealed either a wild excitement or scowling admiration. I passed a middle-aged couple in a metallic-blue Chevelle from the sixties. It was pristine, and I gave them the thumbs-up. They did the same to me.

For the purposes of this project, I would have stayed on I-15, but a friend from home, Fred Poe, had mapped out a more interesting route for me. North of Idaho Falls I turned left onto 33, then cut right on 28. Soon I found myself driving through country of incredible beauty and history. To my right rose the southern part of the Bitterroot Range of the Rocky Mountains; to my left the Lemhi Range. *Bitterroot, Lemhi*—more American words, words that echoed from *Undaunted Courage*. In August 1805, following the low Lemhi Pass over the Continental Divide, Lewis and Clark and their party crossed from present-day Montana into this very valley I was now driving. Then for more than a month they portaged north from here, on the old Nez Perce trail, feeling their way over the daunting Bitterroots toward a water route to the Pacific. Having split from their trail when I turned west toward Lincoln, I now had connected with them once more. It was a provocative thought. Their rugged route had taken them north into the bleak Dakotas, west across the jagged Rockies in Montana, then southwest into Idaho and north again over gameless land and still more mountains. I had shot across I-80, down I-25 to I-70, then over to I-15 and up through Utah into Idaho. I had eaten fast food, slept in chain motels, drunk at sports bars, and paid with plastic. Their leg of the journey took thirteen arduous months. I did it in a leisurely seven days. And yet, I wondered, who was more satisfied upon arrival?

Driving through that magnificent valley, I was aware, too, of another historic figure whose life touched down very near there. Ernest Hemingway had lived and died, by his own hand, just a few hours away in Ketchum, Idaho. In his last years he had moved to that wild land in search of something grand again, something new and idealistic inside himself. He couldn't find it. One Sunday morning in the foyer of the house he had owned for two years, he propped a shotgun to his forehead and tripped both triggers. I remembered the summer night I heard about his death. I was in a car in the driveway of my girlfriend's house in Miami. We were listening to the radio. I was too young then to understand what had actually killed him. Later, in college, I began to know the man who could write the following line to his father: "And how much better to die in all the happy period of undisillusioned youth, to go out in a blaze of light, than to have your body worn out and old and illusions shattered." On that Sunday morning in Ketchum, the great writer believed that his frontier was closed.

Since there were few cars on Highway 28, I decided to see how fast I could go. I also thought that desolate road would be a good place for me to try to stand up as much as possible and look over the rear of the car to see the spoiler. The Porsche was working at 120, but I pushed it to 123. Just by looking at the road, I couldn't tell how much of an incline I was driving on, but it must have been considerable. Clearly, standing up and looking backward in a speeding Porsche was a dangerous idea, so I gave up on the spoiler and concentrated on the road ahead.

Back when I turned onto 28 from 33, the sky seemed to spread for miles. Now the snow-topped mountains were closer, tighter in around the highway, their craggy bluffs dropping down to the Lemhi River to my left. This was the river that not only Lewis and Clark followed, but generations of Native Americans before them. A sign told me that evidence of prehistoric man had been found in this valley—the "Bitterroot People," ancestors of the Northern Shoshones. Eight thousand years ago they settled here in family bands, living off big game such as bison and mountain sheep.

Far ahead I saw a Pepsi sign. Then Seven-Up, too. On this road I had spotted the occasional cloistered cabin and a few secluded ranch houses, but I hadn't expected to find a commercial establishment in such wilderness. I pulled in at the Lone Pine store and cafe and asked to use the restroom. Then I bought a Pepsi and talked a few minutes with the owners. They had moved there from Idaho Falls thirteen years before. "We came to get away from the telephone," the man said.

At Tendoy I passed a historic Lewis and Clark marker indicating that in August 1805, "after passing through Lemhi Pass, twelve miles east of here, Lewis unfurled the American flag for the first time west of the Rockies." I decided to skip the detour and keep on toward Montana. The traffic had picked up, and a state trooper had pulled over a speeding Corvette. Civilization was looming. At the town of Salmon, population 2,941, I connected with U.S. Highway 93. A sign advertised "Betty's Family Dining Room and Car Service." At the Salmon Quick Stop, I pulled in for gas but passed on the "Espresso To Go."

While I was filling up, three teenage boys on bikes came over to look at the Boxster. "Wow! Hot car!" one said.

"How fast you had it?" asked another. A guy in his twenties pulled in and came over, too. "These fifteen-inch wheels?" he asked.

"Yeah," I said, and then turned back to the first kid. "I got it to 125 in Nebraska. But I'm heading to Montana to see if I can get a speeding ticket."

"No, sixteen inches," said the older guy. I ignored him.

"You won't get a ticket unless you speed in traffic," another of the boys said.

"Naw, you can drive 125 all you want."

"I got my dad's Talon up to 136 out on Highway Twenty-eight," the first boy said.

Salmon was a pretty little Western town, the kind of rustic manly place that made me wish I were a fisherman and hunter like Hemingway and his heroes, instead of a writer whose main interest is in exploring the tension between home and the road. Big two-hearted driveway—that's my theme.

North of town, the Salmon River valley was green and lush. The water rushed around logs and over rocks, humming with spring energy. All along the river, cozy log cabins were nestled in among the trees, reminding me of something new urbanist James Howard Kunstler had said during a lecture in Little Rock the winter before. "Little cabins in the woods'—that's a symbol for what we all yearn for," he told his audience. "We're reenacting the frontier melodrama." The reason, he said, is "because our public realm is now a national automobile slum." I was struck by Kunstler's words because I too harbored what I had thought was a secret fantasy—of living in a cabin in the woods. The idea first occurred to me during my years in Chicago. I loved that city, but it was a *city*. Every day was a grind. Then when my wife and I moved to the North Shore suburbs where we could hide out at night, that still wasn't far enough away. "Suburbia," Kunstler said, "has been our fake cabin in the woods." Later, in a relatively new house in suburban West Little Rock, I found myself missing husky old Chicago. My wife went back, but I kept looking for the cabin in my head.

At North Fork, where the Salmon breaks off to the west, I found another Lewis and Clark sign. It told how William Clark, hoping to find that water route to the Pacific, explored the first few rugged miles of the Salmon River Canyon. The river was too fast to be navigable, he reported, so the party pushed northward toward Lost Trail Pass. Today's North Fork is a red-logged encampment of cafes, motels, and general stores catering to the sportsmen who come to fish the swift river. I made a mental note to take Beth there someday.

North of Gibbonsville, not too far past the Lewis and Clark Cafe (how many more of those would I see?), I encountered a sign announcing road work and "intermittent pavement" the next nine and a half miles. There was nothing to do but raise the top and drive on into the cloud of dust churned up by the car in front of me. *Glad I washed the car*, I thought. The driver was kicking up rocks, also, so I hung back out of range. After a series of increasingly dramatic switchbacks, I arrived at the summit of Lost Trail Pass—7,014 feet. On June first there was plenty of snow on the ground. "Welcome to Montana," hailed a rustic placard.

But the marker I was looking for, the main reason I had come to Montana, stood just behind the welcome sign.

SPEED LIMITS		
DAY	REASONABLE AND PRUDENT	
TRUCK		60
NIGHT	ALL VEHICLES	55

Lewis and Clark had continued north from this point, toward Lolo Pass, which I would cross on my way from Montana to Oregon. Now at the Continental Divide I turned right onto Highway 43 and began a long descent into the Big Hole Valley. The road sloped through close-cropped rangeland that gave way to great stands of cedar. Behind the trees rose the mountains. It was beautiful country, sprawled beneath a gigantic sky. In the distance was a rainbow, only the second I had seen on my entire journey. The road was good again. I checked myself cruising along at 87 miles an hour, but who cared? Not Montana.

As the land leveled into a vast grassy valley, I passed a memorial to Chief Joseph, the Nez Perce leader who led a spirited but unsuccessful retreat from U.S. forces in 1877. I thought about going in, but the day was late and the drive had already taken longer than expected. At the little town of Wisdom I turned left along the Big Hole River, a placid silver strip curling through the range. It was a strange-looking river—nearly level to the surrounding ground. A few miles north I turned right again, catching I-15 at Divide. I drove into Butte at 8:00 P.M. and sought out the Finlen Hotel, where my friend Fred had insisted I stay. It was where he and his ex-wife, Tina, had spent their wedding night decades before.

Decidedly non-interstate in location or style, the Finlen was instead a tired old place from this mining town's boomtime past. I parked the Boxster in front and rattled the doors to the lobby—locked tight. I walked down to the corner, peering in windows, detecting not a sign of life. Then I saw a small parking lot surrounded by a little motel connected to the main building. The Finlen, built in the glory days to serve the copper kings who arrived in gilded train cars, had hedged its bets. Now it was the Finlen Hotel and Motor Inn. Many of the rooms were rented by the month to elderly residents. A small sign pointed to the office. The rate was $33. I was skeptical, so I decided to take a room for only one night. I paid and then pulled the Porsche into the parking lot. In fact, the Finlen turned out to be the bargain of my entire journey. It was clean, with pressed sheets and a real tile shower whose water pressure could have cut mildew off Louisiana brick.

Butte, it was soon clear, wasn't chic Montana. This wasn't the glittering place where movie stars went to get away from their adoring masses. In its day, beginning in the 1880s, Butte was the world's greatest copper producer, and by 1917 had become a complex city of 100,000 people. Today you can see the hulking frames of abandoned mines dotting the landscape. In the 1950s, underground mining gave way to open-pit mining, which isn't a pretty sight. One of Butte's main attractions is the Berkeley Pit—7,000 feet long, 5,600 feet wide, and more than 1,800 feet deep. It is a massive gash in the earth. But to Butte's credit, no one has moved in and tried to pretty up the watery hole with cute townhouses echoing boomtown days. The gash remains, a symbol of not just the city's hardscrabble past but something essential at its spiritual core. "This is a town of survivors," a man would say to me the next afternoon.

The Bronx Supper Club was my strange introduction to nightlife in Butte. It was a wash of noirish color, mostly red and black like some Western saloon from the 1890s, but with jarring splashes of clashing tones. A black-tied bartender presided over a stand of amber bottles, while across the room a bank of video poker games emitted an eerie green glow on the pale faces of the players. The back room was marked off by deep wine-colored banquettes and massive mirrors. I took a seat and ordered a glass of cabernet and the veal special. That was the moment I began to understand just how Butte survives.

When the mines were going, this was a city of vibrant backgrounds, tastes, and appetites—German, Asian, Irish, Italian, Jewish, Scandinavian, Finnish, French, Spanish, Lebanese, Dutch, Scottish, Welsh, Hungarian, Yugoslavian, Greek, English, Black, Native American, and more. Today, Butte celebrates its rich past with heaping repasts. With my wine, the waitress started bringing plates of food I hadn't ordered—a cheese and meat plate, bread sticks, carrots and peppers and other vegetables, then a plate piled with ravioli and another of spaghetti. These were the side dishes. When my meal came, it consisted of two giant veal cutlets with a mound of mashed potatoes in the center and plenty of bread. It was a homey end to a long lonely Sunday, although I hardly made a dent. I picked at my comfort food until I could eat no more. Then I went back to the Finlen and crawled between my pressed sheets, where I slept the sleep of the satiated miner, probing the depths of REM until nearly ten the next morning.

Monday brought duties, however, and duties brought their inevitable worries. I had to pay bills and mail them from Butte. That made me wonder about cash flow at home, which made me wonder about everything else there. I never cease to be amazed at home's ambivalent power. When I'm away and lonely, those distant rooms often appear to me through a heart-tugging haze. I think of standing at my front door and looking into our living room, wrapping myself in its deep comforting layers of pattern and fabric, then moving beyond there to the dining room and kitchen, scene of so many warm family dinners. But thinking of home in the context of bills destroys that sweet dream. Paying bills, even from Butte, conjures up home in all its unvarnished reality. The magical haze becomes a layer of dust, oppressive as death, settling over everything in sight, until all I want to do is scream. Sometimes when I'm home the patterns and fabrics choke me with their precious busyness. The family dinners are too often taken in bickering or silence. Home is a radio band on a road trip at night. We fine-tune the dial, and for long moments at a time the beam comes strong and true. Then we cross an invisible line and the signal fades to static.

I also had to phone the Porsche people. When Beth and I had talked from Utah on Friday, she said that Barbara Manha, my contact person at Porsche, had called. It had been weeks since I'd talked with Barbara, and the underlying message in her phone call was *Time's nearly up*. That meant deciding about the car. Bob Carlson had said they would "work with me" if I wanted to keep it. What did that mean? Would they give it to me? Would they make me an offer I couldn't refuse? My agent and I still hadn't smoothed out that snag in the new business, so my financial prospects were cloudy at best.

After a hot shower, I stopped by the hotel office and booked one more night. Then I wandered around the corner to a place called Java John's, where I took a table by the window and sipped strong coffee while working on my notes. There I struck up a conversation with the man behind the counter. I commented on the town's beautiful historic architecture, and he told me the building we were in had once been the office of a doctor who performed abortions on some of the 10,000 "seamstresses" who flocked to Butte during the boom days. Seamstress had been the euphemism of choice.

I told him I was writing a book about cars, so I naturally had come to the state with no speed limit.

"Oh, there is a speed limit," he said. "It's seventy-five." And then he told me a cautionary tale.

It seemed that the state legislature and the highway patrol were at odds about how to deal with Montana's famously open speed limit. The state had never had a daytime speed limit until the 55 m.p.h. forced on them in 1974 by the federal government. When 55 was repealed in late 1995, the politicians, heeding the wishes of their fiercely independent ("belligerent" was the word the Java man used) constituents, didn't dare designate an actual number. So "reasonable and prudent" it became. But the state troopers, whose job sometimes includes scraping dead cowboys off the gouged pavement, had vowed to be the arbiters of what was reasonable and prudent. Searching for a way to spread that message—especially to those outsiders who thought they could breeze into Montana and ride like the wind—they seized upon the opportunity presented by the Mercedes-Benz company, which reportedly used to bring ten or so test cars at a time to Montana to see how fast they could run from point A to point B. The troopers staked them out and caught them tearing along I-90 at 125 miles per hour. They ticketed every driver, penalizing them ten dollars for every mile per hour they were traveling. The troopers also made sure the story got big play in all the newspapers. Before my stay in Butte was over, I would hear the same tale several more times— sometimes the car company was Mercedes, other times it was Porsche. Either way it had become a Montana urban legend.

Sobered by thoughts of troopers lying in wait, I went back to the hotel and faced my bills. Still, I couldn't bring myself to phone Porsche just yet. That call threatened my sense of freedom. If I couldn't buy the car, I would be depressed. If I could, I would be panicked. Sometimes freedom's just another word for not knowing what's going on.

I decided to take a drive around town. In the parking lot, I ran into a man named Jim McInerney, chief Navy recruiter for the area, whose office is in the lobby of the Finlen. He told me Butte now has about 36,000 residents, that it is mostly blue collar, Catholic, very family-oriented. "Whenever Butte's in trouble, everybody pulls together." He suggested I go see the Berkeley Pit and the mining museum.

Butte's thoroughfares bear such names as Quartz, Aluminum, Platinum, Copper, and are crossed by streets named for states. I passed a sign for Clear Grit Road, which easily could have been a candidate for inclusion in old Stephen Vincent Benet's famous poem about American names. "Montana is billed as 'What the West Was,' " said McInerney. I thought about that as I gazed into the infamous Berkeley Pit. I had read a piece in *Outside Magazine* about this place. It told of a hapless flock of migrating snow geese who somehow went off course. Looking for water on which to land, they mistook this pit for a pond and "chose to rest their exhausted bodies in the largest vat of acid from here to Siberia."

The pit didn't hold my attention long. More interesting to me, in light of Western history and the effects of mobility, were the drive-through espresso bars featuring peanut-butter lattes. In one store window a sign read, "Wanted: Old Levis," which reminded me of a story I'd heard in Denver. A man paid $2,500 for a pair of 1950s-era Levis—he had a ready market in Japan. I didn't know what that meant exactly, but it seemed like the kind of thing that ought to mean *something*.

I sought out the post office and mailed my bills. Then as I was getting back into the car, three kids on bicycles came up to admire the Boxster. I felt as though I had seen them before—in Orlando, in Salmon, now in Butte. Three prepubescent boys on bikes—America's ubiquitous auto chorus.

"Great car!" they said in high-pitched unison.

"Thanks."

"It must be *expensive*."

"Well . . ."

"You from Nevada?"

"No, Arkansas."

"Arkansas? Isn't that where Bill Clinton's from?"

"Yeah, it is."

"Do you know him?"

"Well, actually, I do."

"No way!"

"Yeah, really."

"He probably gave you this car."

They told me that if I wanted to see a fancy automobile, I needed to go meet Frank Hall, who owned a bicycle shop called The Mix around the corner. "He's got a low-rider," they said.

It wasn't hard to find Frank, nor was it difficult to persuade him to show me his pearl-gray 1976 Ford Torino which he'd been working on for four years, since his sophomore year in high school. At first I was surprised to find a low-rider in the high plains, but by then I had seen that Butte wasn't so predictable a place. Not really conversant with the ethos of low-riders, I sat back and watched Frank as he took me for a spin around the block. Speed didn't appear to be the point— this was pure showmanship cruising. This was the car as dirty dancer. In his lap, Frank held a box of eight or ten phallic-shaped chrome handles, and by playing with them in various combinations he could make his machine rear, buck, bounce, shimmy, undulate, even hump. Later he showed me the power source, his hydraulic package. It filled the center of his trunk. On either side of the hydraulics were four car batteries, eight in all, packed together to make the pepper pop.

Late in the day I phoned Barbara Manha, who told me Porsche would be willing to knock ten percent off the price of the car. That brought it down from exorbitant to unreasonable, as an old friend of mine used to say. I told her I couldn't do it and made a tentative plan to drop off the Boxster a week or so later on the West Coast.

Predictably, the truth brought me low. Illusions can be useful in keeping us going sometimes. All across this country, I had been able to cling to the faint hope that this might in fact become my car, but there was no way I could justify paying $40,000 for it. Now the hard truth was the old truth: I was still a middle-aged two-van man. The morning after that rainy Arkansas day in 1993 when I'd burned up my Jeep's engine, I sold the carcass to the mechanic who towed it. After that, Beth and I bought the white 1994 Plymouth Voyager and parked it in the driveway behind her bronze 1984 Toyota van. The Plymouth had a CD player and great cup holders, but still. Those had become the cars of my winter's discontent.

As I was getting into the Porsche to scout out a late-afternoon cock-tail, a man walking by the hotel stopped to ask me about the car. "I love Porsches," he said, "and I think this is the best-looking one since the sixties. I had one for a time when I was in the Army in Germany. It was every man's dream." There was a wistfulness to his words. His name was Bill Cain, and he was the one who told me Butte was a town of survivors. Montanans, too, I gathered. "We're like a bunch of Russian peasants: We're tied to the land. My grandfather came here after the Civil War, ten years before Custer's Last Stand. A lot of native Montanans are like that." I was glad I had run into Cain, who pointed out a scenic route to Portland for me. But more than that, he made me realize that the reason I had come to Montana wasn't because of something as simple as speed. It was because Montana was the one place where speed still meant remembering—remembering its independent past—instead of forgetting the crush of modern life.

I drove over to the New Deal Bar and had a couple of drinks while listening to the bartender snort about a group of animal-rights activists who had broken into a mink ranch and set the minks free. Several of the animals later died from exposure. "Hell," said the bartender, decrying the antifur zealots, "that's what minks are *raised* for." Despite the incursion of peanut-butter lattes, I had seen signs— many of them less subtle than the Berkeley Pit—of Butte's old-line stance against such bleeding-heart thinking. "Earth First," read a bumper sticker I'd spotted that day. "We'll mine the rest later."

A man and woman came into the New Deal, and the man commented on the Boxster in the lot. I guess he figured it was mine, since the only other person there was an old guy shuttling from the bar to the poker machines in a wheelchair. As we talked and I told them what I was up to, he said, "You ought to go to Missoula. They're having the same debate between car people and new urbanists there. It's gotten nasty. One faction argues that everybody should ride bikes to work, and the other says we need more auto lanes." The man's name was John, the woman's Laura. I asked where he came down on the issue.

"Well, I live out in the country, so I need my car. In fact, I just parked my new 4Runner next to your Porsche."

He explained that Missoula, home of the University of Montana, is the state's liberal mecca. "More dogs with handkerchief bandannas, more Birkenstocks. One of the quotes is 'More Dykes on Bikes.' But a lot of Montana's economy is tourism, and you run into controversy between tourists and the locals, with the locals taking the self-righteous stance that we really enjoy our parks because we drive to the parks and get out and explore, whereas the tourists only drive through."

I told him about the CNN show I had seen in Lincoln, about outlawing cars in national parks and instituting mass transit.

"We would love mass transit," John said. "In fact there's a bumper sticker here that says, 'Pray for Me, I Drive Highway 93.' It goes north and south out of Missoula, between the Sapphire and the Bitterroot mountains. Absolutely gorgeous. But there's a lot of development—breathtaking scenery, people are moving in in droves. The big controversy is what to do with the highway—go four-lane, or improved two-lane with a turn lane. There's a big ongoing fight about that. And the road *is* dangerous, probably the most dangerous highway in Montana. There's just so much traffic. I read a quote not long ago: 'In this country we used to worry about the out-of-staters coming in with their high-powered rifles. Now the most dangerous thing we worry about is the Californians coming in with their U-Haul trailers.' "

He gave me the names of the combatants, and I thanked him, though I had no real intention of stopping in Missoula. I was ready to get to Portland, but before that I was ready to get something to eat. Remembering the mound of food I'd been served at the Bronx Supper Club the night before, I'd gone easy on eating during the day. Now I actually felt hungry. My friend Fred had told me it was imperative that I go to a place called Lydia's. "Order their sweet potato salad," he'd said.

It stays light forever in the West. I drove south past the cemetery, reading off the names on the stones: Ginsburg, Schwarz, Oppenheimer, Schilling, Kaufman, Schatz, Mueller. At 7:00 P.M., when I pulled into Lydia's lot, the sun was still high enough for me to need sunglasses. But inside the sprawling restaurant, the lounge was so dark that for a few moments I couldn't see. I propped my hand on the door, then fumbled my way to the dim bar by holding on to the chairs. "You're among friends here," said a man's voice, and I thanked him for that even though I couldn't make him out yet. When my eyes adjusted, I had entered a different era. Late fifties, early sixties, Frank and the Rat Pack, ring-a-ding-ding. Had Beth been with me, dry martinis would've been the only appropriate order. But I wasn't up to that. I told the barman that I was required to taste Lydia's sweet potato salad but that I didn't really want a major twenty-course Butte feast. "Can I," I asked, with a hint of pleading, "just have a glass of house red and a couple of appetizers here at the bar?"

Mark Sanderson was the bartender's name, and I suspected he wasn't hired help. "Look," he said, "I've got this little bit of good thirty-five dollar claret left. I'll give it to you for the same as the house wine." He filled my glass and watched me sip it. He was pleased. "How about I fix you a *montage* of appetizers," he said, and it wasn't a question. He disappeared, only to return shortly with his arms loaded with plates. "You gotta try these," he said, and he laid out two plates of homemade ravioli (one light, one in red sauce), a plate of halibut and calamari, a meat and cheese plate, a heaping dish of sweet potato salad, a bowl of fat anchovies. I ate more than I thought I could, and the expensive bottle contained enough claret for two glasses. After that was gone, he poured me a glass of Chilean wine.

While I ate, Mark told me about both Lydia's and Butte. "My step-father was Lydia's brother," he said. "Lydia came over here back in the early part of the century, from a little town south of Rome. By that time her husband had already been here a dozen years, working the mines. Now *that's* fidelity." The restaurant opened in 1946. "Butte was a great old town then, with huge money. As an indication of Butte's power, our fathers had the interstate put right through here—north, south, east, west." Until the last three or four years, the town had been steadily losing population. "We were industrial, and the mines left. Now we're reinventing ourselves. We have great Chamber of Commerce people, and Montana Power is here. That's a major thing. They take care of our town. They're attracting new business. A silicon-chip company is coming soon. That's going to put us on a different level again."

"Tell me about this ravioli," I said, pointing to the empty plate where the lighter dish had been.

"Oh, that one's cooked in butter. It's all-beef ravioli, cooked in butter sauce with a little cheese and pepper. You can taste the real rav. We don't make it with junk, man. We use beautiful, beautiful ingredients. This other is our red sauce, and we've had it since the existence of Lydia's. It's a great sauce, a light sauce, and you don't change it after fifty-one years. But it kind of covers the flavor of the true ravioli."

"Yeah, they're both great, but I believe I prefer the lighter one."

"That's the way my mother likes it."

Mark insisted on charging me ten dollars for everything. I dragged myself to my borrowed Boxster and aimed it toward the Finlen, where I was asleep before dark. Toward midnight my delirious dreams were interrupted by the noise of cars and horns. The next day was high school graduation, and the seniors paraded, with police escort, until two or three in the morning. Then the illusion of freedom dimmed and they all went home to bed.

Tuesday morning I ran into Bill Cain again, this time at Java John's, and we sat for a half hour or so talking about cars, America, and how the dream had turned out. "I don't think there's any more defining icon since World War Two than the automobile," he said. "It has defined what we have become as a people. We've become a land of nomads. It's changed the way we look at families, the way we look at communities. You're no longer tied to the community you grew up in. There are negatives to that—like with anything, technology has its downside. There've been automobile accidents, it's spawned crime, the paving over of America. But on the other hand, look at all the prosperity it's brought us."

I figured Cain, manager of community relations for Montana Power, as three or four years older than me. Not much difference, where cars were concerned. "You go through stages in your life, and they're kind of defined by cars," he said. "Growing up in Missoula in the late fifties, I built hot rods. There was nothing like the freedom of finally getting your own car. I had a great 1940 Ford. I rolled that into the Bitterroot River. But then I had a 1951 Chevy that I customized during high school. And I had a sports car—that Porsche—while I was in the Army. I totaled it in a wreck."

"You know, there's no way I'm going to let you drive this Boxster."

He laughed.

"Then I got married and we had a family, and we had station wagons. A Chevy, a Volvo, a VW. Then, along about 1970, when Datsun came out with a sports car, I got the urge again. I bought one of the very first 240Zs in the country. Serial number 624, I think it was. I had that five or six years, and then I got into the four-wheel-drive stage of my life. I got into steelhead fishing in Oregon. Now, living in Montana, my wife has a Suburban and I have a Ford truck. And then she has an old Toyota Tercel wagon that she drove for years, but we keep it because it still runs good. It's four-wheel drive. And then I drive a company car."

"So the two of you have four cars."

"Yeah. Four cars and two dogs. This is America."

I left Butte shortly after noon, headed west on I-90. Traffic was heavy, bunched up behind a laggard driver languishing at 75. Western Montana's roads really aren't appropriate for the speeds I had imagined when I came there. They are curvy, not straight and flat like Nebraska, and there were an awful lot of cars. Maybe it was different in eastern Montana, but that wasn't where I was.

I pushed the Porsche to 90, then 95, at which time I noticed a highway patrolman in the lane ahead of me. My instinct was to put on the brakes, but I resisted. Instead, I pulled into the passing lane, keeping the speed in the mid-90s. The trooper glanced at me as I passed, but he gave no indication that he considered my speed anything other than reasonable and prudent. Never in my life had I purposefully passed a state trooper at nearly 100 miles an hour. The trooper turned off at the next exit, but I felt guiltily giddy, like a newlywed having sex in a parent's house for the first time.

Just east of Anaconda, I had a split-second perception that the road had opened for me. One moment there were cars, then there seemed to be none. The interstate was straight, too, and I recognized that this was my chance. Very quickly I was at 120, 125, 127, 130, 132, 134, 135, *136!* I wanted to push on, to nudge 140, but suddenly traffic was looming. You catch cars very quickly at those speeds. I dropped back to 114. A shiver went down my spine. It felt wonderful to be driving again after two nights in Butte. I had no idea where I would sleep, or when. Willie Nelson sang, "Why not take all of me?" The road was open. I made the 111-mile trip between Butte and Missoula in just over an hour.

Once there, I found myself deciding, on the spur of the moment, to stop and see if I could talk with the two county administrators embroiled in the new-urbanists-versus-cars feud. Michael Kennedy and Barbara Evans were their names. I didn't want to stay long. In fact, I had noticed toward the end of the trip that I didn't want to stop anywhere much. I just wanted to gas up the Boxster, wipe off the bugs, and keep driving. But this Missoula thing seemed important to what I was doing, and I intended to dip in just long enough to taste the flavor of the conflict. It felt like a gateway to Portland.

After a few miscues (one at the local Chamber of Commerce office, where a woman expressed Babbitt-like *shock* at the idea of any such "debate" going on), I located the county administration building and told the office secretary who I was and what I was doing. Even without names on their offices, it was obvious to me which belonged to Kennedy. I could see the wheel of a bicycle through his open door.

My native ambivalence causes me great difficulty at moments like this. Michael Kennedy was obviously a very bright fellow, and unless he owned stock in a bicycle company, his heart was inarguably pure and in the right place. The tough role he had carved out for himself in late-twentieth-century life was that of Unwavering Grown-up. It's a role my cantankerous soul has problems embracing—unless everyone else is playing Unwavering Child. I'm not sure my fickle soul isn't the more purely American.

Kennedy, I was delighted to find, is a relatively humorless fellow, full of statistics. "I think it's a myth that we're attached to our cars," he said. "What we're attached to is mobility. I look at it this way. The car is a hundred years old. And one reason people came to this country was dissatisfaction with their plight in Europe long before cars were made. They came over here on sailboats and every other way. My sense is that the car is just a blip and all it does is feed the old feeling of mobility that the people who came to this country require. If the mobility is not reduced in any way, I don't know if the love affair would remain with the car."

While he talked, I scrolled back through all the conversations I had had over the past six weeks. I had spanned a country that loves its automobiles. Part of the lure of mobility is *ease* of mobility—the freedom to go when and how you want. Michael Kennedy lives seven miles from work, and he rides a bicycle "because I can't ask others to do something I wouldn't do myself." But I suspected he was simplifying something incredibly deep and complex, because without simplification there was no possible solution. The automobile may take the rap for our sins, but the real culprit lives inside us.

"Here in Missoula, what we have is a unique set of circumstances which brings the car right into the middle of the discussion. We live in a high mountain valley that has some pretty unique topographical and climatological characteristics. We have immersions in the winter time, during periods when people use their cars most, and the result is some pretty horrific air. The more people who crowd into this valley, the greater the problem becomes, because there's no ventilation. We've discovered that seventy percent of the air pollutions that exist in the Missoula Valley are directly attributable to the tailpipe. So what we have embarked on is an overall land-use plan, one of the results of which would be to reduce vehicle miles traveled and not impinge on people's mobility."

"That's a tough one."

"Because what's happened is you have a remarkable increase in convenience driving—not just here, but all across the country. Population increases at the rate of about one percent a year, but driving increases at three or four percent. That growth simply can't be tolerated with any good result. And so, what do you do? Well, sooner or later it's going to get done, even if we do nothing, because cars will become too expensive to drive and fuel will become too expensive to buy. Just two years ago, in 1995, for the first time in the history of record-keeping, the world automobile manufacturers' production capability exceeded market demand. Production capability was fifty-four million cars, and market demand was forty-seven million. That's the first time that's ever happened. One of the reasons it's happened is that they've reached such a cost that people can't afford them the way they once could. We're looking at twenty-one grand a car right now. In Montana, the average salary has been slightly reduced from the 1970 level. So here we are twenty-seven years later, and the average disposable income is less than it was in 1970, and a car then was around five thousand dollars. Now it's more than twenty thousand.

"So you begin to see the enormous problem that we're facing here. Even if we do nothing in respect to land use, the problem will get taken care of because of cost. What we're trying to do is anticipate that and figure out how we can design a city and urban area that requires less reliance on the single-occupancy vehicle so the community doesn't have a depreciated lifestyle—not losing mobility—and it costs them less. Urban sprawl requires people to drive farther to their homes and recreation areas and schools. So you reduce that driving by encouraging development closer to those places. In Missoula, there's about ninety thousand people in the county, and about eighty thousand of them live in the urban area. Those eighty thousand people drive between 1.3 and 1.6 miles a day, and every day they spend about fifty-one man-years in the car. So anything we can do to reduce that, without impinging on their mobility, really does enhance their quality of life, costs them less money, and certainly helps the air quality."

After a half hour with Kennedy, I was ushered into Barbara Evans's office. I could see immediately that she and Michael Kennedy wouldn't agree on much of anything. She struck me as someone who would have been a fine companion on a road trip, singing to the radio and telling life stories, whereas Kennedy would have filled the night with such forboding numbers that the only recourse would be to steer the car smack into a bridge abutment. In Evans versus Kennedy, I felt that I had encountered an outward physical form of our timeless internal debate.

Wry, funny, and tough, Evans had been in office eighteen-plus years. Right away she said she opposed the whole concept of new urbanism. "If to be pedestrian-friendly you have to be auto-hostile, I don't agree with that at all. I don't agree with forcing more density downtown. If people wanted to live as mice in a maze, they would stay in Los Angeles. They wouldn't come to Montana. They come here because they want their little piece of heaven, and they want to be able to drive their cars to work. I've lived here for over fifty years. They had a bus system when I was in high school. It went broke. And that was when people didn't have three cars. Now they have two and three cars per family, and they're not going to stand on a corner in Missoula in the winter, waiting for a bus.

"Hence, you see, our buses are pretty much empty. Yet the system is subsidized, which it wasn't in the fifties, so it's still functioning. And that's fine. I'm not opposed to the buses. I'm not opposed to bicycles. Just don't tell me I have to ride one if it doesn't fit my lifestyle."

"Does this feeling come from a love of cars, or a love of freedom?"

"It's both. I said in my last election, which was in November, they will pry my cold dead fingers off my steering wheel. I choose to drive my car—and I bought a Mercury Grand Marquis, with all the catalytic stuff on it to make it environmentally friendly. For somebody to tell me I need to come to work dressed in a suit and high heels on a bicycle, that's stupid. I'm not going to do that. I'm not putting a helmet on my hair."

She was on her way to a meeting, so we didn't have long to talk. Instead, she handed me a sheaf of photocopied articles about Portland. "I'm not saying I agree with everything here," she said with a wink, "but I wish I had written it."

I left Missoula feeling curiously depressed. After passing through several sprawling miles of fast-food stores, Jiffy Lubes, and discount chains on Highway 93, I finally turned off onto U.S. 12.

Soon I crossed Lolo Pass and descended into the valley that Lewis and Clark and their Corps of Discovery followed through the Bitterroot Mountains on their final leg to the majestic Columbia River and the sea. To my left, the swift waters of the Loscha River sparkled with diamonds of sunshine. The forest beyond was tall and noble, and the distant mountains wore white snow like an eagle's crown. Every few miles, a historic marker announced some pivotal point on the Lewis and Clark expedition. I remembered from my reading that they were exhausted along here—almost to the breaking point. They had been traveling for a year, and the trail grew only more difficult, never easier. I made Lewiston, Idaho, that night, and stayed at a place called the Pony Soldier Motel. The next morning, Wednesday, I pushed across the line into Clarkston, Washington, then followed U.S. 12 through Walla Walla, meeting the wide Columbia at Wallula. Then south again, across the Washington-Oregon line, where I picked up I-84 toward Portland.

But something was wrong, and I tried my hardest to figure out what it was. I had thought I would be exhilarated to reach this point. But instead of being high, I felt a letdown. Perhaps that's natural at the end of any trail, I thought. I remembered the wonderfully simple metaphor of Larry McMurtry's *Lonesome Dove*—the cowboys in that book drove their cattle from Texas north to the Great Plains, and when that epic trip was over there was suddenly no purpose in life.

Even Meriwether Lewis succumbed to depression when his journey was done. He killed himself three years later. For Americans of restless heart, that may be the one great challenge in making and maintaining a home—keeping the promise of a road running through it.

There was something in both Michael Kennedy's and Bill Cain's words that made me think of old Frederick Jackson Turner. "Failures in one area can no longer be made good by taking up land on a new frontier," Turner had written. "The conditions of a settled society are being reached with suddenness and with confusion." Of course, he was writing about the America of a hundred years ago, but I heard his echo in the words of Kennedy and Cain. Kennedy spelled it out almost literally: A hundred years later, he essentially said, we've come full circle. The frontier is closed again.

And where does that leave us? Maybe no worse off—Barbara Evans certainly didn't seem worried, and Alfred Chandler said that Frederick Jackson Turner, in wringing his hands about the closing of the frontier, hadn't pinned enough significance on the coming industrial revolution. Maybe things will work out. But something Bill Cain said haunted me. "I've reached the four-wheel-drive stage of my life," he'd told me, and he clearly enjoyed the kinds of activities that required such vehicles. But after the trip I had just made, I read into his statement a discomforting universality. All across this country, I had picked up a sense that Americans who never venture even *near* the woods had, for some reason or another, decided they too had reached a four-wheel-drive stage of life. Maybe it wasn't just cuteness that compelled Motel 6 to bill itself as "the Road Warrior's view of the world." Late-twentieth-century highways, especially along the frantic corridors between urban and suburban worlds, have taken on more than a hint of apocalyptic desperation. "I think people are feeling threatened by a lot of things these days," David Gartman had told me back in Mobile. "A Range Rover is billed as a vehicle that can withstand the charge of a ten-ton rhino."

Pay attention to the car ads here at century's end. Today, cars often are pitched as places to hide from the world our restlessness has created—from jangling phones, shrilling faxes, downsized corporations, crowded cities, broken homes, salacious headlines, mediocre politicians, mindless movies, arrogant waiters, and cleaners that shred your shirts. Just run to your car, lock the doors, and turn up the music. Somewhere along the line the escape route got jammed and everything became confused. Once upon a time the car was going to take us to our cabin in the woods. Now it's *become* that cabin.

A year or so ago I interviewed a brilliant psychiatrist for an article I was writing. She told me that researchers had detected a greater incidence of depression "in the cohort born since 1940." I asked what that meant, and she said nobody was sure. Later I talked with other doctors who told me they suspected that the greater incidences of depression reflected our increased abilities to *detect* depression today.

Of course, I can't say for sure, but I have this gut feeling. The people born in 1940 would have been sixteen years old in 1956, the year Ike launched the interstate highway system. They came of age with the glorious promise of untold options and opportunities—the greatest in the history of this nation. But despite our lofty expectations, the fact is that the road is long and not always smooth. A lot can go wrong in the distance to the moon.

TWELVE

A Streetcar Named Desire

In some part of my mind I thought Portland would be a walled city, like Avignon, where civilization thrives inside the fortress and angry pagan beasts slouch and belch beyond. So I was greatly surprised to find myself washing into the very heart of the new-urbanist mecca in a rain-soaked rush-hour traffic jam. It *was* as though I were caught in a flood. The Porsche bounced along with the current of cars, and, not knowing where I was headed, I simply stayed with the flow. Portland has a good jazz station, and Ella was singing "Take the A Train"—clearly someone's idea of subliminal advertising. Finally, spotting a Days Inn in the midst of downtown, I tacked left, then right, and docked the Boxster in front of a pair of sliding glass doors that opened wide and welcomed me in.

I booked a room for three nights. Where, besides home, had I spent three nights since Miami? I had to pay very careful attention to Portland. I had to work to understand how this city fit into the great American epic of restless reaching and individual freedom.

Friends from home had provided me with a list of restaurants, so I packed up a new-urbanist tome and some of the literature Barbara Evans had given me and set out in search of sustenance. I decided to take a bus. Partly, that was in the interest of journalistic enterprise, but it was also in the interest of practicality. Portland didn't look like most other cities I had been in outside the northeast United States. It isn't a wide flat sprawling grid of taillights like Dallas or Houston or Los Angeles. Instead, it actually feels dense and *city*like—more on the scale of Boston, I thought, than of Manhattan. Anyway, the restaurant I had decided on, reportedly a good fish place, was just fifteen or twenty blocks away.

The bus stop was at the edge of a park, one block from my hotel. On the way there I saw a bus approaching and ran for it, but it pulled away just as I got to the corner. To get out of the rain, I ducked under the bus-stop shelter, where three other people were already waiting. Once in, I had the immediate sense that my presence had created some invisible molecular gridlock within that space. It was the way the others shifted their bodies and glanced at me from beneath their parka hoods. *One too many,* their stares said. I ended up standing at the edge of the covering, one shoulder in the rain, until the bus came and I got on.

"I only have a twenty-dollar bill," I said to the driver. The subject of change hadn't occurred to me until the moment I boarded the bus. Fortunately, I was the last one on. Back in my Chicago days, the need to carry correct change was one of the most difficult of the urban arts I had to master. In fact, I first had to learn to carry money at all. I've never been one of those people with a pocketful of bills; only because I was on a trip did I have such denominations now. Even when I used to drive to an office, I didn't carry much cash. I paid my parking monthly, so my commute was a non-cash event. At home now, I regularly go a week with, at most, three or four crumpled dollars in my pocket. I can write a check at the grocery, and I can buy gas and wine with credit cards. But in the city, you need to carry cash.

"It's free downtown," said the driver. Obviously, somebody in Portland had encountered people like me.

I got off at Washington Street and walked six or seven blocks north, to a place called Jake's Famous Crawfish Restaurant. It was packed. "An hour and ten minutes," said the maître d', and I said fine. Where else was I going? I tied my parka around my waist and repaired to the bar, where every single stool and table was already taken. There was a palpable hump-night energy to the room. The Jazz and Bulls playoff game made a darting backdrop for the real action. Men puffed on huge cigars and pulled on pints of microbrew. The women, most still in business clothes, perched on stools and sipped their wine, flicking cigarettes with polished nails. "So," said a Barney's model to a pretty brunette next to him at the bar, "do you like good music?"

The bartender finally saw me standing behind the stool perchers and asked what I wanted.

"What's the best local brew?"

"What do you like?"

"I like a bitter beer."

He gave me a taste of three, and to my surprise I preferred the darkest—Full Sail Amber Ale. Leaning forward to receive my glass, I couldn't avoid hearing the bar conversation:

Guy: "I got married when I was twenty-eight. Divorced when I was thirty."

Girl: "I got married when I was twenty-two, divorced when I was twenty-four."

Guy: "You too?"

Suddenly they felt warm toward each other.

Guy: "So, are your parents still together and everything?"

Girl: "My mom's been married a couple of times."

Guy: *"Mine too."*

They were linked by kindred casualties. They'll go home together, I thought.

Frankly, I hadn't expected to encounter such appealingly flawed specimens of humanity in Portland. Read the new-urbanist literature and you come away imagining that everybody in town is level-headed and wears sensible shoes. Portland is billed as a city where light rail passes for instant gratification.

It was hard to read in the bar, with no place to put my glass or book, but I managed to skim over one of the articles Barbara Evans had given me. It was a piece called "The Great Wall of Portland," by a man named Alan Ehrenhalt, recently published in a magazine called *Governing*. The title referred to the strict Urban Growth Boundary (UGB) that Portland—and, in fact, all Oregon cities—must by state law respect. Past that line you cannot build. The result is an outlying area of protected forest and farmland and a philosophy of ever-greater "density" within that boundary. The article mentioned that planners from as far away as China and Botswana have come to Portland searching for answers to their own urban ills. "But," wrote Ehrenhalt, "it is the official delegations from other American cities that fall for Portland the hardest. And it isn't difficult to figure out why. They arrive from places where the downtown is dead, the neighborhoods are crumbling, and the strip malls sprawl for fifty miles across the suburban asphalt. They see a place where the downtown has a thousand retail stores, the outlying neighborhoods are healthy and growing, and the sprawl ends at a greenbelt twenty minutes from the city line. And every land-use decision is made under the aegis of an elected metropolitan government in accordance with the dictates of a tough and explicit state law."

Wow, I thought, ordering up another Full Sail. Why would Barbara Evans give me *this* article? Portland sounded perfect. Don't we *all* want booming downtowns? Healthy neighborhoods? Rolling farmland in lieu of more Taco Bells? Then I got to the end of the piece, in which the author explained that the regional government—Metro—determines the number and, largely, the type of housing units to be added to the areas within its purview. "The question," Ehrenhalt wrote, "is whether the voters who have to absorb the density—and who elect the Metro council—will accept it. Early in the discussion process, when Metro penciled in nearly 4,900 new units for Lake Oswego [a Portland suburb], the local paper complained that 'a suburb that looks like downtown Hong Kong could be planned for the heart of . . . Lake Oswego, and the city would have to sit on the sidelines and brood.' "

Pondering Portland, I thought back to Miami in the fifties, when nothing succeeded like excess. It was a swinging, toe-tapping time. Now, forty years later, there I was in Portland. I worried that I was about to meet the foot binder.

After an hour and a half, my booth was ready. Feeling homesick, I ordered Jake's étouffée with shrimp and chicken. "You came at the right time," the waitress told me. "This weekend is the Rose Festival."

"What's the weather supposed to do?"

"Oh, like today. We have warmer or cooler, but mostly it rains."

After dinner I walked in a light drizzle the six blocks back to the bus stop, where I waited for five minutes. The first bus sped by with a "Not in Service" sign above its windshield. Then a second arrived, and it also zoomed by—but then stopped at the end of the block, where there was another bus stop. I ran for it and was again the last one on. A young bearded man sat high behind the wheel.

"Does this bus go to the Days Inn?" I said.

"I dunno," he said. "Where's the Days Inn?"

"I have no idea," I said, and I could feel that old heat boiling up from deep inside. "Fifth or sixth or something."

He shrugged, and off we went. I tried to stuff a dollar bill in the coin receptacle. "Is this how this goes?" I said.

"This is a free zone."

"What?"

"You don't need to put that in. It's free here."

"Oh yeah, I forgot." Old Chicago habits die hard.

I settled into a seat and watched for the Days Inn, but I was disoriented. The driver turned, finally, and said to the entire bus, "Who wants Days Inn?"

"I do," I said, standing up.

He pulled the bus to a stop. "Whether you believe it or not," he said, "Days Inn is one block that way," pointing to the left.

You jerk, I thought. *You knew where it was all the time.*

"You've been a great help," I said, and as I went down the steps I tripped. I cursed aloud and then turned to see all the expressionless faces watching me from the well-lit bus, looking like characters in Hopper's "Night Hawks." I'm sure they thought I was a pitiful stumbling drunk, one more hopeless urban loser, unable even to negotiate a simple bus ride.

On the walk back to the hotel, I remembered what a dream analyst once had told me about automobiles. If you dreamed about cars, you were dreaming about how you were progressing in the world. "But it's very important," she added, "to see *yourself* in the driver's seat."

Damn right, I thought. *Damn* right.

On Thursday I heard my first California joke. I was at a laundromat trying to wash the road from my clothes, when I struck up a conversation with the woman who oversaw the place. Sally was her name. I had asked whether she lived in the city or commuted from the suburbs. She lived near work, but she knew a lot of people who came in on the

MAX. This isn't a commuter train or a subway, like Washington's Metro or New York's subway. This is a system of light rail, which is essentially a streetcar system. In the sixties, when Portland was still on the brink of deciding what kind of city it wanted to be, the planners had mapped out a system of freeways around the city—a system big and elaborate enough to give Portland the title of most freeway lanes per mile of any city in the country. After coming to their senses, they scrapped those in favor of light rail, which is one of the favorite new-urbanist ideas. "It's slow," said Sally, "but they make parking in the city very, very expensive."

That led to a broader discussion of just *who* makes parking expensive (Metro), and why (they want to discourage driving), which in turn led to her mentioning the name of Tom McCall, the former Oregon governor who started this entire revolution against the American spirit. It was only the first of many reverential invocations of McCall that I would hear in my short time in Portland. "Tom McCall *moved a highway*," Sally said, and anyone could have heard the lingering astonishment in her voice. "Where it was, he turned into a riverfront park." If true, that was indeed impressive. It made me think back to my erstwhile meadow in Kansas City, now a roaring expressway.

"McCall used to talk about what he called 'Californication,' " she said, laughing. "He didn't want Portland to become sprawling and car-dependent, like Los Angeles. Oh, that reminds me of a joke. There's this Oregonian, this Texan, and this Californian. They're out target shooting. So the Texan comes up with a bottle of tequila and takes a single sip out of it. Then he throws the bottle really high and shoots it out of the air.

"The Californian says, 'Oh, wow, why'd you do that? That was a great bottle of tequila.'

" 'Don't worry about it,' says the Texan. 'There's lots of that stuff where I come from.'

"So the Californian gets up, with a really fine bottle of merlot from the Napa Valley. He takes a sip of it, throws the bottle up, and shoots it out of the air.

" 'Aw, man,' says the Texan, 'that was a *great* bottle of wine. Why'd you do that?'

" 'Hey,' says the Californian, 'there's tons of great wine where *I* come from.'

"So then the Oregonian gets up to shoot. He pulls out a bottle of Widmer root beer, which is a famous brand around here. He opens up the root beer and drinks it dry. Then he shoots the Californian.

" 'Oh, man,' says the Texan, 'why'd you do *that?*'

" 'Well,' says the Oregonian, 'there's lots of those where I come from, and I can get a nickel for the bottle.' "

Sally thought it was the funniest thing she had ever heard.

That afternoon, after a long pleasant walk around downtown Portland, I sat in my room making calls and trying to line up interviews. I also phoned Beth, who informed me that she had booked a beach house at Pawleys Island for a week in August. The house happened to be the most expensive one on the beach and was (not surprisingly) the only one available. Forty-two hundred dollars for the week. We were sharing it with two other families. Our portion would be fourteen hundred dollars. Fortunately, my agent had straightened out the other mess, so I probably would have a little cash. But I wanted to pay for *this* trip before embarking on another one. Still, I decided not to protest. "The bill always comes," said Hemingway—another quote I found myself remembering quite often.

I managed to make an appointment to see one of the Metro councilors, Ed Washington, on Friday morning. He was chairman of the transportation committee. I also hooked up with Mike Hoglund, Metro's manager of transportation planning. Finally, I got in touch with one of Metro's most vociferous opponents, an environmental writer named Randal O'Toole, whose articles Barbara Evans had given me. I was confused about the way divisions formed in this conflict. I would have thought an "environmental writer" would be on the side of Metro against the automobile, but O'Toole brought other considerations to the table. He was involved with something called the Thoreau Institute, "a non-profit organization that is finding ways to protect natural resources without big government."

Late in the day, I gazed out my window for a long time, watching the trench-coated workers coming and going at the bus stop across the street. They carried newspapers, briefcases, backpacks, coffee cups. They didn't talk with one another much. I guessed they were like commuters everywhere, preoccupied with their days, with the wounds they'd sustained, with the dreams they'd seen soar or sink. Or maybe they were thinking about what they faced when they got home—needy spouses, unruly children, dinners to fix, dishes to wash, maybe a half hour of a vapid TV show or a formulaic bestseller, then bed and more of the same tomorrow.

I chuckled at myself, at my bleak existential take on the world. But I believed I had a bone-deep understanding of why statistics show more American workers commuting alone in cars than any other way. "During the 1980s," wrote Brad Edmondson in *American Demographics,* "Americans spent tens of billions of tax dollars to promote car pools, buses, and other alternatives to driving alone. It's hard to say what the money really bought. According to the Census Bureau, the proportion of employed Americans who usually drive to work alone rose from 64 percent in 1980 to more than 73 percent in 1990."

The dry statisticians point to various explanations, including the increasing presence of working women and something called "trip chaining," which basically means that people stop at the cleaners on the way home from work. But at the end of his piece, Edmondson echoed what I sensed was true: "To those who drive the most, cars are havens of solitude in an increasingly hectic world. . . . More than three-quarters of Americans describe themselves as 'environmentalists,' but when Roper Starch Worldwide asked them which environmentally friendly actions they would consider taking, changing their personal driving habits ranked dead last."

Watching the trench coats dutifully boarding the bus, I decided I would bet on the heart over the head any day. Even in Portland.

That evening I had dinner with my friends Hope Dlugozima and Tom Lombardo, people I had met during a period in the late eighties and early nineties, when I did consulting work for Whittle Communications in Knoxville. In 1994, after Whittle's self-destruction, Hope and Tom moved to Portland and got into the new-media business. I knew them as liberal thinkers, and Tom was an avid bicyclist—the kind of man who thinks nothing of riding a hundred miles on a weekend. They and their new baby, Lucy, live in a beautifully refurbished old house on a quiet leafy street on the east side of the Willamette River, about a seven-minute drive from my hotel. The neighborhood reminded me of Hillcrest, the area where I live in Little Rock. I'm sure there were ways for me to get there besides taking the Boxster, but of course I wanted to show it to them. Also, I didn't want to have to deal with getting home late at night by foot or mass transit.

The evening was clear, and we sipped beers in their manicured back yard. Curious to know about life in the great Northwest, I asked if people in Portland talked much about the issue of cars. "Actually," said Hope, "I've been *amazed* by how much people do talk about it. Back in Knoxville, they bitched about traffic—'It took me forty-five minutes to get to work'—that sort of thing. But here, at work and at parties, they talk about bike paths and traffic calming."

"Traffic what?"

"*Calming*. Traffic calming. I'd never seen it before, but there are these big signs by the side of the road: 'Traffic Calming Project.' "

"You'll get a technical explanation when you talk to Metro," said Tom, "but what it means in a practical sense, from a driver's standpoint, is putting obstructions in to slow traffic." He gave as an example little "runarounds" in the center of a street—small circles of grass and flowers or sculpture to make speeding more difficult. "There's a huge one-way artery into the city—a street called Broadway. A few months ago, to make the area more 'livable' and 'shoppable,' they cut out a whole traffic lane. They put in a bike lane, and they're widening all the sidewalks. So what they've done is taken away space for cars, and they've made space for bikes and pedestrians. That's traffic calming."

"And nobody's been complaining," said Hope.

"In other cities," Tom said, "people would *scream*. 'You're going to add five minutes to my commute to work! Not here."

"But the benefits go beyond what you might think, which is biking or walking. It's also really good for business. Because what they've proven is that it generates more excitement around the street. Kind of like Georgetown in Washington being popular because it *feels* popular. It makes people want to shop more. It makes it feel *congested*."

I could feel my old ambivalence rising. Intuitively, I could grasp the physics of Metro's thinking: When you squeeze something tight, you create more energy. Molecules get mashed up next to one another, and the friction causes heat. But if you loosen your grip, energy dissipates. It's the difference between, say, Manhattan, New York, and Manhattan, Kansas. Or a full restaurant and one that's nearly empty. Still, this conversation felt surreal, like a cosmic joke: Go West, Young Man—and when you finally get there, you discover the West wants to be the *East*.

Over dinner, Hope and Tom told me that local companies offer free passes to employees who are bus or rail riders—but they won't provide parking for people who drive to work. Echoing Sally at the laundromat, Hope talked about how expensive parking in downtown Portland is—a quarter gets you eighteen minutes, and the cheapest all-day parking ("in a place where drug dealers do business") is $5.75. The urban planners at Metro pull the strings that create that situation. Through Metro, they wield the clout to make companies support The Cause. "More and more companies have showers now," Hope said, "and all new buildings are required to have bike racks sketched in as part of their plans."

"I hate to generalize," I said, "but do Portlanders just flat-out hate cars?"

They looked at each other, not quite sure how to answer.

"A lot of the people I work with are twenty-year-old bike riders," Hope said. "They're very anti-car."

"Well, I don't think the people in Portland *hate* cars," Tom said. "We all have cars, we all drive."

"*I* drive," said Hope. "I just can't work it out otherwise. I can get from here to there, but I can't work out how to get to my yoga class."

"Well, I don't use my Saab between April 1 and October 31, when the time changes. I don't like to bike at night. But in the summer, my car battery goes dead. I think the attitude here is 'Let's try something different.' There's a sticker that says, 'One Less Car.' I see that around here a lot. People put them on their bikes. It's a ripoff of a sticker the buses use: 'Two Hundred Seventy-nine People Are Not in Their Cars Because I'm Driving This Bus.' "

On my way back to the hotel that night, I pondered the conundrum that was Portland. Even though it was a lively, attractive place, it seemed somehow less an organic city than a life-sized lab for experiments in social engineering. Despite my fondness for crowded restaurants, didn't the very concept of congestion (never mind *orchestrated* congestion) go against the whole of American history? It occurred to me that the new urbanists want not merely to build for tomorrow but to erase yesterday—namely, the twentieth century. Their big plan for the twenty-first century is for us to live in nineteenth-century neighborhoods and use nineteenth-century transportation.

I understand, better than most, how nostalgia for a bygone time leads people to old houses. Our imaginations are fertile. We yearn for eras we never even lived in. But I began to wonder if new urbanism is some kind of institutionalized nostalgia cult. And who *are* all these happy bicyclists and light-rail riders, these patient trench-coated bus passengers, in a city where rain is a fact of everyday life? I couldn't wait to visit Metro headquarters. As I pulled the Boxster into my space at the Days Inn, a very strange idea popped into my head: *What if there's a room deep inside the Metro building where earnest urban planners implant obedience microchips in the soles of Birkenstocks?*

Early Friday morning I went for a run in Tom McCall Waterfront Park. It was a clear day, just in time for the Rose Festival. After covering the entire length of the park, I stood and watched the traffic go by. It was 7:30 A.M. There was no gridlock, but even more astonishing was the silence. No one honked a horn. It reminded me of something Hope and Tom had told me the night before. Portlanders are very polite, they said, and they expect others to be. They won't jaywalk, but if you do they'll give you a dirty look. They wait for the green light. If you edge your car into the pedestrian crossing, they'll smack your hood with their hands. They'll say things like, "You must be from the East Coast. We don't *do* that here."

Jogging back along the riverfront, I noticed that vendors were getting their booths set up. A Coast Guard cutter was docked at the park, presumably for public tours, and the crew was making everything shipshape. A man wielding a dolly was unloading cases of beer from his truck, then wheeling them into a pavilion. By noon it would become a lively riverfront beer garden. It was a nice place for a morning run, and I wasn't the only one who thought so. I wished I had brought money so I could stop and buy coffee at one of the already-open booths.

At mid-morning I parked the Boxster on a side street near Metro headquarters, a big, white, modern glass building on the south side of the Willamette. A Land Rover dealership was just across the street. I was early, and so waited for Councilor Washington on a sofa upholstered in fabric featuring Matisse cutout designs. In the lobby I picked up a brochure about the Metro building. "Resourceful Renovation" was the title, and then this cover text: "In 1992, Metro, the agency responsible for solid-waste disposal and recycling in the Portland metropolitan area, began renovating a vacant Sears department store into earth-wise offices." I opened the brochure and read about all the ways the building was efficient: Floor tiles in restroom levels one, two, and three were made from waste glass; ceiling tiles throughout the building were made from newspapers; landscaping soil was made from yard debris. "The paint, used as primer throughout the building, is reprocessed locally from household latex paint Metro collects at its household hazardous-waste facility. The wallboard is made locally with gypsum recycled from construction sites." It was all very impressive, though something in the tone—or was it in my disposition—brought to mind that smug girl with glasses who sat next to me in third grade and always got the A+ while I had to settle for the A. I found her insufferable.

Finally, Ed Washington emerged from a meeting. We shook hands, and he escorted me into his office, where for the next hour we discussed Metro and its mandate. Metro councilors are elected officials, he explained, "the only elected regional government in the country," with the possible exception of Minneapolis. He wasn't sure about that. Of the three counties in the Portland metropolitan area, each county has its government; each of the twenty-four cities in the tri-county area has *its* government; and then there's Metro. "We have governance over the tricounty area, but only in specific things: Our primary function is land use and transportation planning."

Covering most of one wall of Washington's office was a multicolored map of the metropolitan area with the logo "2040" on it. "That's our growth plan for the next fifty years," Washington said. The predominant color was green, listed on the legend as "Rural Reserves." That's the vivid face of the Urban Growth Boundary. The plan for the next half-century doesn't provide for pushing back that boundary but instead calls for more and more and *more* density within it. Oregon is a place where they grade hard on coloring inside the lines.

"I tell people that the thing that made all this possible was Senate Bill 100," said Washington. "For every Oregon city over five thousand people, the UGB is state mandated. That was twenty years ago. Would it be difficult to get that done today? Yes. Were we lucky? Yes. We had the right people in place at the right time. Also, our population wasn't that big then. We were gobbling up farmland, and somebody noticed. 'Wait a minute,' they said. 'If we don't manage this growth, we're going to be like Los Angeles or Miami or all the rest.' Suburbs were exploding. So-called inner cities were being paved over to accommodate freeways. Twenty, twenty-five years ago, we were destroying the heart of our cities. The car was king. Even here, I'm sure people envisioned eight- to ten-lane freeways someday."

"Do people in Portland hate cars?"

"I don't think they hate them. People in Portland love their cars just as much as people anyplace else. But I think you have a lot more people here in Portland who are willing to look at alternative forms of transportation, such as light rail."

"Maybe that's due to twenty years of conditioning."

"Part of it is conditioning, but I think part of it is just commitment.

Part of it is just those people's psyches. They're really committed to riding their bikes."

"Are you telling me there's a certain *kind* of person who moves here?"

"Yeah, I think so. You have the original Oregonians, and then you have the transplants. And the transplants range from people like me, who have been here fifty-three of my sixty years. I came from Birmingham, Alabama, in the forties. But probably the great majority of transplants are coming here now. They're strong advocates for the environment, and for livability. Many of them are coming from New York or California or New Jersey, or from Arizona or Texas. They come here because they hear it's a great place. They hear we have good land-use laws. Those who've come over the past five or six years are the most vocal. As soon as they get here and discover the place, they want us to close the border. *Don't let anybody else in.*

"People here still love their cars. The freeways are not going to close down. But I think Portlanders in the years ahead are going to have to make some real decisions as to whether they want to get on public transit, or whether they want to sit on the freeway. Because our freeways are small compared to L.A.'s."

"And I bet you're going to keep them that way, aren't you?"

"Oh yeah. There will be minimal—*minimal*—expansion of the freeways. I'm the chairman of the transportation committee, and one of the things I've learned is that you cannot build your way out of this mess. It's an overwhelming issue, and if we don't get our arms around it, it will get its arms around us. That's all there is to it."

"I had dinner with friends last night, and they told me about some of the things Portland does to subtly squeeze the car. Tell me about that."

"Right now they're subtly squeezing the *hell* out of the car. Because what's happening on the major streets is you have to have bike lanes, and that's a helluva squeeze. They're also widening the sidewalks. And then on many of the major streets you've also got to have a *turning* lane. So cars have about two lanes to drive in. What's going to happen, I think, is that slowly but surely people are going to say, 'Hey, this isn't worth it.' And they'll start getting on light rail and buses. I don't know if that's by design—"

"You *don't?*"

He laughed. "Well, it isn't so much predicated on hurting the car. The thing is, if you look at the total transportation picture, it should be pedestrian-friendly, because people transport themselves; it should be bike-friendly, because people do ride bikes; it should accommodate the automobile; and it should provide for handicapped people. It's got to be balanced. When you consider what it costs to build a freeway to accommodate a car, you can do that for so much less by having a good mass-transit system."

I told him what Sally at the laundromat had said about the MAX.

"Well, on a scale of one to ten, we're probably a high six. There's room for improvement. But it's not because we don't have a good system or it's not managed well. It's just money."

"So tell me, if somehow I found myself plopped down in Portland in the year 2040, what would I see?"

"In 2040 we're anticipating another half million people. The present population of the region is 1.5 million. In 2040 there will be much greater density. People will live much closer together. Your lot size will go from 50-by-100 to maybe 30-by-70. People are going to have to rely on mass transit a lot more. They'll walk a lot. You'll probably see commuter rail from the far-out distances. Probably by that time you'll have a spine of light rail going north and south. One is proposed, and one is already under construction. You'll probably also see some form of congestion pricing. That means if you want to get in the car and zip up and down the freeway, you're going to pay for it. You're given only so many trips per day. So if you're lazy, like some of us, you're gonna pay."

"How do you get to work?"

"Oh, I drive. I come and go so much."

After my hour with Councilor Washington, I went across the hall to see Mike Hoglund, the transportation planning manager. If Washington was the politico, Hoglund—who appeared to be in his late thirties, early forties—was the transportation pro. He showed me an old Portland map from the sixties, with all the proposed freeways. The city-to-be looked like a spiderweb, which may tell us something about freeways. In contrast was the new 2040 plan, with its wide swath of green. I asked if any of the new-urbanist gurus were involved in shaping that happy future. He named Peter Calthorpe and Andres Duany. I was curious as to which came first, Portland's land-use philosophy or the new-urbanist philosophy.

"I don't know if those guys would tell you this, but I think in the backs of their minds they've benefitted from Portland. Back in the seventies, when the statewide land-use planning came up, there were nineteen goals that every comprehensive plan had to be consistent with. You had to have good transportation, economic development, open spaces, housing, growth management, and so on. One of the first plans that came out was the downtown plan for Portland. It was key, because it was one of the first plans that called for a good mix of housing, commercial, and retail activity. It laid out where we wanted the transit. We had an inkling we were going to get light rail. The plan said light rail should probably go in this certain area, and in that area is where we should put the most density of buildings. Every building got bonuses for putting the parking underground, and the first floor of every building was required to be retail. There were limits on blank walls and sky bridges and things like that. It became a real interesting, people-oriented, friendly downtown. The other thing it did was that it said, 'Well, we're not going to get everybody to take transit—we need to accommodate cars.' So there was a strategic parking-management component to it that said where we wanted to locate parking garages to encourage short-term visitor parking downtown.

"So when we came in at the regional level, Portland's downtown plan was a good example for us in expanding that notion to the outlying areas. You know, there's bad density and there's good density. There was bad density done under Model Cities in the early urban-renewal programs, where they wiped out old neighborhoods and put up highrises. They threw in low-income people and the issues those people have, and they put it all in one area. Of course, nobody wants to live in that type of area—not even the low-income people. What's going on downtown is that there are requirements to provide single-occupant-room housing for people who can't afford something better. So there's a good mix of housing types, a good mix of retail types. It all kind of comes together. It's a community within itself."

Community. I thought about that slippery concept early that afternoon as I drove to the Portland suburb of Oak Grove to see Randal O'Toole. I had liked Ed Washington and Mike Hoglund. They didn't strike me as megalomaniacs, or as robots. The moment that had put me off the most was when I asked Hoglund how he gets to work and he said, "I'm multimodal." His wife drops him off on Mondays, he tries to walk on Tuesdays, and he drives three days a week. He justifies the latter this way: "I only live two miles away, so if I single-occupant-vehicle three days, that's only six miles of VMT (vehicle miles traveled). Whereas, if you live in Beaverton and you drive only once a week, that's twelve miles away. That's twenty-four miles of VMT. By living closer to work, I get to drive more."

But Washington and Hoglund seemed to be doing a job they believe in. Creating community, I suppose you could call it. They were wrestling with the hard choices three centuries of American individualism had wrought. Until I read the new urbanists and heard about Portland's plans, I would have defined community as people coming together in a comforting way. What I didn't understand was how great an effect the infrastructure has on people's communal behavior. Metro's goal is to create and implement that infrastructure. It is a job best done behind the scenes, I thought, with minimal horn blowing, lest the manipulation spook the American spirit.

I had asked Hoglund what the prognosis is for all those other cities that have sent emissaries to Portland—cities that don't have twenty years of smart planning under their belts. "It's hard," he said. "The stars kind of aligned for us in the seventies. The hard part to figure out is, could you do this without the urban-growth boundary? It kind of jump-started things. The economy and the livability are good here, and so, whether you like it or not, Portland is a place people want to come to. And businesses want to locate here because their execs like it. And plus, we've got good cheap electricity here and plenty of water. That's why a lot of the microchip plants are here. We've got a pretty good high-tech base now. So it's a nice place to be, and the market has had to react to our rules whether they like it or not. Some innovative developers have started working downtown, building row houses, smaller lot sizes. I come back to the urban-growth boundary. It creates a certain positive tension."

As I was driving toward Oak Grove, a man in a Mercedes pulled up on the left and made a gesture with his right hand. I wasn't sure what he meant. Then he did it again, and this time I recognized his gesture as a thumbs-up. It was such a timid one that I hadn't been able to

make it out. I gave him one back. We were two underground opera-
tives speaking code in an occupied land.

I wasn't quite sure what to expect from Randal O'Toole. I'm uncomfortable with ideologues. My heart and my head seldom agree on
anything, so for someone to take an unwavering stand—resisting any
arguments thrown his way—is an amazing and unsettling spectacle.
O'Toole and I met in the living room of his suburban home, and to
my great relief I found that he had a sense of humor.

"I went down to Metro this morning," I said.

"That's fun."

"Yeah, I was delighted to see a car dealership across the street."

"Oh, they've got a huge parking garage. Did you notice that?
Their staff was given a choice of either a reserved parking space or
free Tri-Met passes, and they all took the parking spaces." He found
that very, very funny.

"Why do you oppose Metro?"

"The simplest explanation is that everybody in Portland agrees on
one thing. They don't want this city to become another Los Angeles.
So Metro has this great plan for increasing population density, building light rail, building pedestrian-friendly design, and so on. And they
did an analysis, Metro did, and they looked at the fifty largest U.S.
cities. They looked at densities, they looked at the number of highways per capita, and all these other factors, and they said, 'Which city
is closest to what we're trying to turn Portland into.' Guess which one
it was—Los Angeles! They say right in a document called 'Metro
Measured': 'Los Angeles represents an investment pattern we desire
to replicate.' Los Angeles has the highest density of any metropolitan
area in the country. New York City has a high density, but the New
York metropolitan area includes northeastern New Jersey. The density of the overall metropolitan area is 4,100 people per square mile,
in 1990. The Los Angeles density is 5,600 people per square mile.

Miami has about 5,400, and from then on it goes way down. Portland is 2,800. The density that Metro expects Portland to reach, under their 2040 plan, is 5,000 people per square mile. Just a little short of Los Angeles, and well above what New York is now.

"Metro says their goal for Portland is to add all these people, but to build no new freeways. They might widen the lanes in a few areas, but they aren't going to build more. Now what *is* it that we *really hate* about Los Angeles? What we hate is the *congestion!* And that's what Metro's trying to do here!"

O'Toole has a funny way of talking, kind of a W. C. Fieldian raising of the voice when he wants to make a point. *What we hate, my little chickadee, is the congestion!* Even with all the numbers he peppers you with, his manner is entertaining. In the seventies, he entered the University of Oregon's Department of Urban and Regional Planning, but he took economics courses on the side. When the UGB was passed, O'Toole disagreed with the forecast for it. It was supposed to save farmland, but his economic model showed that the trade-off would be more cars in a tighter area—more congestion. He tried to convince his fellow urban-planning students and his professors, but they told him he was wrong. "That day I decided I was an economist, not a planner.

"Metro says, in the technical appendices to their 2040 plan, that Portland will have four times the congestion in the year 2040 as it did in 1990. See, the whole idea of new urbanism is that if we have transit-oriented development, pedestrian-friendly design, and if we pack 'em in—they like to say, 'Grow Up, Not Out,' but one county commissioner here, who tends to favor them, says it's called 'Stack 'Em and Pack 'Em.' Anyway, if they pack 'em in, if they build ninety miles of light rail, thirty miles of commuter rail, build transit-oriented developments, require pedestrian-friendly designs all over the city— they do all that, and the share of trips that use automobiles, which is currently around ninety-two percent, will fall *all the way down* to eighty-eight percent.

"That's using a computerized transportation model that the Department of Transportation told me the other day was the best in the nation. I looked at the model, and I thought it was kind of optimistic. They have all these assumptions, you know. If two people live in a house like this, they're going to have two automobiles. But if they live in row houses, there's a much greater chance that they'll have only *one* automobile. All these assumptions. It's based on a survey of three thousand people, and there's a significant bias there. If you survey people who already *live* in apartments or row houses, maybe the people who are willing to live with fewer automobiles *choose to live there.* But that doesn't *mean* if you take people who are *not* willing to live with fewer automobiles and put them in row houses or apartments that *they're automatically going to start living without automobiles.*

"Metro's survey assumes that. So I think their numbers are optimistic. And yet, as optimistic as they are, the numbers only go from ninety-two to eighty-eight percent! So why are we spending *billions of dollars* on light rail, nothing on highways, getting *four times* the traffic congestion, *ten percent more* smog (because congested traffic causes more pollution), *all for this ideal called new urbanism?*"

After that, a drink sounded ideal to me. I parked the Boxster at the Days Inn and walked down to McCall Waterfront Park to see how the Rose Festival was progressing. That tent where I'd seen the man wheeling in cases of beer had now been transformed into a fresh-air bar. It was crowded with businessmen in ties and shirtsleeves, sipping microbrews, smoking cigarettes, having a fine old Friday afternoon.

I found a place at the end of the bar and soon was in a conversation with a portly man wearing big amber sunglasses and a pinkie ring.

He was a transplanted Californian from Pasadena—a developer. "I love it here," he said when I asked him why he moved. "People in California used to have values. Now they're shallow. Cars, crime. I hate it. I *love* this place." He ordered another gin and tonic.

"A developer, huh?"

"Yeah. I made a lot of money. Lived in Malibu. Had to give some of it back, but got away with a little. Now I don't want as much."

"Scale down."

"You bet."

"You're a developer—what do you think about the UGB?"

"Hey, I say, 'When in Rome . . .' "

Some of his buddies showed up, and he turned to them. I ordered another brew and worked on my notes. What a day. What a *mess*. I was feeling the old urge to crank up the Porsche and drive on.

That evening I stopped by the Heathman Hotel bar for one of its famous martinis. Nice and dry, very cold. At the bar, an NBA playoff game was on—Jazz 79, Bulls 62, fourth period. After that drink, I decided to take a walk. It was a nice night, no rain for a change. Someone was looking out for the Rose Festival. I wandered around the central part of the city, watching the people at sidewalk cafes, peering in store windows, stopping to sit on one of the terraced stones in Pioneer Square. It was a city park, with steps rising like a Roman coliseum. Bricks bore the names of donors. Teenagers waded in a fountain, pretending to try to push one another in. By now the daylight was fading. I could hardly make out a sign in the park, an old-fashioned signpost putting this place in the context of a wider world. "Mount Hood, 70 miles." "Timbuktu, 6,726 miles." "Mutare, 10,115 miles." "Sapporo, 4,456 miles." "Walden Pond, 2,530 miles."

Downtown Portland had a nice energy on that summer night. There were all kinds of people out—teens with pierced noses, the grunge crowd, yups in linen slacks, outdoorsy types in safari vests from

Banana Republic. One woman pushed a shopping cart full of bottles to cash in. People in cafes were smoking and drinking, laughing, having a good time, while just a few feet away on the curb, entire families were unpacking their lawn chairs and blankets and thermos jugs, claiming prime spots for tomorrow's Rose Festival Parade. It was like an all-night tailgate party. I ate at a Greek cafe on the corner of SW Forth and Washington. Calamari and wine, extra feta on my salad. Then I wandered back to my hotel, dead tired, and fell asleep before ten.

The next morning, Saturday, I woke up late. I looked out the window and saw scurrying crowds carrying their blankets, headed toward midtown. A bus was parked in the Days Inn lot, ready to transport tourists to the Rose Parade. Some internal timer told me I should get on the road. There was one other place I wanted to go. I showered and packed, then checked out and loaded the car. The day was slightly overcast, but not raining. I dropped the top on the Boxster and put on my sunglasses. A couple cutting through the parking lot stopped to tell me how great-looking the Porsche was.

At 11:30 I pulled the car onto Market Street, headed toward the Willamette River. On the other side I would connect with I-5 south, toward California. I was stopped at a light when my ear picked up the distant tinny sound of a brass section, and I glanced into my rearview mirror to see what it was. There, framed by the fan-shaped Porsche mirror, a slice of life marched into view between buildings two blocks away. It was a red-uniformed band with bright brass tubas swaying to the insistent *click-clickety-click* of a snare drum tilted to the edge. They had taken over the street. In the foreground, crowds cheered and waved. Fathers held their children high. I watched for a few seconds while I waited for the light to turn green. In my rearview, the scene became a diorama, a jewel-like re-creation of a perfect Norman Rockwell America.

Then the light changed, and I drove away.

The Sculpture Garden

The only wreck I saw on my entire trip was on June 7, on I-5 north of Eugene, Oregon. I didn't actually see the wreck itself; I saw its aftermath. Traffic backed up for miles and was stalled for nearly an hour. People got out of their cars and congregated in little knots of conversation. Several came over to look at the Boxster. Word was passed back from down the line that there had been an accident and that there was a fatality. In the next lane and a few cars behind me, an RV erupted in flames while we were waiting. People scrambled into their vehicles and pulled them onto the shoulder, as far away from the RV as possible, in case the gas tank exploded. Fortunately, another driver had a fire extinguisher handy and doused the fire. Finally the traffic began moving again. Just north of Eugene I saw a scorched place on the interstate, silent testament to a life snuffed out. Soon there would be flowers propped against a mile marker.

At Eugene I caught Highway 126 to the coast. I stopped to look at the Oregon dunes, which were beautiful in their barrenness. They reminded me of Nebraska. Someone had told me that the state of Oregon, wanting to restrict development of the dunes, declared the beach a part of the state highway system. So it's legal to *drive* on most of the state's beaches, but you can't build houses or condos on them.

After the dunes, I headed south on Highway 101, past hulking boulders that looked like giant water buffalo sunning themselves in the cold Pacific. It had been a full month since I had seen an ocean. All afternoon and into early evening I drove south, through Oregon logging towns and seaside resorts. The Pacific turned from blue to black as the sun sank farther west. I spent that night in Crescent City, just across the California state line. In the motel, the TV and phone were chained to the furniture.

The next day I got up and drove into the astounding Redwood Forest. It was a bright Sunday morning, and the light filtered through the giant limbs like sun streaming through a cathedral window. Somewhere near Orick I paid three dollars to drive the Boxster through a redwood tree. Some people tried to do it in a van but couldn't make the squeeze. At Eureka the road cut back inland, away from the coast. I stopped and ate breakfast, a crab omelet, and then paid $2.60 a gallon to fill up at the only gas station I had seen in miles. By that afternoon I was in wine country, passing vineyards whose names I knew from my table at home. That night I stayed in Santa Rosa with Beth's oldest friend, Elizabeth, and her daughter Madeline. "I hear your wife is mad at you," Elizabeth said.

On Monday I washed the car in Santa Rosa, then went south to Petaluma to have lunch with my old friend Erich Braun. I was early, so I bought Beth a couple of gifts in an antique shop. Then Erich arrived, and thirty years vanished as if they had never happened. We sat an an outdoor cafe reminiscing about Mendy Briscoe and Bill Ballentine, talking about our wives and children, speculating about cars and the

American dream. Erich, a car salesman's car salesman, had owned several major dealerships—Cadillac, Chevrolet, Mercedes, BMW, Porsche, Audi, and others, in Orlando and Nashville—since I last had seen him. Now he owns a company that helps the automobile industry retrain for the new American trend in car selling—giant, buyer-friendly dealerships where no unpleasant horse-trading is allowed. Erich is keenly aware of the irony in that. "The car replaced the horse and buggy. Car selling came *out* of the great American tradition of horse trading. It used to be fun for both seller and buyer, especially when cars were inexpensive and you were only haggling over twenty-five dollars." But with car prices in the stratosphere, the halcyon days when the pure American love of automobiles was evenly matched with the pure American love of selling them are gone forever. As I listened to Erich talk, I couldn't help thinking of what Olin McKenzie had told me in Miami: "The joy is gone."

"When I got into the business in 1963," Erich began, "there were forty-two salesmen on a three-car showroom floor. We had six or seven of us to one desk, and we worked shifts. There were tons of customers walking through the door then, and we had all kinds of terms we used in dealing with them. They were obnoxious terms—for example, we called a customer who came into the dealership an 'up.' What it meant was that we had to get up and go wait on him. *'Hey, there's an up outside.'* A 'flake' was a customer who had bad credit or took up a salesperson's time and didn't buy. 'Wouldja-take' and 'If-I-could-wouldja' were methods to start negotiations for a car. A 'high ball' was a ficticiously high value for the customer's trade-in. A 'be-back' was a customer who said he'd be back or who came back to the dealership for a second or third visit. A 'conquest sale' was one in which you persuaded the customer to switch to your brand from a different make of automobile. A 'lot lizard' was somebody who walked the sales lot and looked at every car and still didn't buy.

"Training was nonexistent. Chevy made a Bel Air and they made a Biscayne. 'There it is, go sell it,' the sales manager would say. But while there was no training, there was a definite strategy to the selling. If I couldn't sell you, I had to introduce you to one of my teammates. If he couldn't sell you, he had to introduce you to another salesman. If he couldn't close you, he brought in a manager. If the manager couldn't sell you, he got another manager involved. We had to have what we called six 'turns'—turnovers from one salesman to another—and the customer couldn't leave until we had gone through all that. One of the first things we were told was 'Get their keys.' We had your car keys, so you couldn't get away. It was real easy to do. Most of the time we'd be standing outside when you'd drive up. You'd pull up in your Audi, and I'd say, 'Boy, have I got a customer for *that* car. Let me have your keys, because you know what makes a good deal is how much I can get you for *your* car—you agree with that, don't you? I'm gonna have somebody looking at it so you can buy another one.' We didn't throw the keys up on the roof or anything, but some dealerships just about did. You were going to drive out in a new car or you weren't going to drive out at all. It was that atmosphere that created the reputation car salesmen have today."

Erich was silent for a moment.

"It was a good time while it lasted," I said.

He smiled. "Yeah, it sure was."

I spent three hours with Erich, then pushed south under a cloudy sky toward San Francisco. At the entrance to the Golden Gate Bridge, I pulled next to a Volvo covered with bumper stickers. The driver could tell I was trying to take his picture, so he slowed and waved and shouted that he liked my car. I shouted that I liked his, too.

That night I stayed in Los Gatos. I could have driven farther, but

I didn't want to miss the sights. The next morning I stopped and watched the sailboats in Monterey harbor. I thought about old John Steinbeck, who grew up near there, and about the mixed feelings with which he ventured home again. In Carmel I cruised along the doll-like main street, jammed with tourists eager to part with their cash. At the beach I turned back and got out of town as fast as possible. Dropping the Boxster into manual, I wound along Highway 1, past Big Sur, Cape San Martin, Ragged Point. The sun was up, the sky clear. The ocean was crisp blue with crashing whitecaps. Some people stopped and crossed a meadow to see seals lying on the sand forty yards away. I passed dozens of open-air Chrysler Sebrings, the best news for convertible lovers since the mid-seventies. They're sleek, like fine slippers, and not terribly expensive. Of course I loved the name. I decided that maybe Beth and I should sell her old van and buy her a Sebring when I got home.

At Cambria I left the ocean and turned inward on 46, toward Paso Robles. I was surprised at all the vineyards there, so far south. At Paso Robles I bore right. When I saw a sign for Cholame, I knew I was on the right track. At first I missed the cafe and drove on into the wide valley, past cows grazing, past where the highway Vs to the left across a section of flat land before climbing into the hills again. It was late in the day, nearly 6:00 P.M. The sun had turned the dry range to amber. The hills were golden where the sun touched them, and deep blue in the crevasses. The sky was still bright, the clouds white and fluffy.

I stayed on 46, following it up into the hills and around a curve. Then the road went straight for a very long time. At some point I decided I had gone too far, so I turned around and retraced my steps. Later I would confirm, as I flew west at 90 miles an hour, that the hills straight ahead and the desolate flat rangeland whizzing by on either side of the Porsche were the very last views of this earth that James Dean ever saw. The landscape there—undeveloped farmland—

couldn't have changed much in forty-two years. On September 30, 1955, just before 6:00 P.M., Dean and a friend emerged from the very straightaway I had just driven, accelerated into the curve I had just negotiated, and shot down the sloping hill I had just descended toward the valley below. At the same moment, a student named Donald Turnipseed was traveling east on 46. At Cholame he came down a hill and made a gentle curve to the right. When he was in the flat of the range, Turnipseed turned left where the highway splits. The two cars collided. Dean's silver 550 Porsche Spyder ended up as a snapshot on my wall: *twisted next to a barbed-wire fence, the hood flayed open and hanging out like a tongue.*

I retraced both drivers' routes several times that day, coming out of the hills west, then east, my heart racing each time I neared the point of impact. Later I went to Cholame to Jack's Ranch Cafe, where outside in the gravel parking lot, shaded by a tree of life, a Japanese devotee had erected a memorial to James Dean. Inside the cafe, the walls are decorated with photographs from Dean's three movies. I ordered a beer, bought a few postcards, and sat at a booth scribbling notes to friends and family.

It had been a good trip, I told them. Had driving this beautiful Porsche across this car-crazed country changed me? In some ways, surely. I would always have North Platte. I would always have Pocatello. I would always have the roar of the wind as I descended Loveland Pass. And I would always have—at least on videotape, shot with one backward-reaching hand as my other hand steered the Porsche at 80 miles an hour along a California highway—a glimpse, finally, of the Boxster's rear spoiler fully engaged. By the end of my trip I had begun to think of that spoiler as a kind of testament to our native need to speed and our coexisting desire to remain grounded. Without home, the road isn't much fun. Without the road, neither is home. I was ready to go back to Little Rock and see Beth, no matter what my hubris in Miami had cost me.

I had found this to be a country of unexpected generosity, I wrote. The Porsche had seemed to bring that out in people. Never mind that most of them had long since surrendered, at least on the surface, to the desperate domesticity of minivans or SUVs or four-door sedans. The Boxster was a machine that matched their deepest dreams. They hadn't been offering thumbs-ups just to the car—they'd also been reaffirming a part of themselves.

There's no doubt that I would miss driving that sexy car, but I was already coming to terms with that. The Boxster wasn't really me. It was too new, too flashy, too expensive for me to justify. *Too many people try to live up to their cars,* I remembered Dano saying back in Miami. *They need to choose a car that's right for who they are.* Maybe my father's mantra about my wanting, wanting, wanting had had some effect, but over the years I had become more preservationist than consumer. That didn't mean, however, that I no longer could lust for a Porsche. It meant just that I would still lust for an *old* one.

As for that terrible photograph I kept taped to my wall when I was a boy, the photograph that essentially prompted my Porsche lust, I still found it disturbing—and no less so for my having driven thousands of miles to stand in the very spot where the picture had been taken. I wrote a postcard to a friend: "The wreck seemed so unnecessary, and yet so *inevitable.*" The resulting twist of steel seemed to have a life force of its own. Now, with what I had learned about this country traveling from 1950s Miami to 1990s Portland, I interpreted it as a peculiarly twentieth-century kind of American presence, marked by desire, glamor, speed, selfishness, excess—and inevitability. Like with any piece of abstract sculpture, you could read many meanings into it. You could say that it was a depiction of freedom, which always comes with trade-offs. Or that it was a brilliant comment on the clashing forces of restlessness and consequence. As I sat there writing at Jack's, I even found myself imagining the wreckage, wherever it is today, being transported across the country to the Museum of Modern Art in New York, where it would find a prominent place in the outside sculpture garden. Art lovers would approach quietly, respectfully, bending over to read the crisp clear brass label: "American Century."

I spent that night in a small Motel 6 near a truck stop in Buttonwillow, California. The next day I drove into Los Angeles and checked into a Ramada Inn on Sunset Boulevard. On Thursday, June 12, I was to turn in the Porsche in Torrance. That day I got up early and went for a run. Later in the morning I bought Beth a present at Bloomingdale's in the Beverly Center—a pair of very sexy shoes. Before I checked out of the hotel, I called her in Little Rock. By then I had realized I would be arriving home on Friday the thirteenth. I groveled shamelessly on the phone: I told her I loved her, told her I had missed her, told her I would be bearing wonderful gifts.

"They'd better be nice ones," she said.

After lunch with an old friend from *Playboy* days, I took my last drive in the Boxster. At first I couldn't find the address for the drop-off, so I drove back and forth on the main drag of Torrance for half an hour. Finally I saw it, a small sign on a side street. The warehouse was a nondescript metal building protected by a chain-link fence. I pulled the Porsche into the driveway and parked outside an open garage full of fancy cars earmarked as loaners for journalists. When I got out, I checked the odometer—9,501 miles. Then a man came and held out his hand for the keys.

An employee there was leaving work early, so I caught a ride to the airport with him. On the way, I mulled over what had just happened. It seemed a humble end to such an ambitious forty-seven-day odyssey. Ashes to ashes, vans to vans. Just like that I had been returned to the mundane concerns of any traveler. I had a lot of baggage—all my clothes and equipment, plus books and papers I had picked up along the way. My flight didn't leave until 1:35 A.M., so I planned to check most of my bags and go over to the futuristic LAX lounge, Encounter, for drinks and dinner. One last treat, one last fling. The lounge, hovering above the parking lot like a flying saucer, looked like L.A. circa 1960 as imagined for the 1939 World's Fair.

But when I got to the ticket counter, the agent told me I couldn't check my bags until three hours before flight time. It was then only 5:00 P.M.—eight and a half hours till takeoff, more than five hours of lugging these emblems of home around like an albatross. I thought about stowing them in a locker, but one of the bags was much too big. So for an hour or more I sat in the Delta lounge, my suitcases stacked all around me.

Finally I couldn't stand it: I slipped a dollar in the cart dispenser and loaded all my bags onto it. They filled the bottom rack and overflowed the basket on top. Occasionally, I had to stop and boost a slippery bag back onto the pile. Still, I didn't have to carry them.

I rolled the cart toward the elevator and squeezed in next to it. On ground level I headed toward the sliding glass doors and glided down the sidewalk slope and into the crosswalk. Limos and taxis whizzed by. Several people stood on an island, waiting for rental-car vans.

Once I crossed the street, I veered into the parking lot toward the restaurant. For a while I had to weave in and out around parked cars, but then I found a clear stretch where I could get up some speed. I was moving along at a nice clip when a woman in a shiny new Jaguar suddenly emerged from a row and we almost collided. I careened left to miss her, then quickly regained control of my cart. When I looked at her, she was just sitting there, gripping her wheel and staring at me. The expression on her face wasn't the one I had become used to.

I laughed, at both her and myself, and gave her a big thumbs-up. Though the day was still light, a pale sliver of moon seemed to hang over the spaceship bar. I aimed my cart toward it and pushed on.

Acknowledgments

I owe a great deal of gratitude to scores of people for helping me complete this dream journey. The names of many already appear in the narrative, along with their wonderful stories about cars and life. In many ways, they and their stories *are* the narrative. But I must single out three men for special thanks—Thomas Adams, who told me how it felt to be the adman behind Chevrolet in the heyday of the American century; Frank Turner, who recounted his battles in building the highways for Adams's Chevys to drive on; and Alfred Dupont Chandler, the historian who explained why those cars and those roads were an inevitable result of America's restless spirit.

I also want to acknowledge many people who played vital roles behind the scenes. William Jeanes, editor of *Classic Automobile Register* (and publisher emeritus of *Car & Driver*), pointed me in the right direction in the Detroit phase of my background research. One of his good ideas was that I talk with Tom Adams. Mark Patrick, curator of the National Automotive History Collection at the Detroit Public Library, and his staff were very helpful on the long winter days I spent in their reading room. There I found everything from automobile-production charts to an account of the first car trip on the streets of Detroit. The archival staff at the Henry Ford Museum in Dearborn also were very helpful, especially in my research on Harley Earl and automobile design. Susan Stepek, manager of the reference center at Campbell-Ewald Advertising, provided information on Chevrolet ad campaigns through the years and guided me to an overview of auto-mobiles and American culture in general. In Washington, D.C., Richard Weingroff, historian at the Federal Highway Administration, produced a bibliography and stacks of reading material about high-ways and American driving habits. Weingroff also helped me make contact with Frank Turner. Stephanie Faul of the AAA Foundation for Traffic Safety responded promptly to requests for statistics about road rage and other craziness that afflict the commuting public these days. I would be remiss if I didn't also thank editor Richard Snow and his *American Heritage* magazine staff, who happened to publish a splendid issue on the automobile just as I was beginning my research.

Beyond those specific contributions, many other people helped me in ways too numerous to recount here. I'll simply list their names and trust that they know how much I appreciate their assistance: Bill and Betty Allen, Sidney J. Blatt, Max Brantley, Erich Braun, Mendy Briscoe, Marguerite Burgin, John Burnett, Hope Coulter, Ed Cromwell, Augusta Day, Hope Dlugozima, Elizabeth Evans, David Gartman, Blair and Bret Graves, Matt Lane, Tom Lombardo, Olin McKenzie, Lisa Matthews, George Millar, David and Erin Morgan, Matthew Morgan, Pat Morgan, Phil and Joyce Morgan, Ted Neuweiler, Fred Poe, Tina Poe, David Sanders, Buddy Slate, Polly and Paul Spear, Ed Strohm, George Wittenberg, and Katherine Har-rison Wyrick.

Finally, I offer deepest thanks to my agent, Joseph Vallely, who rep-resented this project so well; to editor Cindy Spiegel, who commissioned it (and who went to bat for me once again, even when I was late); to Bob Carlson of Porsche Cars North America, who said yes to lending me the Boxster; to Barbara Manha, who made the car materialize; and to Chris Knutsen, my excellent hands-on editor, who made a retracing of the trip in manuscript not simply beneficial but fun.

First, last, and foremost, however, I thank my wife, Beth. When my confidence wavered, she continued to believe in the book. When my plan for buying an old car went awry, she suggested I appeal to Porsche. And when I finished my time on the road, she let me come home again—in spite of everything.

About the Author

A former magazine editor, James Morgan is the author of *If These Walls Had Ears: The Biography of a House*. His articles and essays have appeared in such publications as *The New Yorker, The Atlantic Monthly, GQ, The Washington Post Magazine, Playboy, Outside, Preservation, Men's Journal, Travel & Leisure,* and many others. He lives in Little Rock, Arkansas.